Microsoft Publisher 365

A Step by Step Practical User Guide to Learn Microsoft Publisher with Professional Tips, Tricks, & Shortcuts.

Crystal Gibson

Copyright © 2024 by Crystal Gibson

All rights reserved. This book or any portion thereof should not be reproduced or used in any form whatsoever without the express written permission of the publisher except for the use of brief quotations in the book reviews.

Printed in the United States of America

TABLE OF CONTENTS

TABLE OF CONTENTS III

INTRODUCTION VIII

CHAPTER ONE 9

UNDERSTANDING MICROSOFT 365 9

ADVANTAGES OF USING MICROSOFT OFFICE 365 9
SIGN IN OR CREATE AN ACCOUNT WITH MICROSOFT 10

CHAPTER TWO 13

GETTING STARTED WITH THE PUBLISHER 13

LAUNCHING MICROSOFT PUBLISHER 14
PIN PUBLISHER TO THE TASKBAR FOR EASY ACCESS 15
STUDY PUBLISHER MAIN SCREEN 16
THE MENUS TAB (RIBBONS) 17

CHAPTER THREE 20

CONSTRUCTING A NEW PUBLICATION 20

CREATING YOUR NEW PUBLICATION 20
OPEN A NEW PUBLICATION 21
STUDYING THE MAIN SCREEN 23
CREATING GUIDES 24
KEY ELEMENTS OF PUBLISHER 25
INSERTING A TEXT BOX 26
ADDING TEXT TO THE PUBLICATION 27
FORMATTING YOUR TEXT 27
CHANGING THE FONT OF YOUR TEXT 27
CHANGING THE FONT SIZE OF YOUR TEXT 27

BOLD, ITALICIZE, AND UNDERLINE YOUR TEXT	28
CHANGING THE TEXT COLOR OF YOUR TEXT	29
SPECIFYING TEXT ALIGNMENT	29
CHANGE CASE	30
ADDING TYPOGRAPHY FEATURES	31
USING DROP CAP	31
USING STYLISTIC SETS	32
USING LIGATURES	33
USING STYLISTIC ALTERNATES	34
WORKING WITH TEXT EFFECTS	35
APPLY SHADOW/REFLECTION/GLOW ON THE TEXT	35
ADDING TEXT OUTLINE	35
USING WORDART STYLES	36
FORMATTING THE TEXT BOXES	37
APPLYING BACKGROUND COLOR TO THE TEXT BOX	38
APPLYING BORDER TO THE TEXT BOX	38
APPLYING EFFECT (SHADOW, GLOW, OR REFLECTION) TO THE TEXT BOX	39
APPLYING STYLE ON THE TEXT BOX	39
ADJUSTING TEXT BOXES	41
RESIZING THE TEXT BOX	41
MOVING THE TEXT BOX	41
ROTATING TEXT BOX	42
CHANGING TEXT DIRECTION	42
TEXT AUTOFIT	43
ADJUSTING TEXT BOX MARGIN	43
SPECIFYING TEXT BOX ALIGNMENT	45
LINKING TEXT BOXES	45
CHAPTER FOUR	**47**
INSERTING TABLES	**47**
RESIZING THE TABLE	48
MOVING THE TABLE	49
FORMATTING TABLES	49
ADDING A COLUMN	50
ADDING A ROW	51
RESIZING ROWS AND COLUMNS	51
MERGING CELLS	52
ALIGNING CELL TEXT	53

CELL BORDER	54
CHANGING CELL COLOR	55
CHANGING TEXT DIRECTION	56

CHAPTER FIVE 57

GETTING STARTED WITH GRAPHICS 57

ADDING PHOTOS	57
ADDING PHOTOS FROM THE INTERNET	59
INSERTING CLIPART	61
ADDING EFFECTS TO YOUR PICTURES	63
ADDING A CAPTION	63
CROPPING PICTURES	64
CROPPING TO SHAPE	66
ADJUSTING PICTURES	67
WRAPPING TEXT AROUND PICTURES	69
CUSTOMIZING WRAP POINTS	70
INSERTING SHAPES	72
ADJUSTING SHAPES	72
CHANGING SHAPE COLOR	72
CHANGING SHAPE BORDER	73
APPLYING SHADOW TO A SHAPE	74
ALIGN OBJECTS ON THE PAGE	75
DISTRIBUTE OBJECTS ACROSS THE PAGE	76
GROUPING AND UNGROUPING OBJECTS	77
ARRANGING OBJECT LAYERS	78
USING PUBLISHER PAGE PARTS	80
INSERTING BORDERS AND ACCENTS	82
INSERTING CALENDARS	84
ADDING ADVERTISEMENTS	86
INSERTING WORDART	87

CHAPTER SIX 91

GETTING STARTED WITH MAIL MERGE 91

MAIL MERGE ENVELOPES	91
MAIL MERGE AN INVITATION	96

CHAPTER SEVEN 100

GETTING STARTED WITH PUBLISHER TEMPLATES 100

LOCATING AND USING AN IN-BUILT TEMPLATE 100
CREATING YOUR OWN TEMPLATE 102

CHAPTER EIGHT 106

MANAGING YOUR PUBLICATION 106

SAVING DOCUMENTS 106
SAVING DOCUMENT AS A DIFFERENT FORMAT 107
OPENING SAVED DOCUMENTS 109
PAGE SETUP 110
CREATING BOOKLETS 111

CHAPTER NINE 114

GETTING STARTED WITH THE PARENT PAGE 114

EDITING MASTER PAGES 114
CREATING MASTER PAGES 116
APPLYING MASTERS 117
USING THE LAYOUT GUIDES 119

CHAPTER TEN 122

PUBLISHING YOUR PUBLICATION 122

PRINTING YOUR DOCUMENT 122
PRINTING AS A BOOKLET 123
SHARING A FILE 125
EXPORT DOCUMENT AS PDF 126

CHAPTER ELEVEN 128

MICROSOFT PUBLISHER TIPS AND TRICKS 128

CHANGING INTERFACE SCRATCH AREA TO DARK GRAY 128
TIPS ON WORKING WITH SHAPES 129

CHAPTER TWELVE 133

SHORTCUT KEYS FOR ENHANCED EFFICIENCY 133

COPYING, CUTTING, PASTING OR DELETING OBJECTS 133
NUDGING AN OBJECT 133
ZOOMING 133
EDITING AND FORMATTING SHORTCUTS 134
LAYERING OBJECTS 135
SELECT OR GROUP OBJECT 135
SNAP OBJECTS 136
SHOW OR HIDE BOUNDARIES OR GUIDES 136
DEALING WITH PAGE SHORTCUTS 136
CREATING, OPENING, SAVING OR CLOSING A PUBLICATION 137
WHEN USING PRINT PREVIEW 137
WHEN USING DIALOG BOXES 137

CONCLUSION 139

INDEX 140

INTRODUCTION

Microsoft Publisher empowers you to craft numerous publications with its array of features and tools, catering to creations like banners, posters, flyers, letterheads, certificates, and beyond. These tools are neatly organized into tabs along the Ribbon tab, situated at the top of the screen.

This software proves invaluable for fashioning diverse publications conveniently from the confines of your room or office, enabling the creation of high-quality materials with ease. However, proficiency in using Publisher's tools requires a level of mastery if you must create flawless and effortless publications.

Whether starting from scratch or using preformatted templates, you can effortlessly tailor designs to your preferences. Yet, mastering the Publisher's tools is pivotal to exploring its full potential for crafting exceptional publications.

This comprehensive guide encompasses both fundamental and advanced techniques, addressing potential challenges that users might encounter while navigating the Microsoft Publisher application. Among the plethora of benefits this book offers, key highlights include mastering the Publisher interface, designing and reformatting publications, setting up pages, adjusting views, managing textboxes and overflow text, effectively incorporating colors, shapes, and text, manipulating margin guides, ruler guides, and gridlines, selecting appropriate fonts and design elements, creating envelopes and mail merge invitations, handling objects and images, as well as managing pages efficiently, and much more.

I passionately endorse this illustrative guide to anyone seeking to explore the full potential of Microsoft Publisher with minimal struggle. It equips readers with fundamental insights for exploring the Publisher's capabilities comprehensively.

CHAPTER ONE
UNDERSTANDING MICROSOFT 365

It is of utmost importance to understand Microsoft Office 365 before moving ahead to discuss Publisher 365.

Microsoft Office 365 was originally known as (Office 365) when it was released in 2011, but it has been renamed (Microsoft 365) since April 2020. Microsoft 365 is an online-based version of the Microsoft Office suite that grants users access to over 20 Microsoft applications like traditional office suites such as Word, Excel, PowerPoint, Publisher, Outlook, and others via the cloud (internet).

In contrast to the classic Office Suite, Office 365 does not need installation to function. Furthermore, Office 365 does not need physical storage to keep its information since it offers email hosting and a cloud storage space that enables users to host their files online and access them at any time and from any location as long as they have an internet connection.

Microsoft 365 has seemed to be a substitute for conventional office suites over time due to its prominent advantages, one of which is the accessibility and editing of the same document both at the workplace and at home, regardless of the device you use.

ADVANTAGES OF USING MICROSOFT OFFICE 365

There are several parallels between Office 365 and the conventional Office Suite. Despite these similarities, Office 365 offers certain unique features that set it apart from the standard Office suite. However, these are the primary benefits that will entice you to adopt Office 365. Let us now emphasize these using the table below.

ADVANTAGES	EXPLANATIONS
Easy Accessibility and Online Storage	Office 365 enables you to access your files from any device, at any time, using an internet connection. Office 365 is hosted at a Microsoft data center; therefore, users must connect to the internet to use the program.
Automatic Upgrades	Applications including Word, Excel, Publisher, and others are automatically updated at predetermined periods. With this in place, the worry and expense of purchasing new software are

	eliminated since updates are included in the Office 365 license subscription.
Software Update	Another benefit of using Office 365 is that customers may get regular software upgrades. These upgrades provide access to the most recent features, such as security patches and bug fixes.
Secured Cloud Storage	Office 365 provides a secure working environment with high-security safeguards in place, such as two-factor authentication, which prevents authorized users from accessing your data even while they are on your devices. Your sensitive data are protected with this in place, as there is no security danger or breach.
company Continuity	No matter what happens to your physical equipment, emails, files, and data, threats such as catastrophes and thefts cannot disrupt the flow of your company. This is because all files and data required for workflow are kept and routinely backed up in the Office 365 cloud.
Mix and match options	There are a variety of Office 365 subscription options available, each with its own set of plans and features. As a result, not everyone will need the same strategy. As a result, you may mix and match plans to avoid paying more or less than you need to.

SIGN IN OR CREATE AN ACCOUNT WITH MICROSOFT

To access Publisher 365 program, you must first sign in to Microsoft's official website and then subscribe to the Microsoft 365 package that includes Publisher. Follow the steps itemized below to access Microsoft Office 365 applications:

1) run any **web browser** that is installed on your PC.
2) To access Microsoft's official website, type **www.office.com** into the address bar.

3) On the Microsoft website, click the **sign-in** button.

4) Enter your **username** and tap the **Next** button if you already have a Microsoft account; otherwise, tap the **Create One** button and follow the **on-screen** instructions to create one.

5) Enter your **password** and click the **sign-in** button.

Note: when you have successfully completed the registration and subscription, you can click on the Publisher icon to begin the exploration.

CHAPTER TWO
GETTING STARTED WITH THE PUBLISHER

You must have heard of Microsoft Publisher. It's a desktop publishing program crafted by Microsoft, tailored for users seeking basic desktop publishing capabilities, primarily aimed at schools, households, and small businesses for internal printing needs. However, it's worth noting that Publisher isn't the go-to choice for commercial printing ventures.

What distinguishes Publisher from Microsoft Word is its emphasis on page layout and design over text creation and proofing. This focus enables users to craft an array of publications with diverse features and tools, such as posters, banners, flyers, letterheads, certificates, and more. These tools are neatly organized into tabs along the Ribbon tab at the top of the screen, enhancing accessibility and ease of use.

Unlike advanced publishing applications like Adobe InDesign, Publisher adopts a "WYSIWYG" (What You See Is What You Get) interface, ensuring that your printouts mirror what's displayed on the screen. This user-friendly approach allows users to visualize and refine their designs effortlessly.

Publisher enables you to easily arrange your designs on the page using elements such as text boxes for headings and main text, and photo placeholders for pictures and shapes.

The publisher also has preset templates and building blocks for designing larger publications known as "page parts".

Proofing tools such as spell and grammar checks enable you to proof your work as you type. Possibly misspelled words are indicated in red, and grammar errors are ticked in green. Auto-correct features correct regularly misspelled words, phrases, or sentences.

In Summary, Publisher allows you to conveniently create business cards, greeting cards, booklets, flyers, and personalized calendars using your graphics, text, and photographs.

LAUNCHING MICROSOFT PUBLISHER

The user of Publisher with the traditional version can get started on Publisher with any of the listed steps:

- Type **Publisher** into the Search box and click the **Publisher** icon as indicated in the screenshot below.

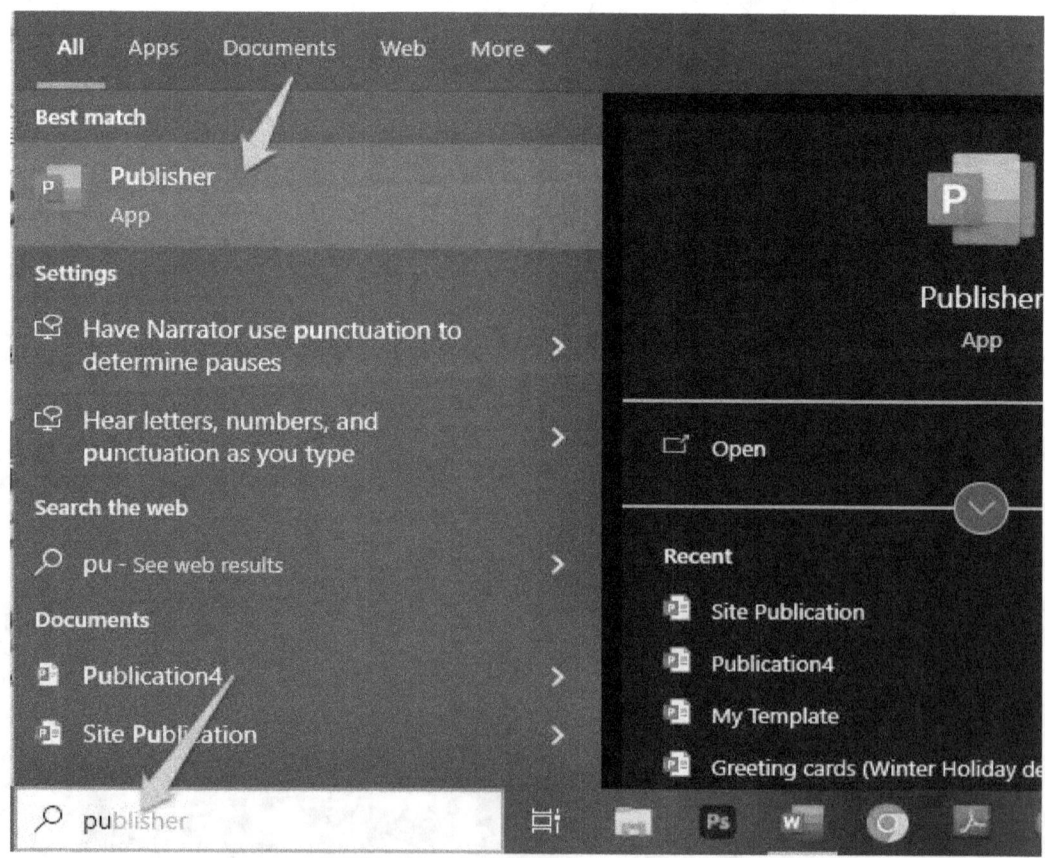

- Click the **Start** button and scroll through the apps you have on your PC, then click the **Publisher** app to get started.

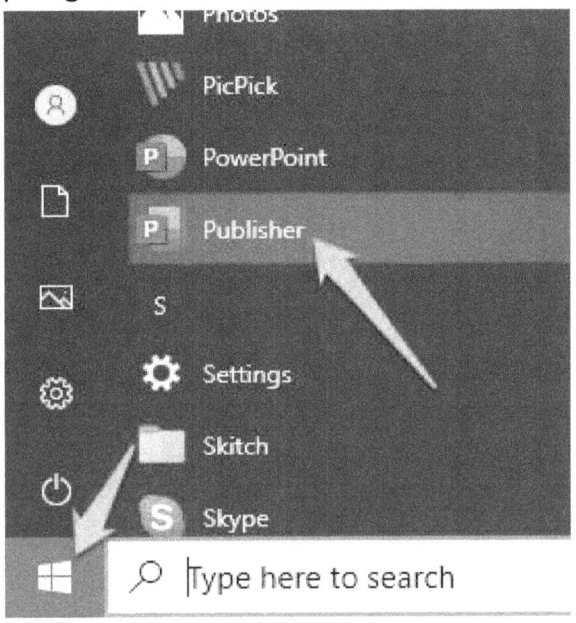

PIN PUBLISHER TO THE TASKBAR FOR EASY ACCESS

You can pin Publisher to the taskbar to give you free access anytime you want to use Microsoft Publisher. Follow the steps itemized below to pin Microsoft Publisher:

1) Right-click the **Publisher** icon on the **taskbar**.
2) Choose "**Pin to taskbar**" on the fly-out. now Publisher is pinned to the taskbar, you simply need to click it for subsequent access to Publisher.

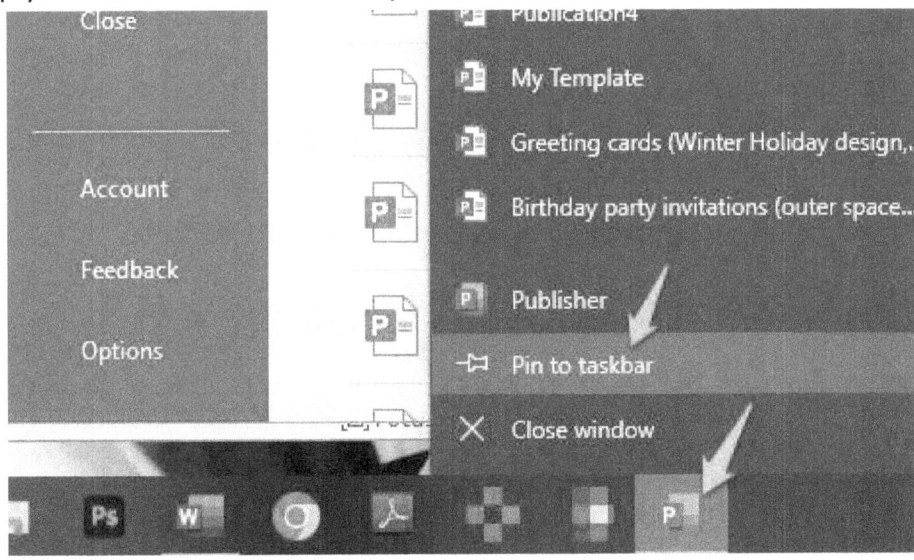

When you launch Publisher, the **Start Screen** will appear, The most recently saved publication appears on the Recent tab on the Start Screen.

choose a **template** from the **thumbnails** at the top of the window. Click over any **template** to get started. You can click More Templates to access the entire templates.

STUDY PUBLISHER MAIN SCREEN

The publisher's main screen is split into sections as shown in the screenshot below

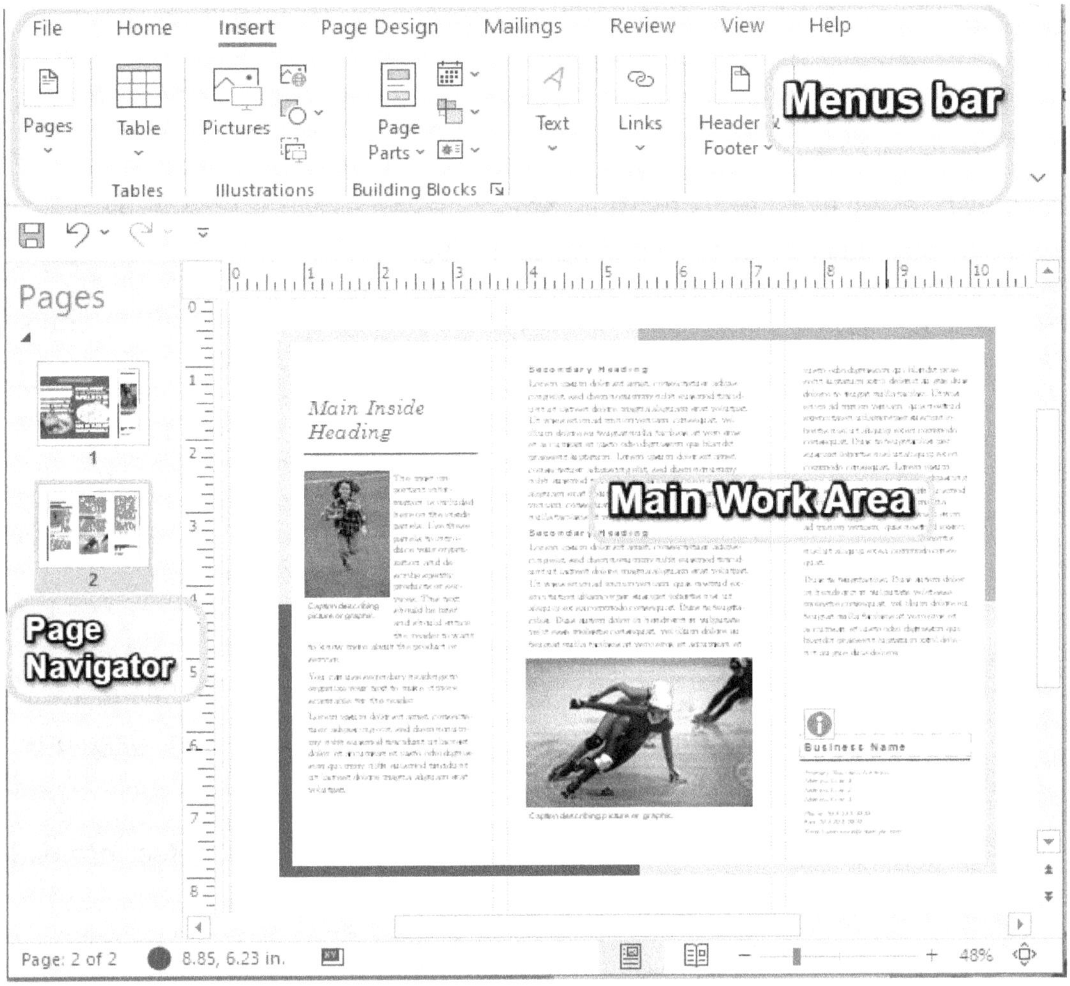

THE MENUS TAB (RIBBONS)

Ribbons are arranged into tabs otherwise known as menus tab across the top of the window. Ribbons are arranged based on their functions.

HOME TAB

The Home tab includes tools for text formatting, for instance, you can change **fonts**, **bold text**, **change text color**, and the regular tools for text alignment.

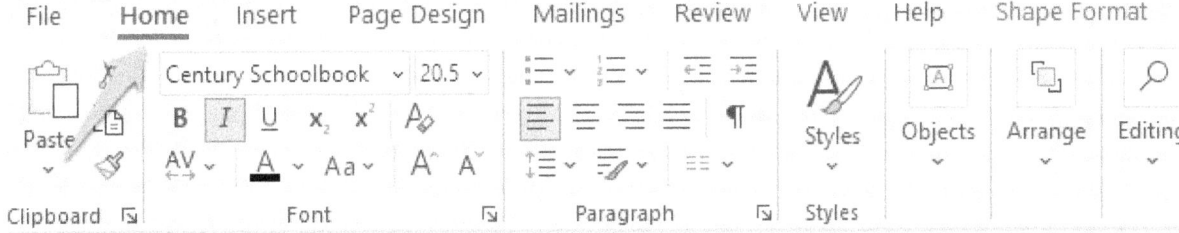

INSERT TAB

The Insert tab includes tools for inserting tables, charts, photos, borders, shapes, and so on.

You can also insert word art, equation, smart art, and graphic "page parts" using the "building block" and illustration grouping of the Insert tab.

The Text group of the Insert tab can be used to insert text boxes, word art, and symbols.

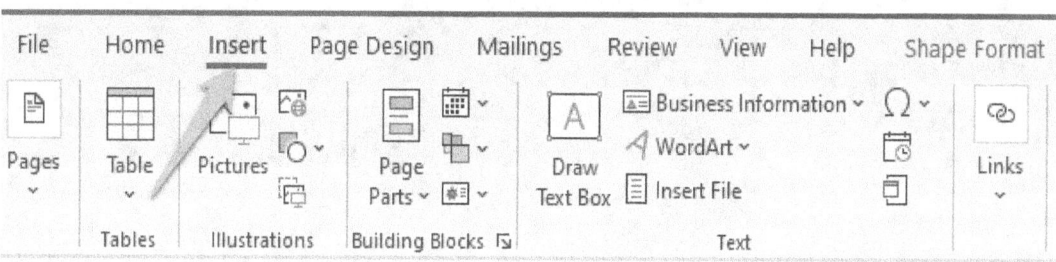

PAGE DESIGN TAB

The Page Design tab is used for adjusting margins, changing templates, page orientation, and setting up design guides for aligning the objects on your page.

You can also change the background, set up page masters, and select premade color schemes.

MAILING TAB

The Mailing tab lets you create mail merges and link them to a data source in a database or spreadsheet.

REVIEW TAB

The Review tab allows you to check your words with a thesaurus, spell-check your document, translate text to a different language, and carry out other research.

VIEW TAB

The View tab allows you to switch to different views, add rulers, open master pages, and zoom.

FILE TAB

When you click the File tab, it leads you to File Backstage. The File Backstage allows you to execute common commands such as open publications, save publications, share or export publications, print, and preference settings.

You can also access your Microsoft Account, change your Microsoft Account, log in and activate your Microsoft Office, and so on, using the **File Backstage**.

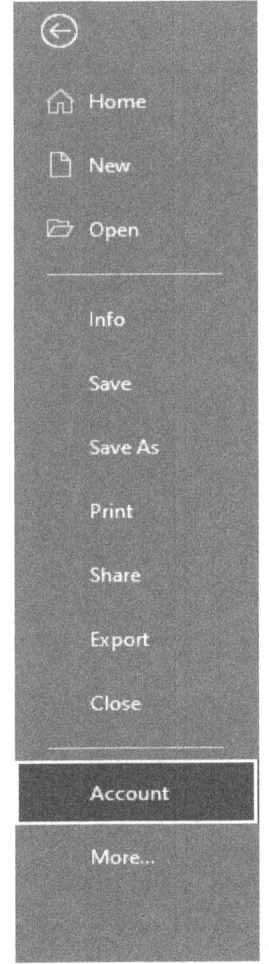

CHAPTER THREE
CONSTRUCTING A NEW PUBLICATION

Publishers permit you to create diverse designs, you can start your design from scratch or use one of the multiple different templates provided in Publisher.

CREATING YOUR NEW PUBLICATION

Before we get started to create a new publication, there are certain options you need to specify such as **paper type**, **paper size,** and **page layout**. Those options are explained below.

SPECIFY SIZE

Publications come in different sizes, posters always come in bigger sizes such as A1 or A3 while flyers can come in smaller sizes like A6 or A5.

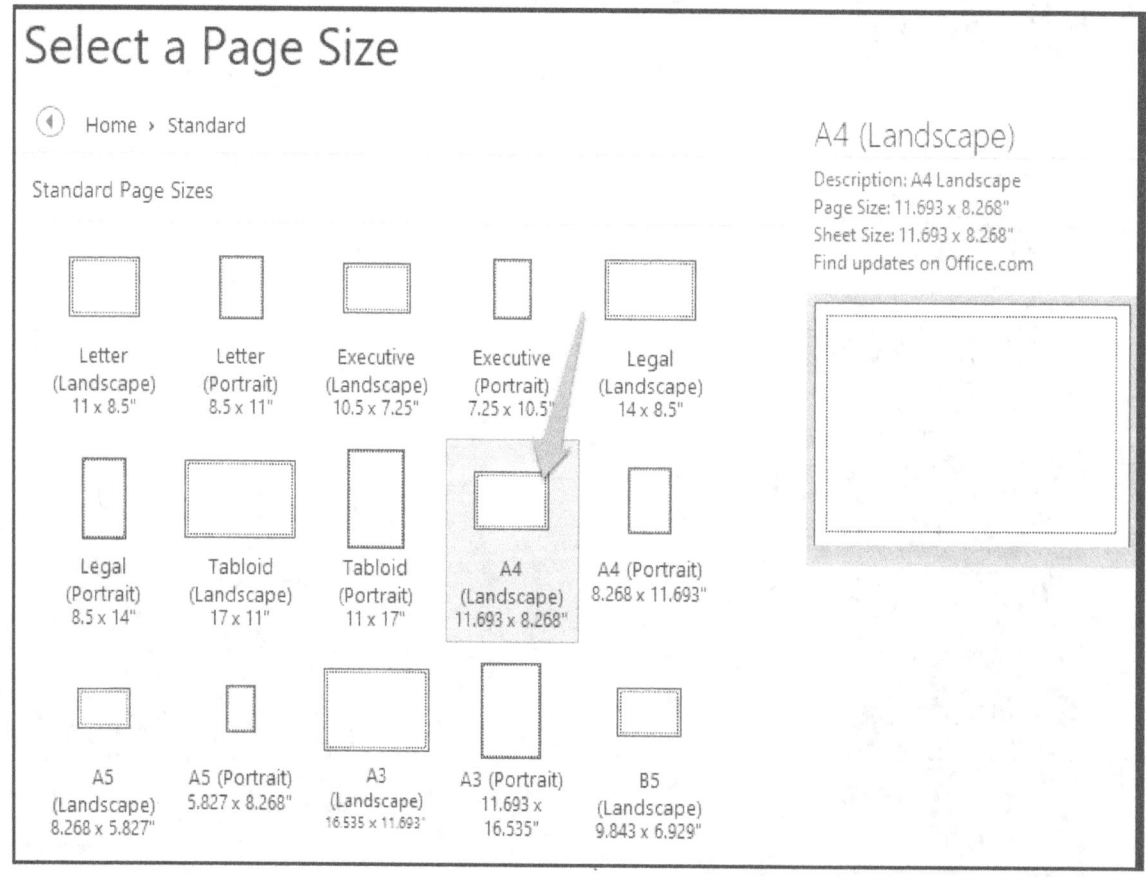

Note: to specify page size, go to **Page Design** > **Size** > **More Preset Page Size**.

SPECIFY ORIENTATION

Orientation comes in Portrait or Landscape, you can use both portrait and landscape for Greeting cards. Certain fliers are portrait and most of the posters are portrait as well.

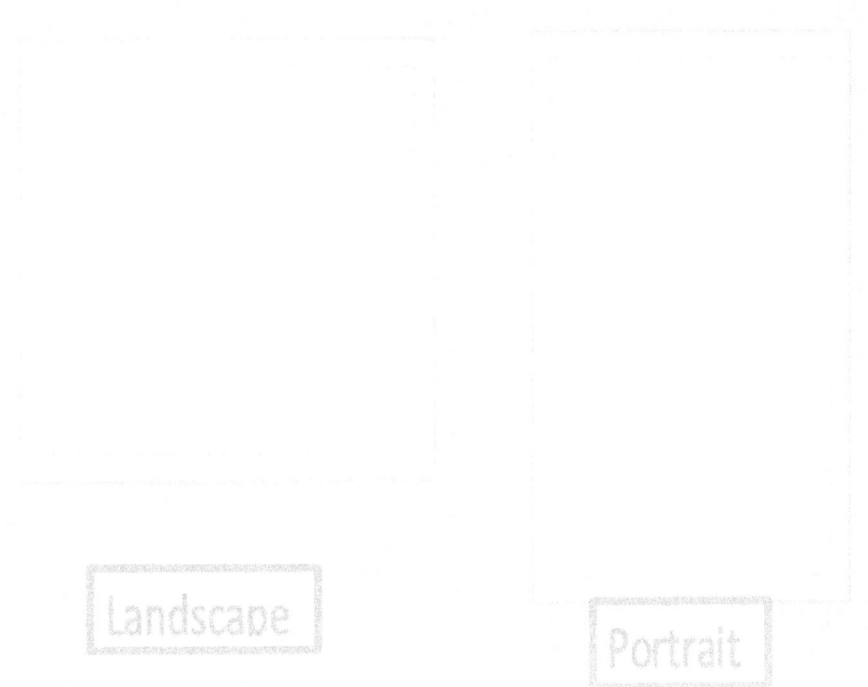

Note : to specify orientation, go to **Page Design** > **Orientation** > **Portrait or Landscape**

MARGINS

Margins are the blank space areas across the top, bottom, right, and left edges of a printed publication.

Note: To set the margin for your publication, go to **Page Design** > **Margin**

OPEN A NEW PUBLICATION

When you launch the Publisher application, you can create a new publication using a blank publication or choose a template to begin with. To open a new publication, follow the steps itemized below.

1) Click the **File** tab on the main screen of Publisher and select **New** on the File Backstage.
2) Choose a **template** on the right pane.

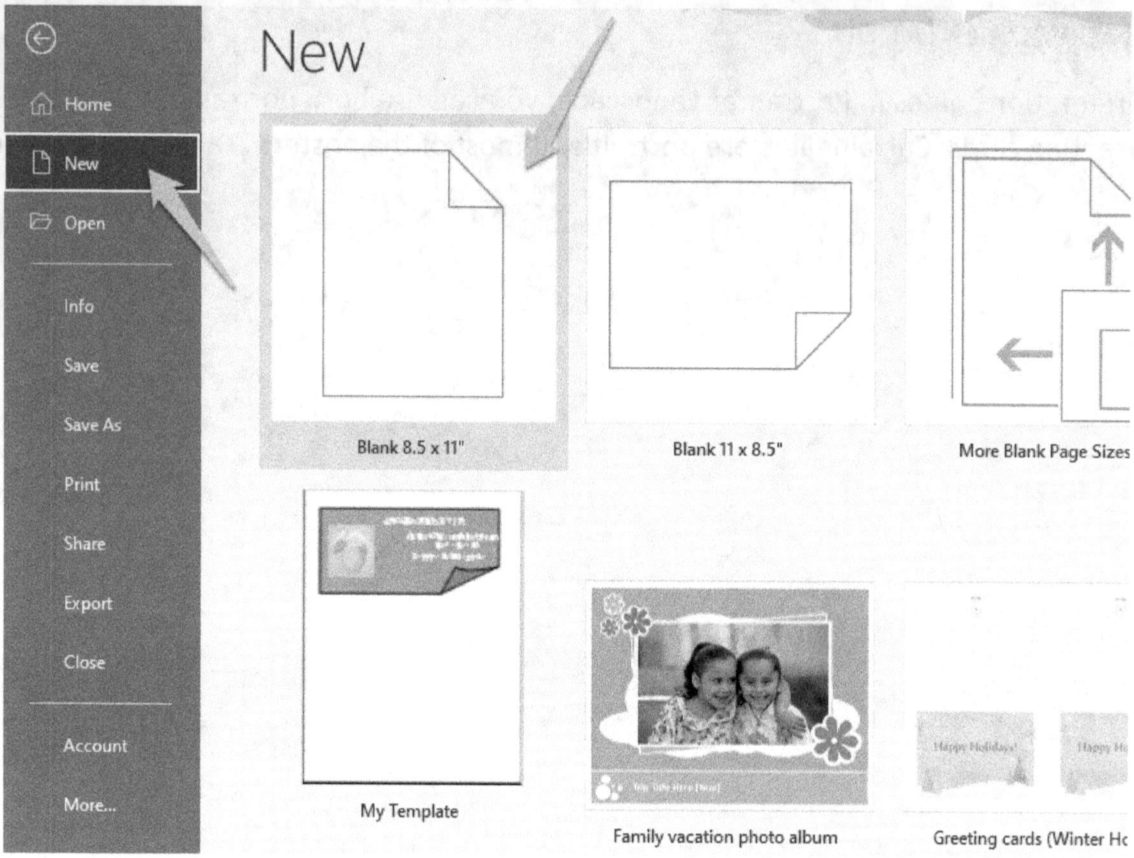

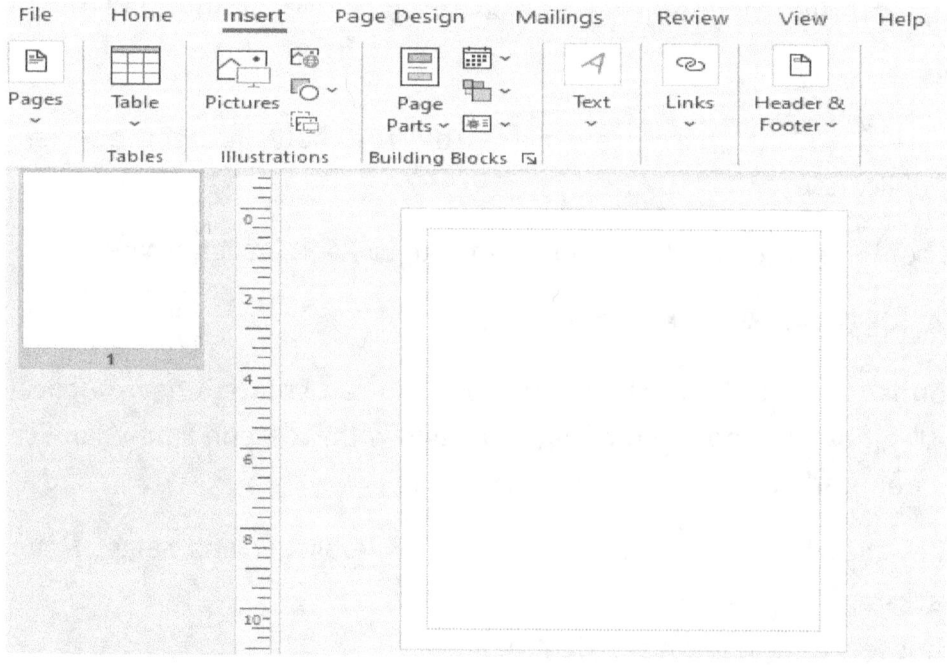

3) You will be moved to the **publisher's work area** where you can start to build up your publication.

STUDYING THE MAIN SCREEN

On the left side of the Publisher main screen, you have the **Page Navigation** pane. Each page thumbnail has a page number to differentiate it from others. When you click a **page thumbnail** in the navigation pane, the Publisher moves you to that page.

On the lower left side of the main screen, there are **three components:**

1. The **first component** displays the current page number; click this button to close and open the page navigation pane.
2. The **second component** displays the position of the top left corner of the selected object on your page. The selected object in this case is 3.68cm down from the top border of the page and 0.9cm from the left border of the page.
3. The **third component** displays the size of the selected object.

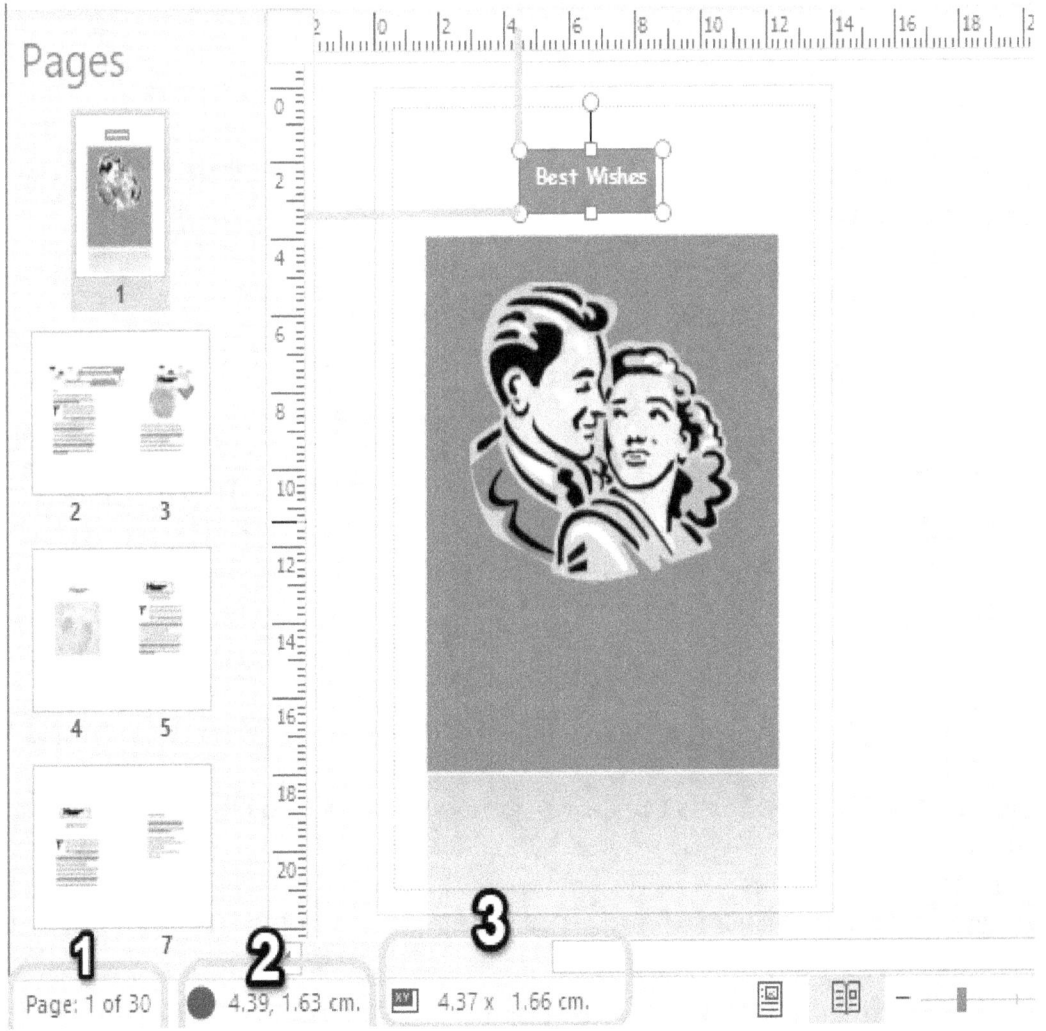

Note: If your measurement is showing a different measurement unit aside from centimeters (cm), you can change it using these steps: Click **File** tab>**Options**>click **Advanced category**. Then choose **Centimeter** on the menu beside the "**Show measurements in units of**" heading in the **Display** section.

At the bottom right side of the main screen, you have a page view switch and page zoom control.

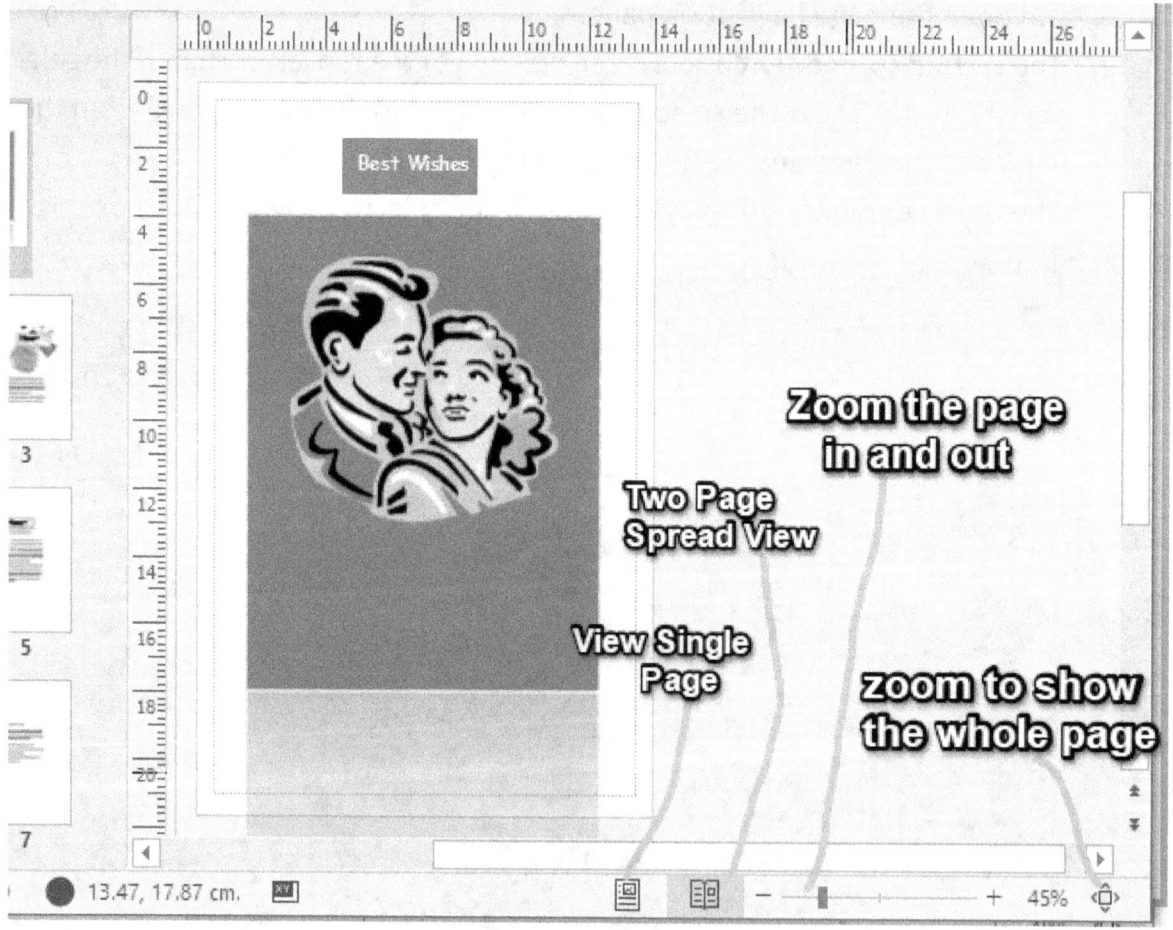

CREATING GUIDES

Guidelines help to align objects on your page. Follow the steps itemized below to create guidelines:

1) Click either the **vertical or horizontal ruler** and then drag the mouse pointer to any position you want on your page
2) Click and drag the **guide** to reposition the guide if that is required.

Note: if the ruler is not visible around the work area, go **View** menu and tick the Ruler checkbox.

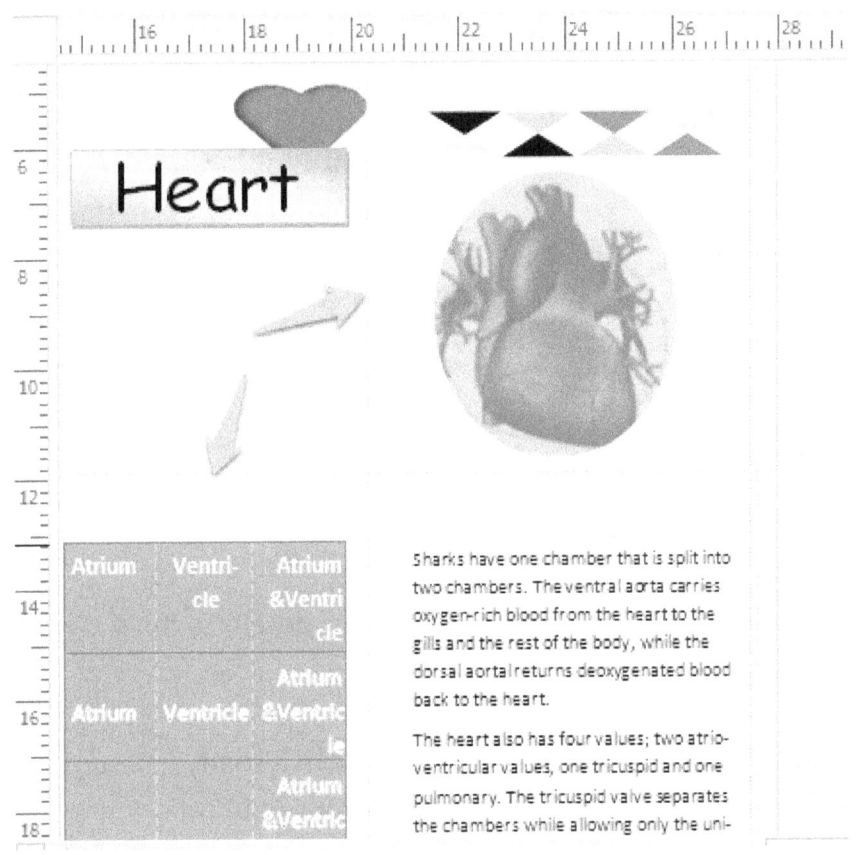

KEY ELEMENTS OF PUBLISHER

Publisher documents are built and fashioned using some key elements. The first element is the **text box**. The **text boxes** include text that you can add to your design and position separately anywhere on the page.

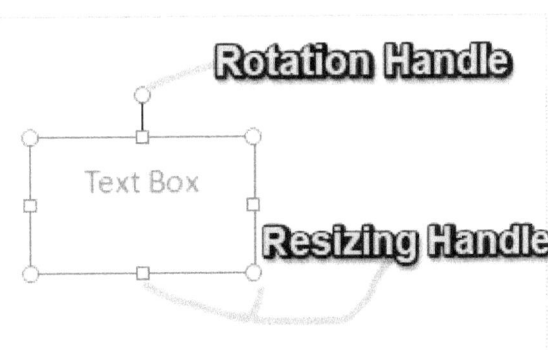

There are also **picture placeholders** for adding photos to your design and placing them on any location within the page.

In some contexts, **text boxes** and **photo placeholders** are called **frames**. When you click a frame, small circles display across the border known as the handles. You can click and drag the handles to resize your text box or image placeholder.

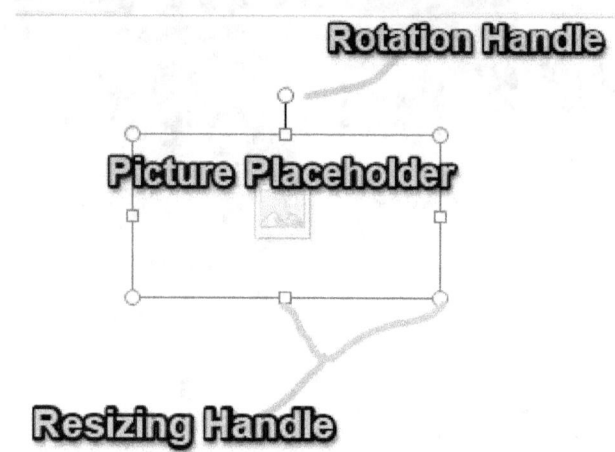

You can also add tables, shapes, and charts to your design to build up your publication.

INSERTING A TEXT BOX

You can only add text to your design after you have already inserted a text box. Follow the steps itemized below to insert a text box on your publication page:

1) Click the **Home** tab and click the **Draw Text Box** button.

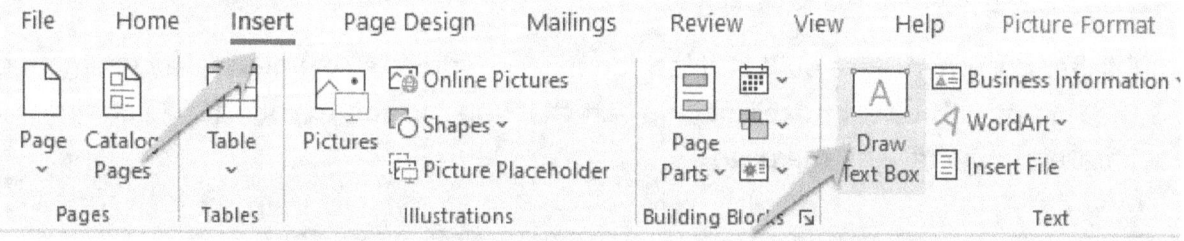

2) Click and drag to draw the text box across the page.

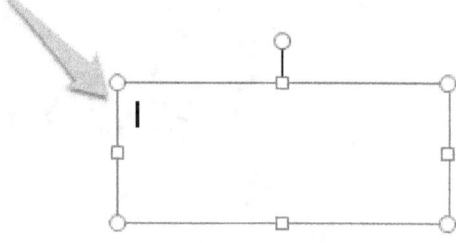

ADDING TEXT TO THE PUBLICATION

After you have inserted a text box, you can begin to add some text to it as shown in the screenshot below.

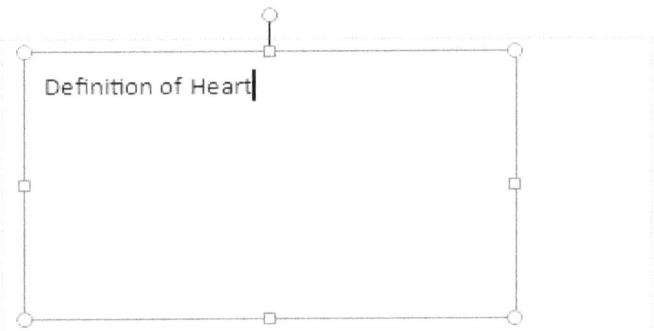

FORMATTING YOUR TEXT

You can format the text inside your text box. There is basic and advanced formatting. Next, we will be looking at elementary text formatting using the formatting tools in the home tab.

CHANGING THE FONT OF YOUR TEXT

1) Highlight the **text** whose font you wish to change.
2) Click the **Home** tab, click the **Font** menu, and select the **font** you prefer.

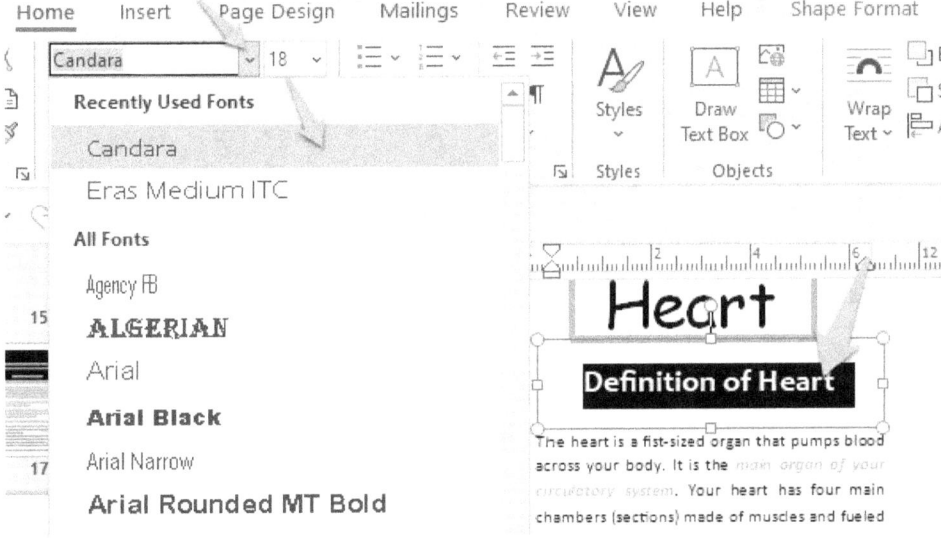

CHANGING THE FONT SIZE OF YOUR TEXT

1) Highlight the **text** whose font size you wish to change.

2) Click the **Home** tab, click the **Font Size** menu, and select the **size** you prefer on the drop-down menu.

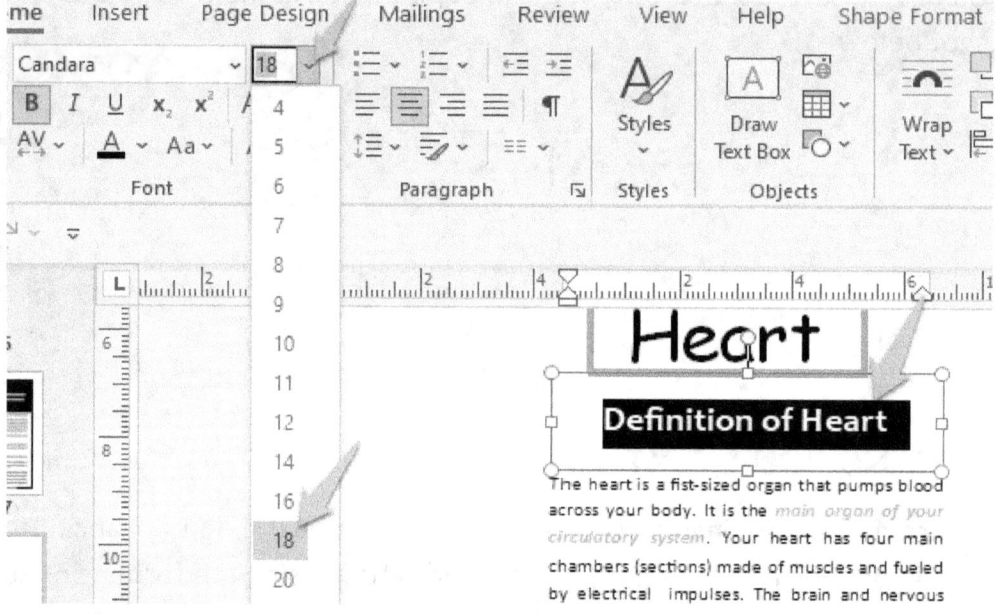

BOLD, ITALICIZE, AND UNDERLINE YOUR TEXT

1) Highlight the **text** you want to apply with the aforementioned formatting.
2) Click the **Home** tab, and click the **Bold**, **Italic**, or **Underlined** according to how you want to format your text.

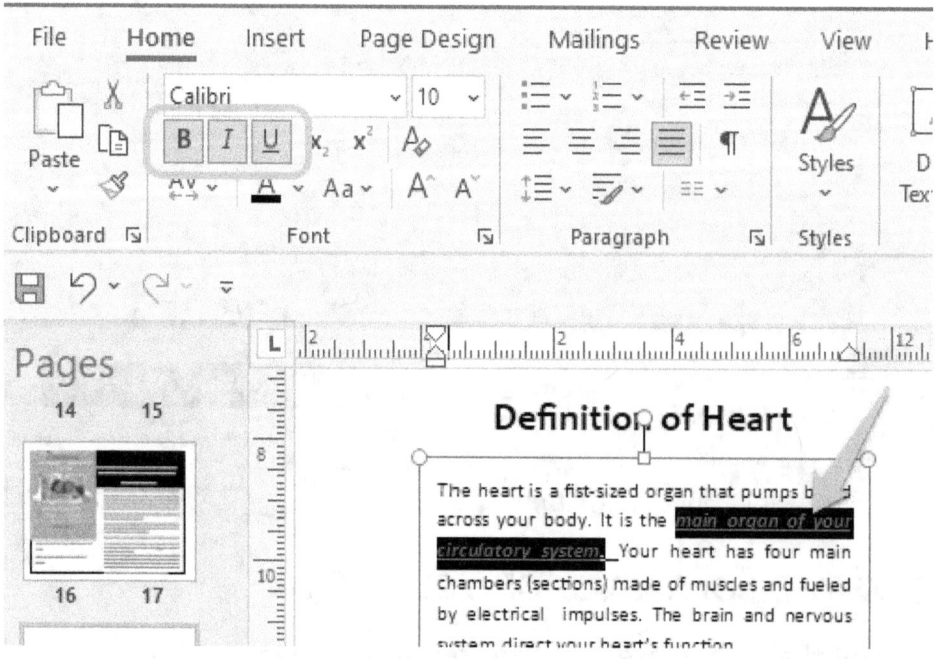

CHANGING THE TEXT COLOR OF YOUR TEXT

1) Highlight the **text** whose text color you wish to change.
2) Click the **Home** tab, click the **Font** color menu, and select the **color** you prefer on the drop-down menu.

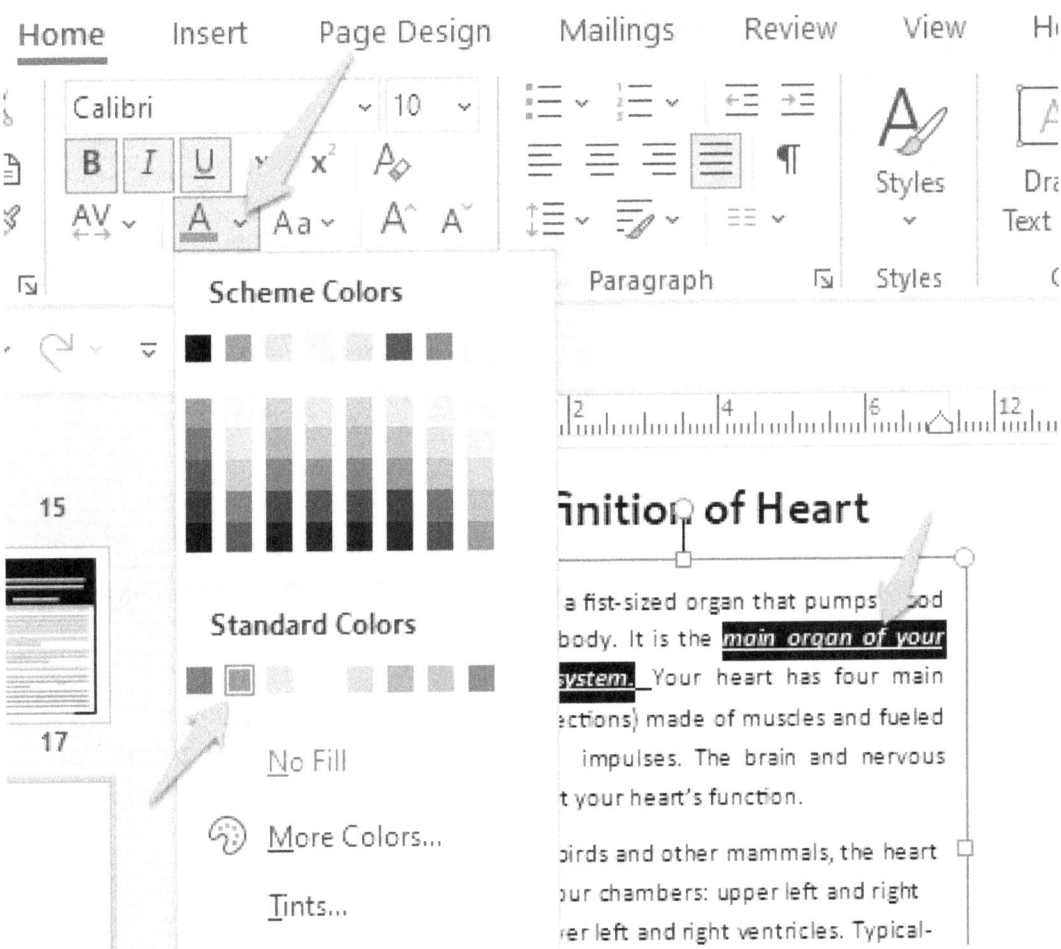

SPECIFYING TEXT ALIGNMENT

You can specify the alignment you want for the text inside the text box; the alignment may be to the right, middle, left, or Justify to align text to the left and right of the text box.

Follow the steps itemized below to align text within the text box.

1) Highlight the **text** you want to set alignment for.
2) Click the **Home** tab, and choose the **alignment** you want in the Paragraph group.

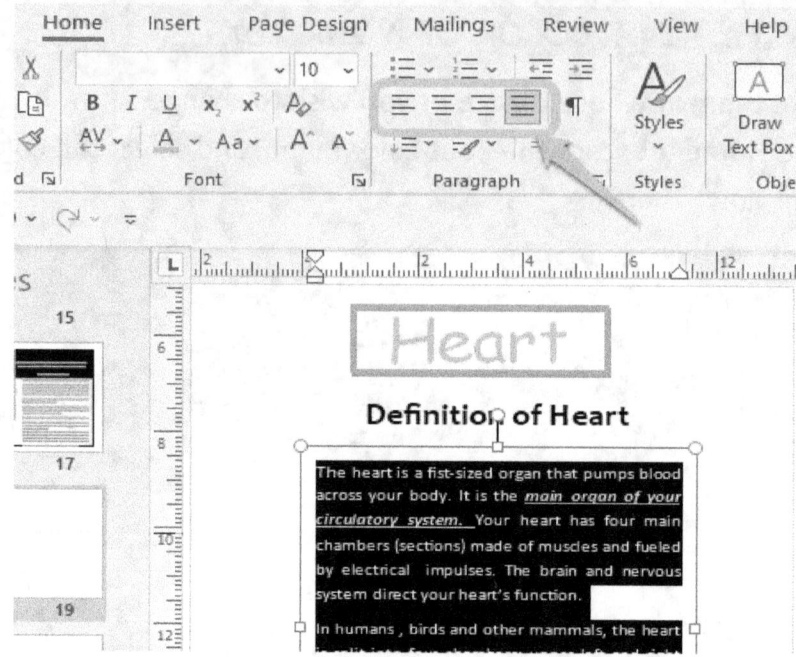

CHANGE CASE

You can change the case of your text to any case that suits your design, the case can be **UPPERCASE, Sentence case, or lowercase**. Follow the steps below to change the case of your text.

1) Highlight the **text** whose case you wish to change.
2) Click the **Home** tab, click the **Change Case** menu in the Font group, and select the case you want on the drop-down menu.

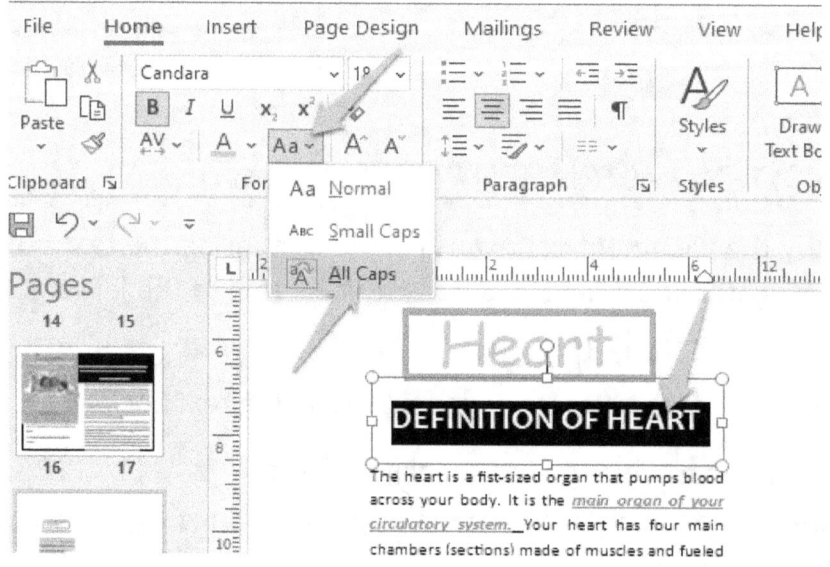

ADDING TYPOGRAPHY FEATURES

There are different typography features you can apply to your text for creative design. However, these features work with specific fonts that are listed here; **Cambria, Garamone Calibri, Zapfino, and Gabriola.**

USING DROP CAP

A drop cap expands the first letter of the selected text, the drop cap is majorly used at the beginning of a chapter or the beginning of a paragraph. Follow the steps itemized below to apply the drop cap feature:

1) Click anywhere around the paragraph you want to format with a drop cap to drop the insertion pointer.
2) Click the **"Text Box"** tab and click the **Drop Cap** menu in the Typograph group.
3) You can choose a **predefined style** on the drop-down menu or click the **Custom Drop Cap** to open the Drop Cap dialog box.

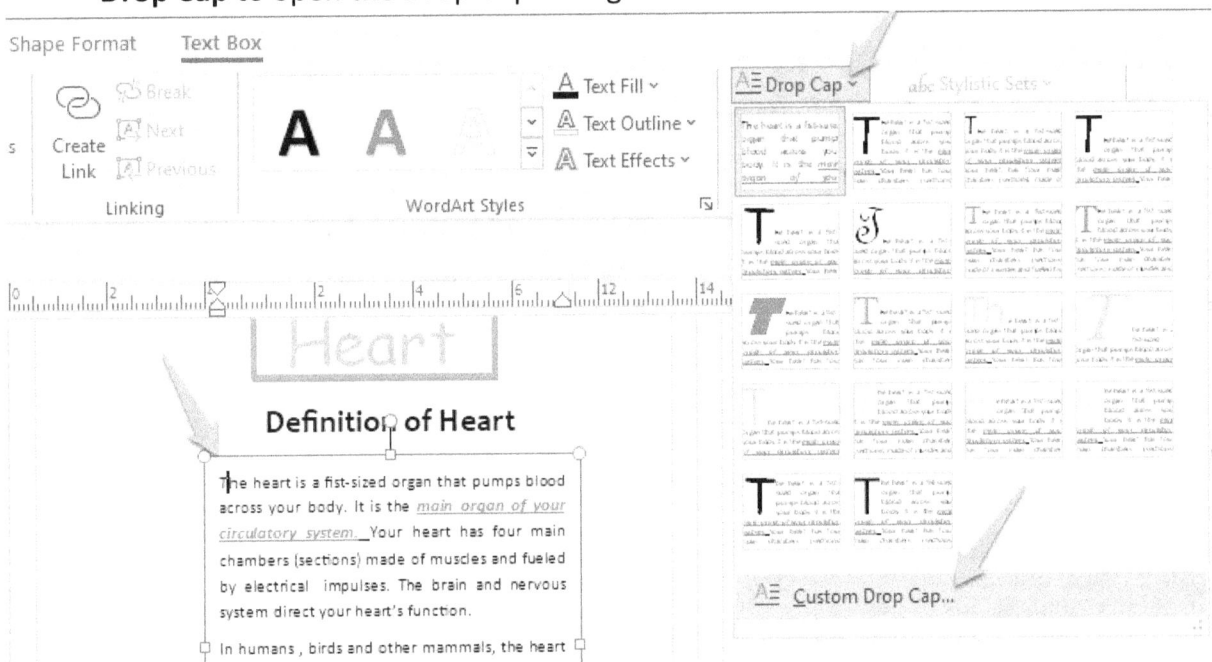

4) You can alter the **size of letters** to fit the drop cap into the paragraph inside the Drop Cap dialog box, you can also change the color and font of the letters by unchecking each option.
5) Click the **Apply** button to apply the drop cap feature and **OK** to close the dialog box. You play along with the Drop Cap dialog box.

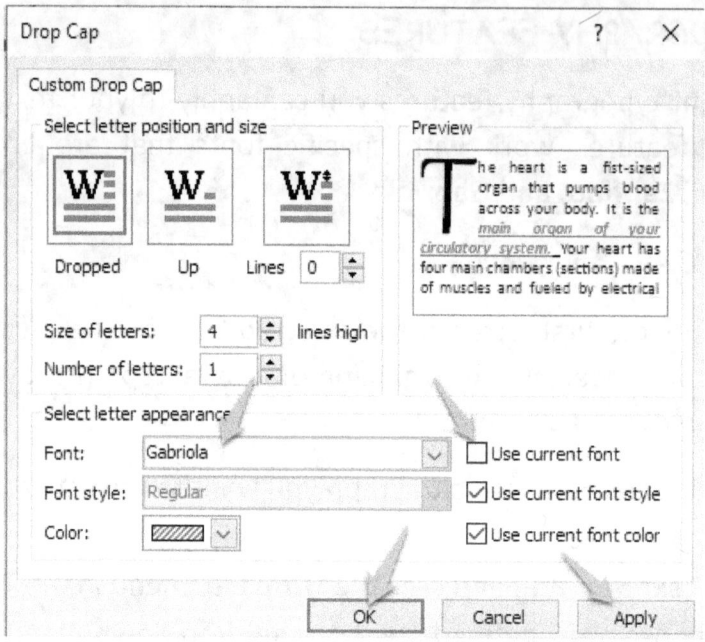

USING STYLISTIC SETS

The stylistic sets let you select one of the various styles for fonts, mostly in the sort of excessive flourishes or serifs. Follow these steps to use the Stylistic set.

1) Highlight the **letter** and click the **"Text Box"** tab.
2) Click the **Stylistic Sets** menu in the Typography group and pick one option on the drop-down menu. I used **Gabriola** font in this case. Stylistic Sets don't work for all the fonts.

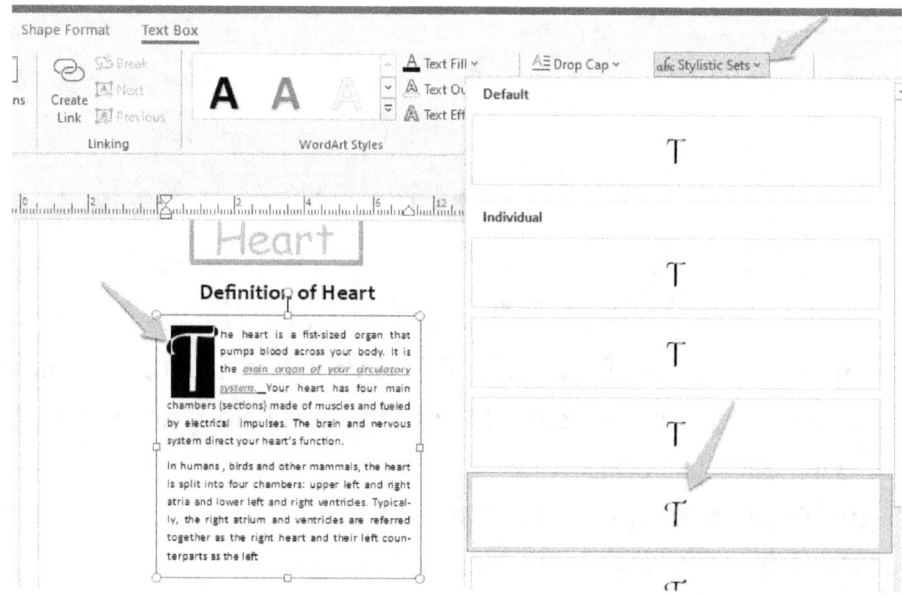

3) You can also use stylistic sets on words. it is very good for headings and titles. I used Gabriola font in this case as well. You can try other fonts

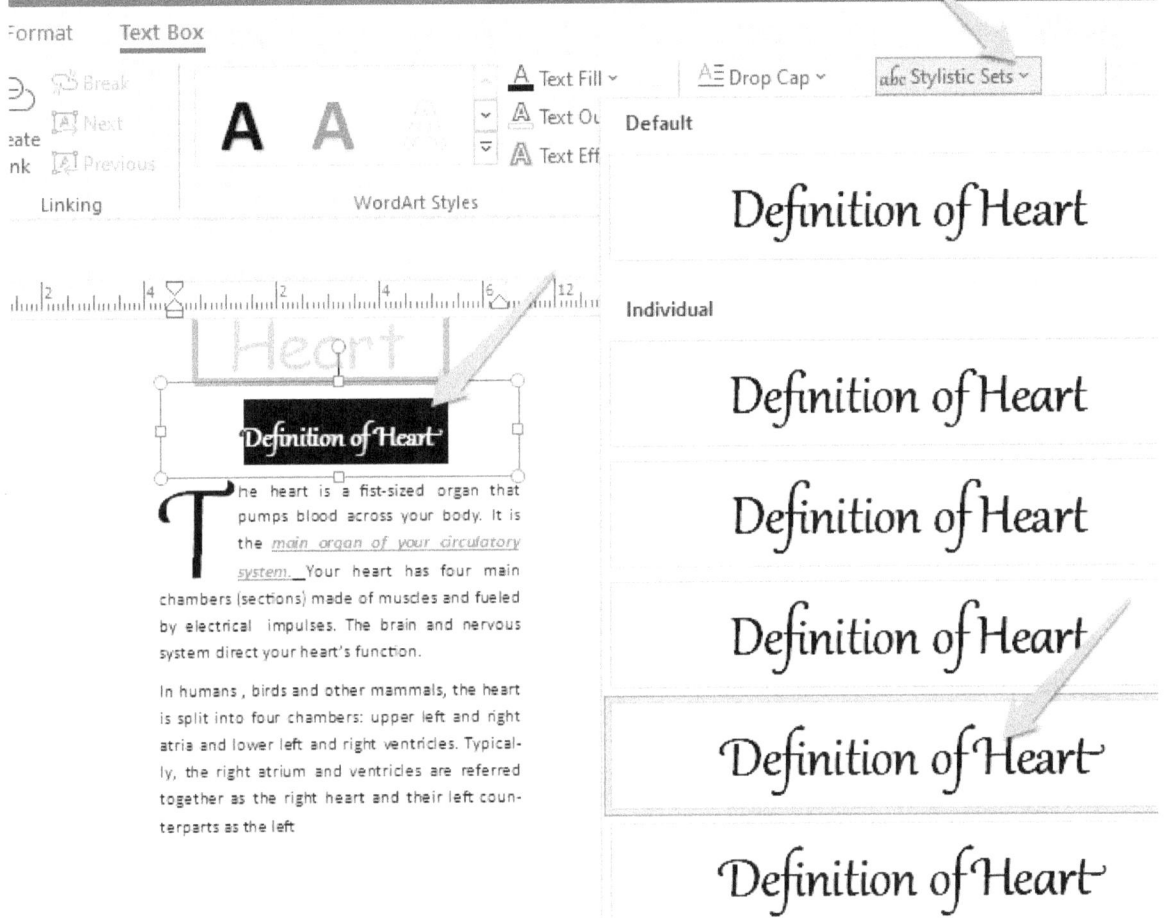

USING LIGATURES

Ligatures join a specific combination of letters for convenient reading. There are many ligatures, the most common are the following: **st, th, ff, ct, fi, sp, ffi,** and so on.

$$AE \rightarrow \text{Æ} \quad ij \rightarrow ij$$
$$ae \rightarrow \text{æ} \quad st \rightarrow st$$
$$OE \rightarrow \text{Œ} \quad ft \rightarrow ft$$
$$oe \rightarrow \text{œ} \quad et \rightarrow \&$$
$$ff \rightarrow ff \quad fs \rightarrow \text{ß}$$

do the following to use Ligature:

1) Highlight the **character** and click the **"Text Box"** tab.
2) Click the **Ligatures** menu and choose the ligature type you want.

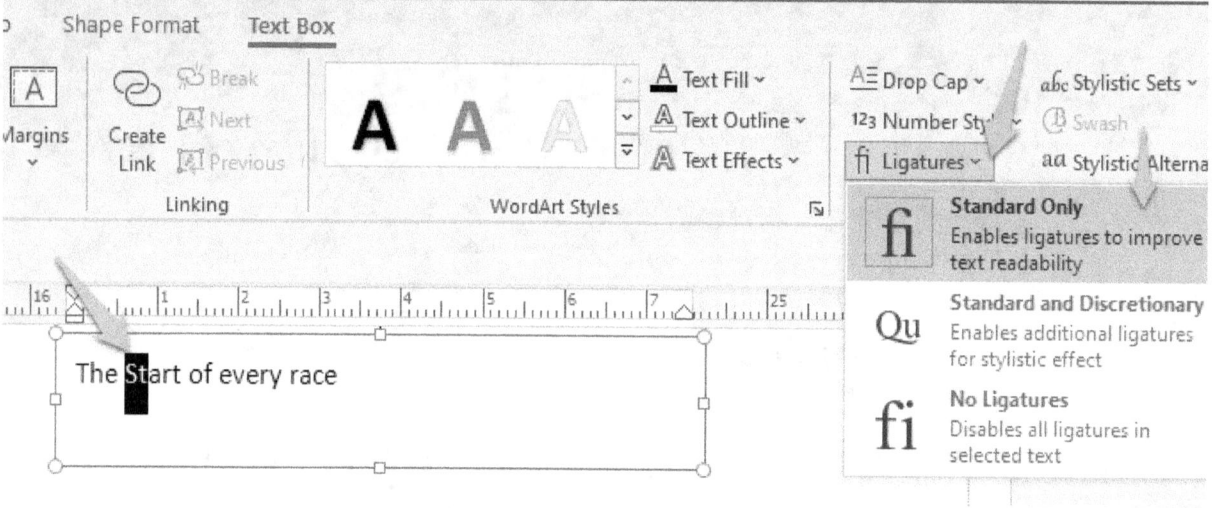

USING STYLISTIC ALTERNATES

The Stylistic alternates offer various versions for certain letters. Follow these steps to use the stylistic alternates:

1) Highlight the **character** and click the **"Text Box"** tab.
2) Click the **Stylistic Alternates** menu and choose any style on the drop-down.

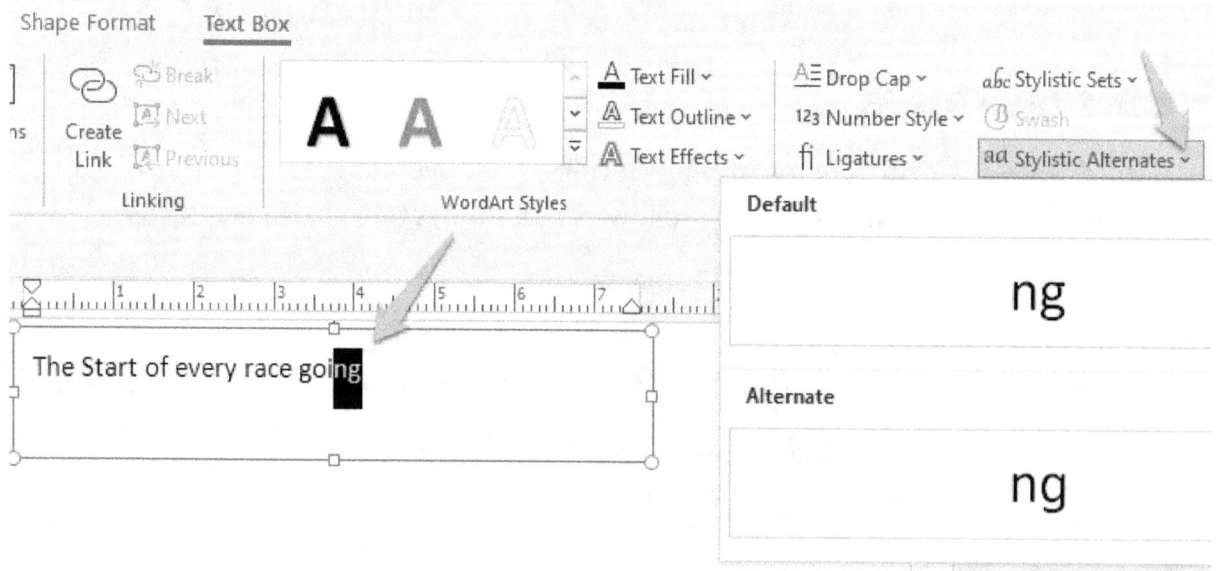

WORKING WITH TEXT EFFECTS

There are various text effects you can apply to your text, some of the text effects are drop shadows, bevels, and reflection on your text, you can also add fill and outline color and change the style of the text.

APPLY SHADOW/REFLECTION/GLOW ON THE TEXT

1) Highlight the **text** on which you want to apply shadow.
2) Click the **"Text Box"** tab and click the **Text Effect** menu.
3) Choose an effect from the list and add a **shadow, reflection, bevel, or glow** to the text.

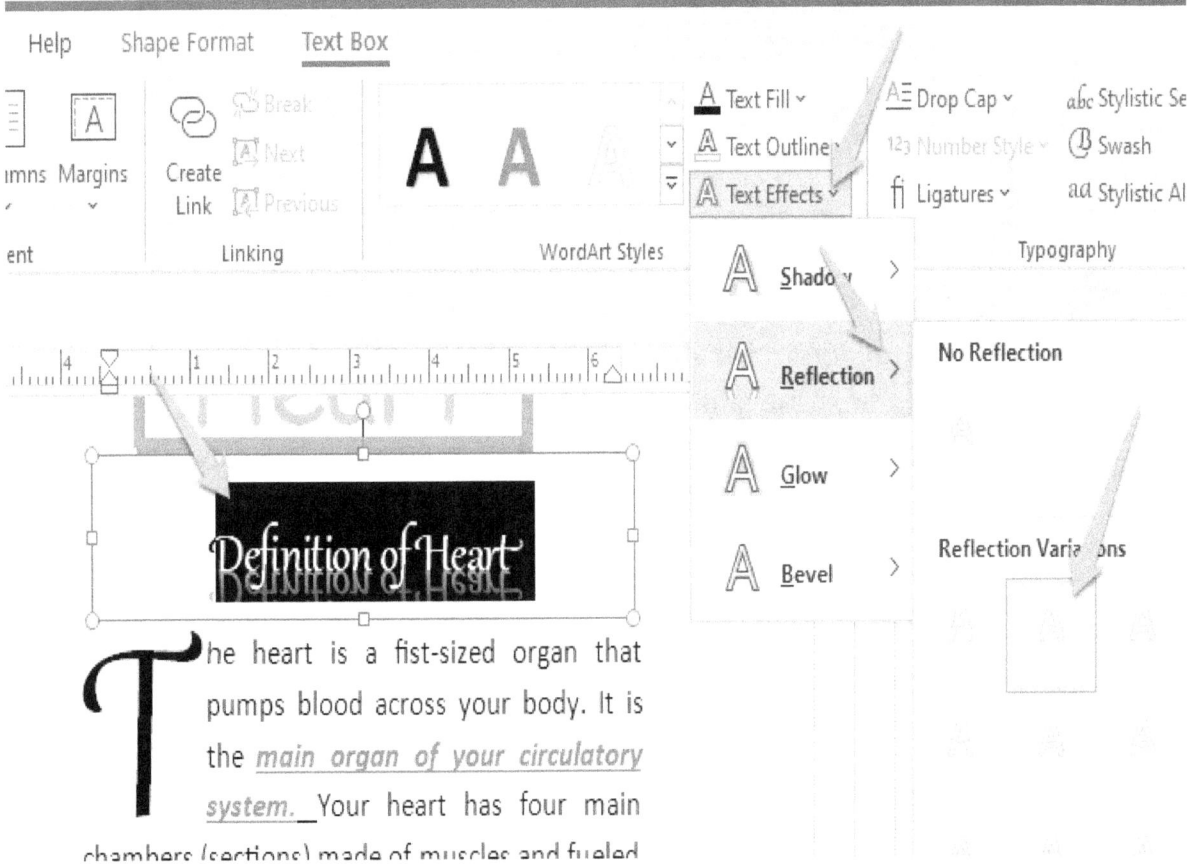

ADDING TEXT OUTLINE

1) Highlight the **text** on which you want to apply the outline.
2) Click the **"Text Box"** tab and click the **Text Outline** menu.
3) Choose a **color** from the **Text Outline** drop-down menu.

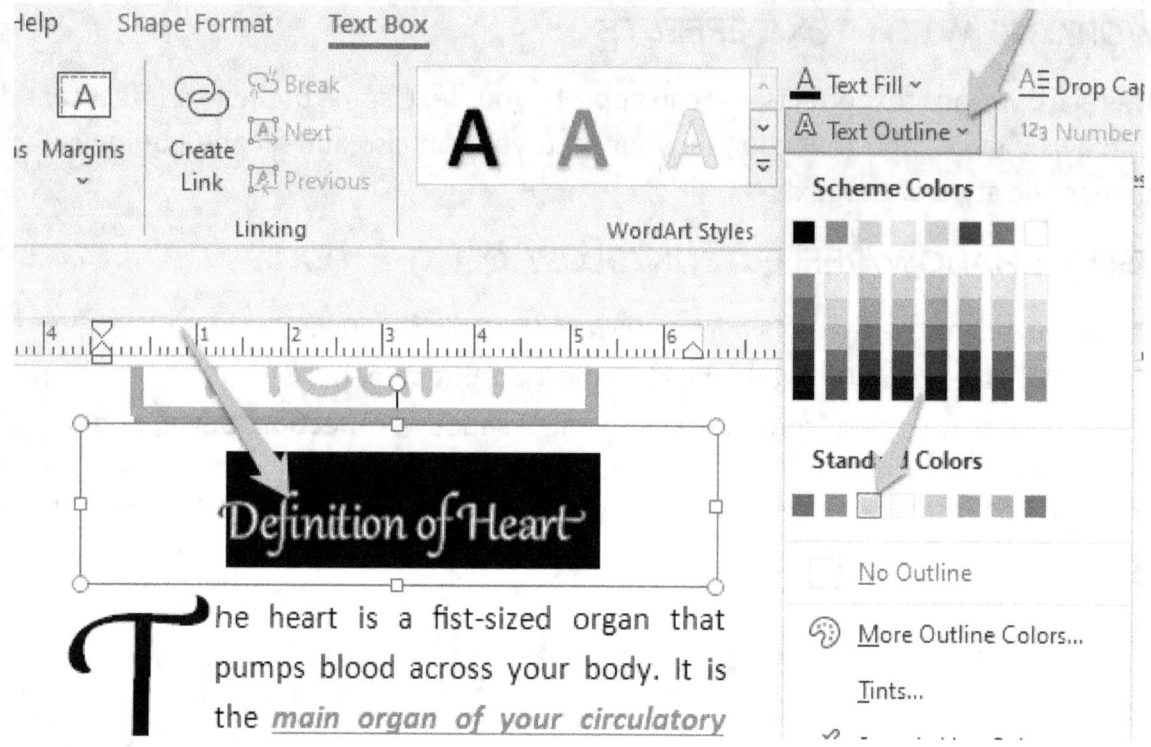

USING WORDART STYLES

1) Highlight the **text** on which you want to apply wordart style
2) Click the **"Text Box"** tab and choose a **style** from the wordart.
3) To access more wordart styles, click the **More** button (down arrow) in the Wordart group.

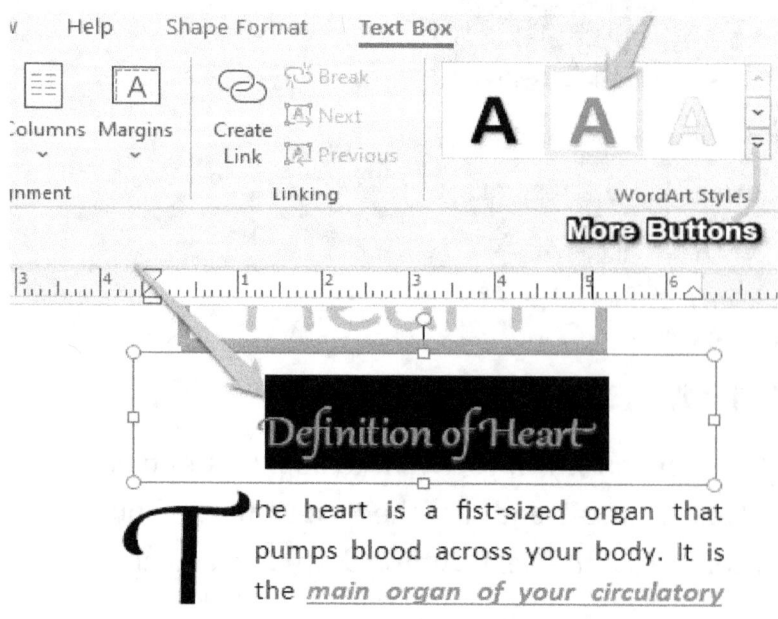

4) The complete list of the wordart styles displays on the screen.

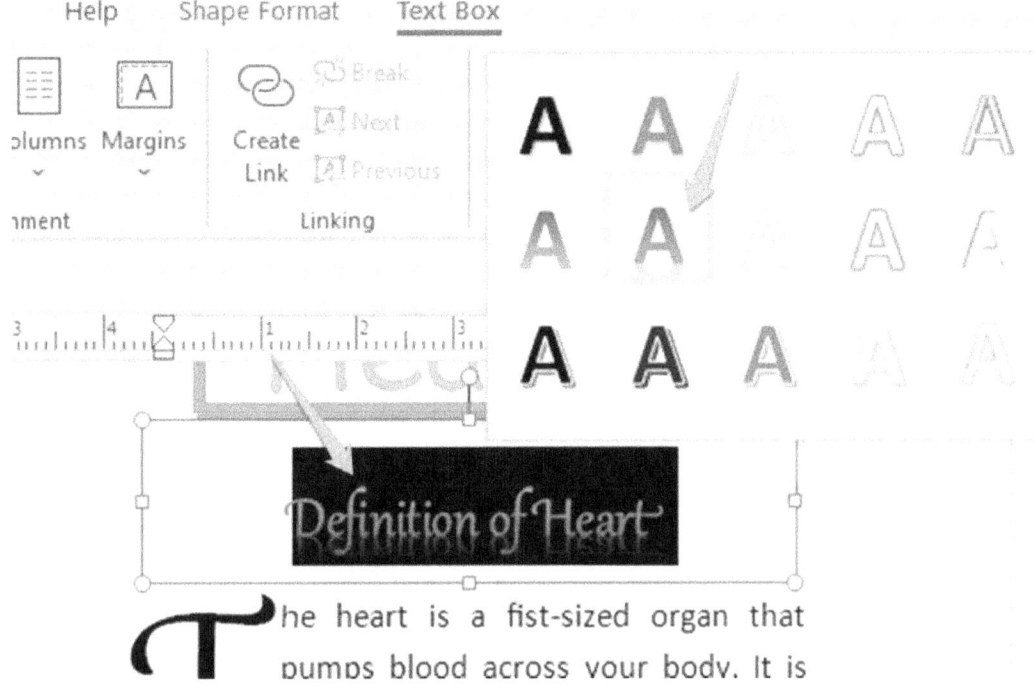

5) Choose your **preferred style** from the available preset styles.

FORMATTING THE TEXT BOXES

Just like the text, you can also add a **shadow, bevel,** and **reflection** to your text boxes. You can add a fill, outline, and change the style of the text box.

APPLYING BACKGROUND COLOR TO THE TEXT BOX

1) Select the **text box** you want to format with the background color.
2) Click the **"Shape Format"** tab and click the **Shape Fill** menu.
3) Choose the **color** you want on the drop-down menu.

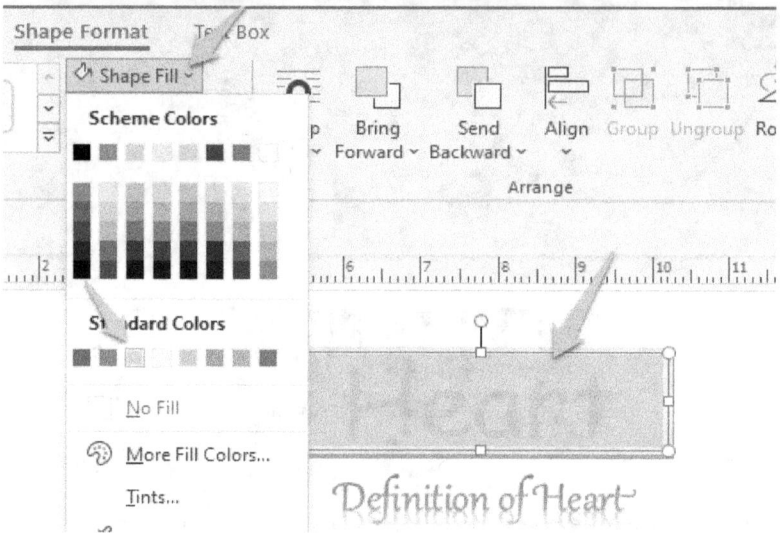

APPLYING BORDER TO THE TEXT BOX

1) Select the **text box** you want to apply with the border
2) Click the **"Shape Format"** tab and click the **Shape Outline** menu.
3) Choose the **color** you want on the drop-down menu.

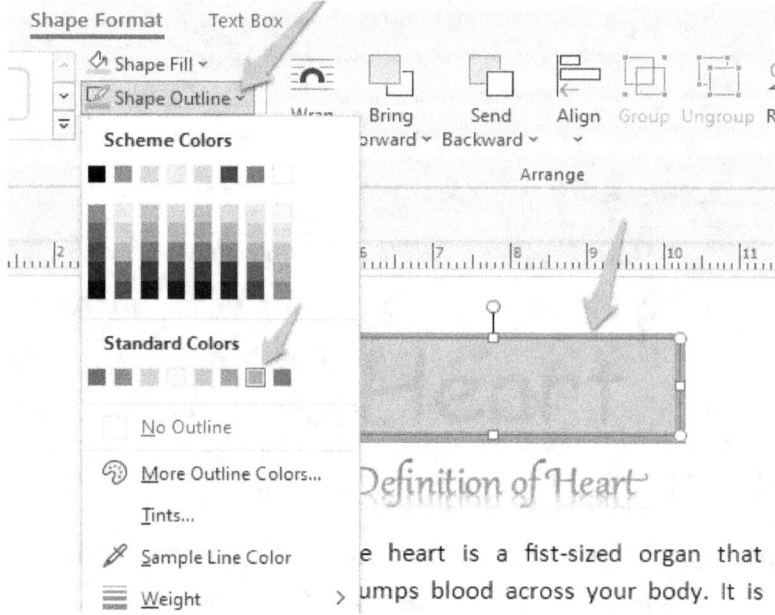

APPLYING EFFECT (SHADOW, GLOW, OR REFLECTION) TO THE TEXT BOX

1) Select the **text box** on which you want to apply shadow.
2) Click the **"Shape Format"** tab and click the **Shape Effects** menu.
3) Choose any effect (**shadow, glow, bevel, or reflection**) on the drop-down menu.

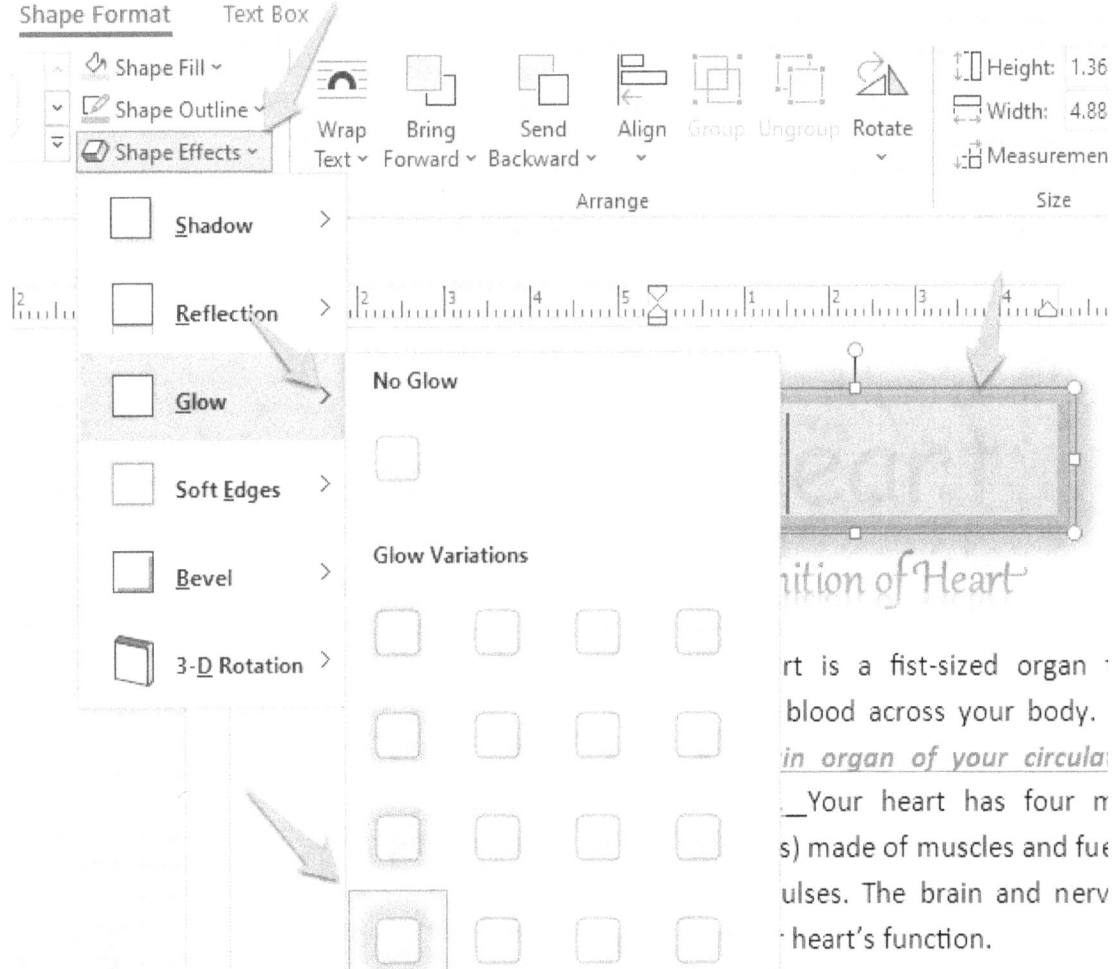

APPLYING STYLE ON THE TEXT BOX

Publisher offers you preset styles you can use to beautify your text boxes. Use these steps to apply the style to your text box.

1) Select the **text box** you want to format with style.
2) Click the **"Shape Format"** tab and click the down arrow beside **Shape Styles** to access the whole style.

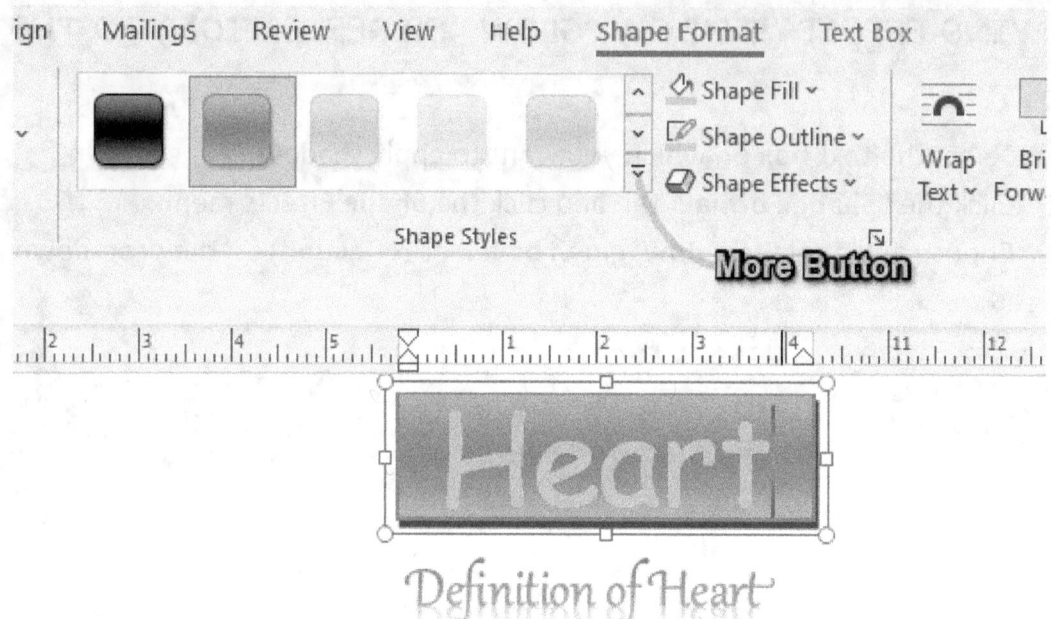

3) Choose the **style** on the fly-out list.

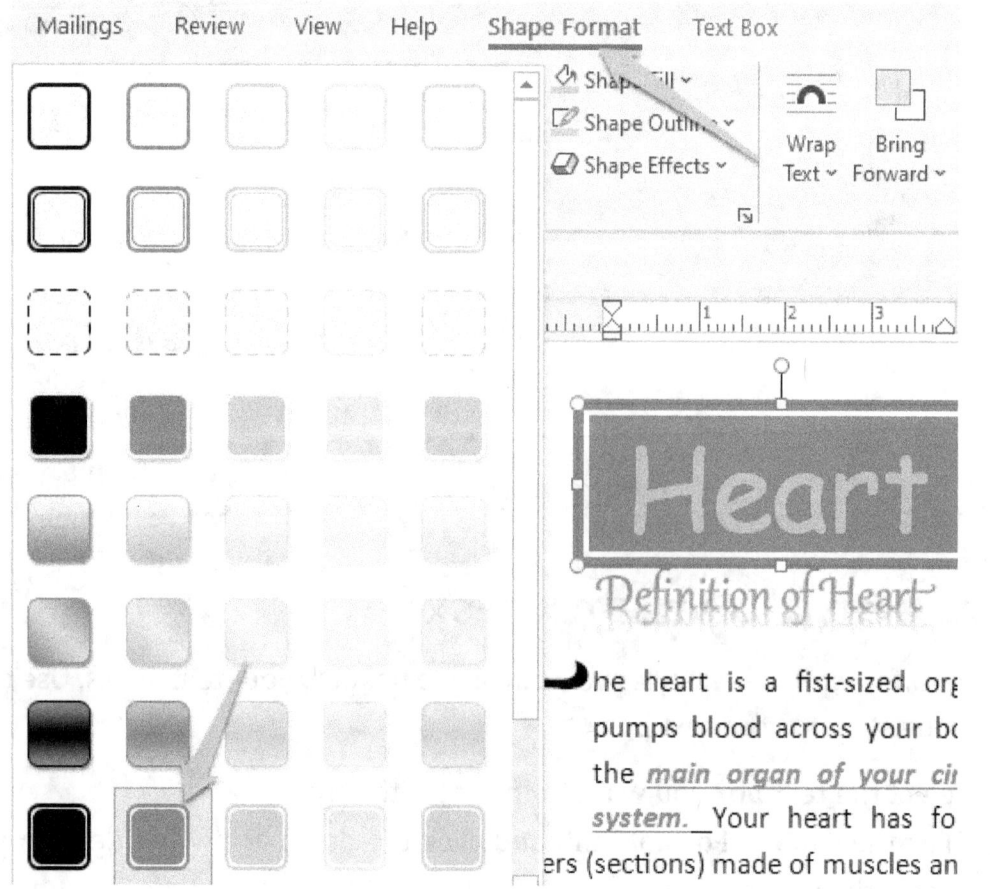

ADJUSTING TEXT BOXES

You can rotate, resize, and move your text boxes, you can also change the **text direction, margins,** and **alignment**.

RESIZING THE TEXT BOX

1) Select the **text box,** the handles appear around the text box.
2) Click and drag any of the **handles** to resize the text box to the size you want.

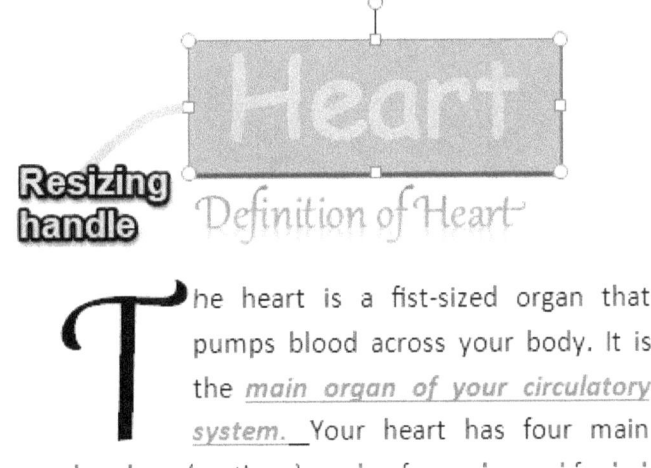

MOVING THE TEXT BOX

1) Click to select the **text box**, place the cursor around the text box, and wait until it turns into a **four-headed arrow.**
2) Drag the text box to any location within the page.

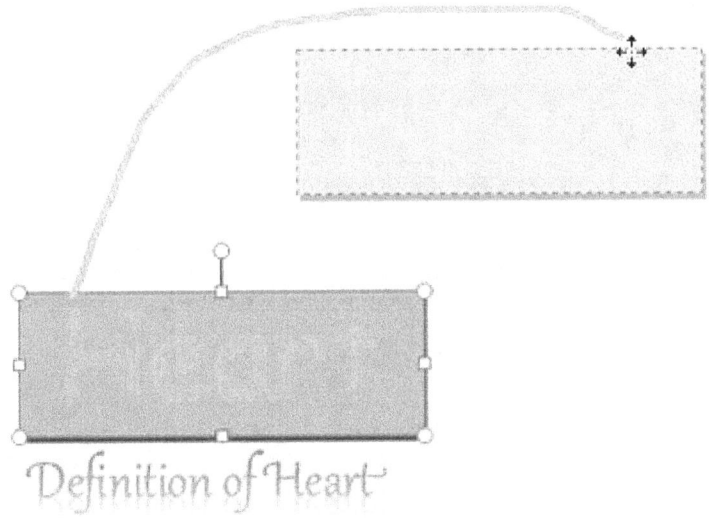

ROTATING TEXT BOX

1) Click and drag the **rotate handle** at the top middle of the text box.
2) Drag the **mouse** to the right or left to adjust the rotation.

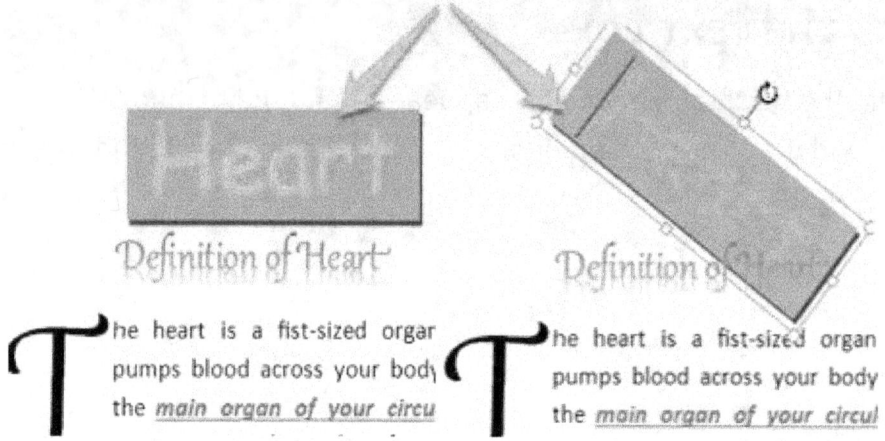

CHANGING TEXT DIRECTION

To change the text direction with the text box with the following steps:

1) Select the **text box** and click the **"Text Box"** tab.
2) Click **Text Direction** in the Text group.

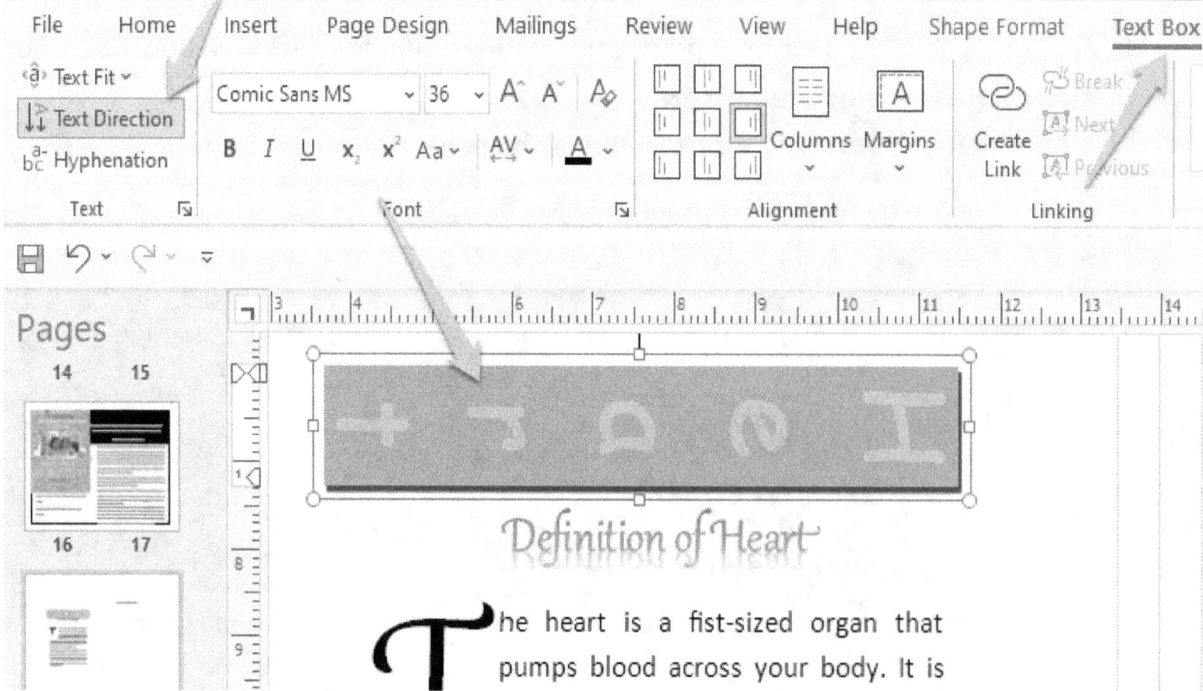

TEXT AUTOFIT

You can conveniently auto-size and fit text within the text boxes. Follow the steps below to Autofit text inside the text box:

1) Select the **text box** you want to adjust and click the **"Text Box"** tab.
2) Click the **Text Fit** menu and select any of the options on the drop-down menu as explained below:

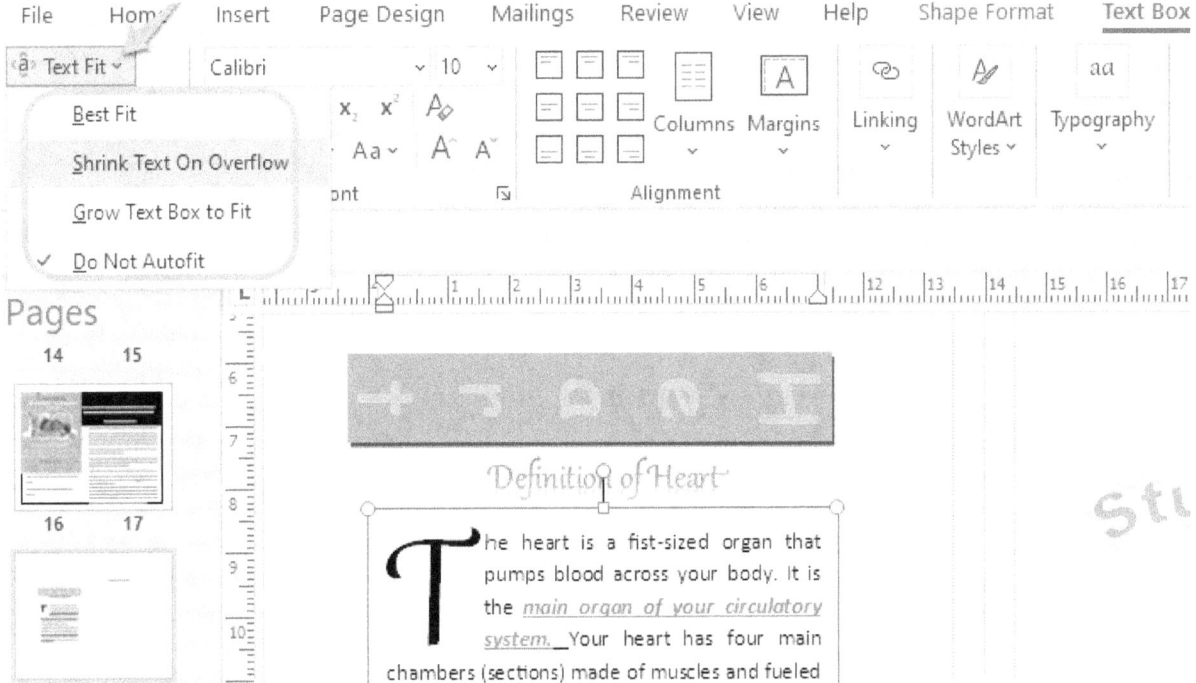

- **Best Fit** increases or decreases the text to fit it within a text box.
- **Shrink Text** on Overflow shrink the text automatically as you type to fill the size of the text box.
- **Grow text box** automatically increases the size of the text box based on the size of the text.
- **Do not Autofit** does not change the text or text box size. It is the default option.

ADJUSTING TEXT BOX MARGIN

Margins represent the space between the text and the edge of the text box. You can alter the margin of a text box.

1) Click the **text box** whose margin you want to adjust

2) Click the **"Text Box"** tab and click the **Margins** menu.
3) You can choose one of the four **Presets** or click the **"Custom margins"** to access the **Format Text Box** dialog box.

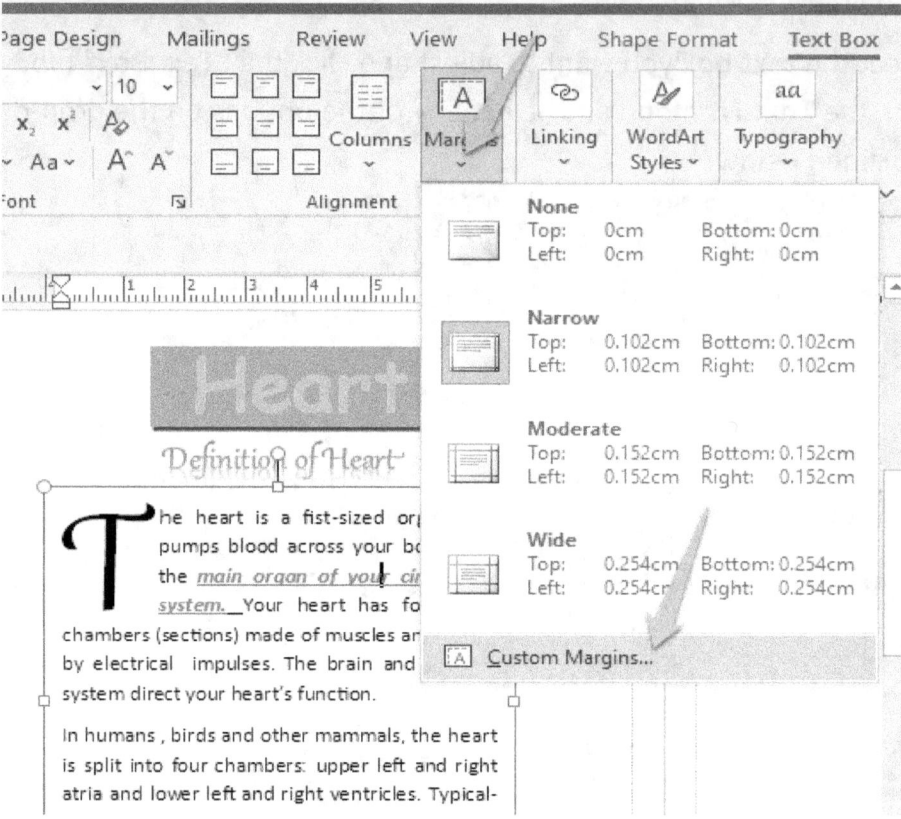

4) You can adjust any of the four margins in the Text Box Margin heading.

SPECIFYING TEXT BOX ALIGNMENT

You can specify the alignment you want for the text inside the text box; the alignment may be to the right, middle, left, top, center, or bottom.

Follow the steps itemized below to specify text box alignment.

1) Click the **text box** and click the **"Text Box"** tab.
2) Choose the **alignment** icon you want on the Alignment group.

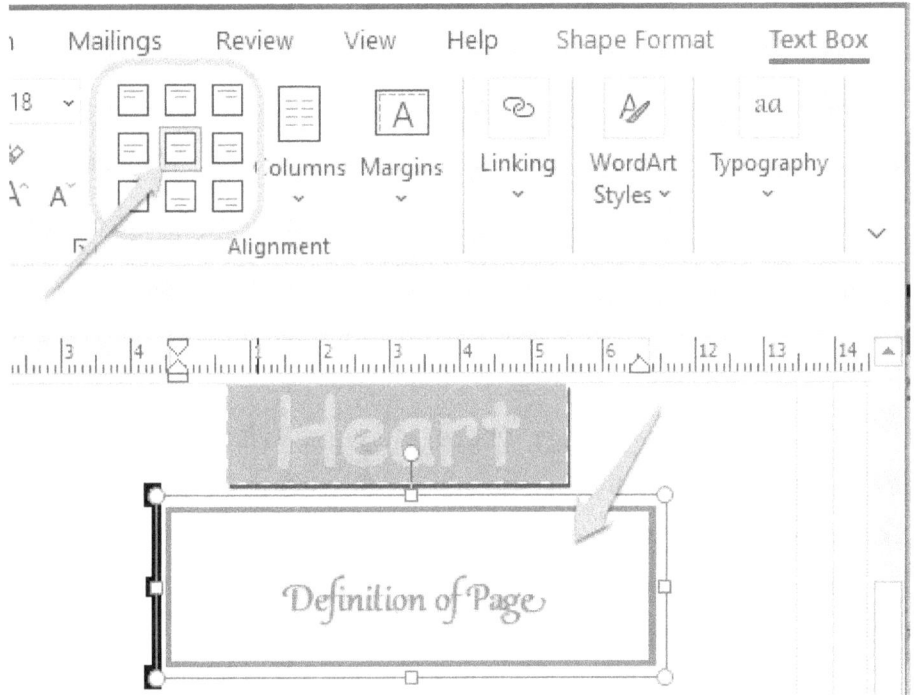

LINKING TEXT BOXES

Sometimes, you will realize that a text box isn't big enough to accommodate all of the text you want to add. When you consume all the room for text, you can link the text boxes. When two or more text boxes are linked, the text will overflow or continue from one text box to the next one. Follow the steps below to link text boxes.

1) Select the **text box**, click the **"Text Box"** tab, and click **Link**.
2) The **cursor** instantly turns to a **"link icon"**.

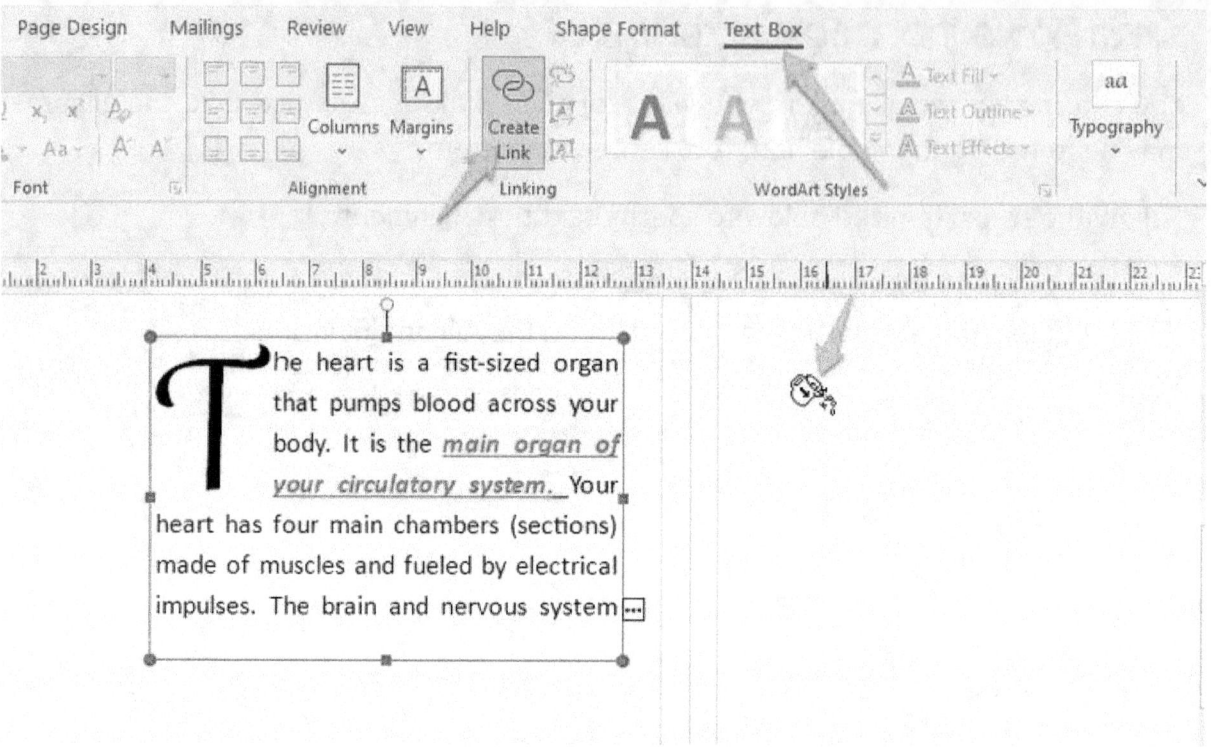

3) Click the position on your page where you want to link to.
4) A new text box will display. As you type your text, the text will flow onto the other text box or if the text box has overflown text already represented by **More Options (...)** at the lower left corner of the text frame, the extra text will flow onto the other text box.

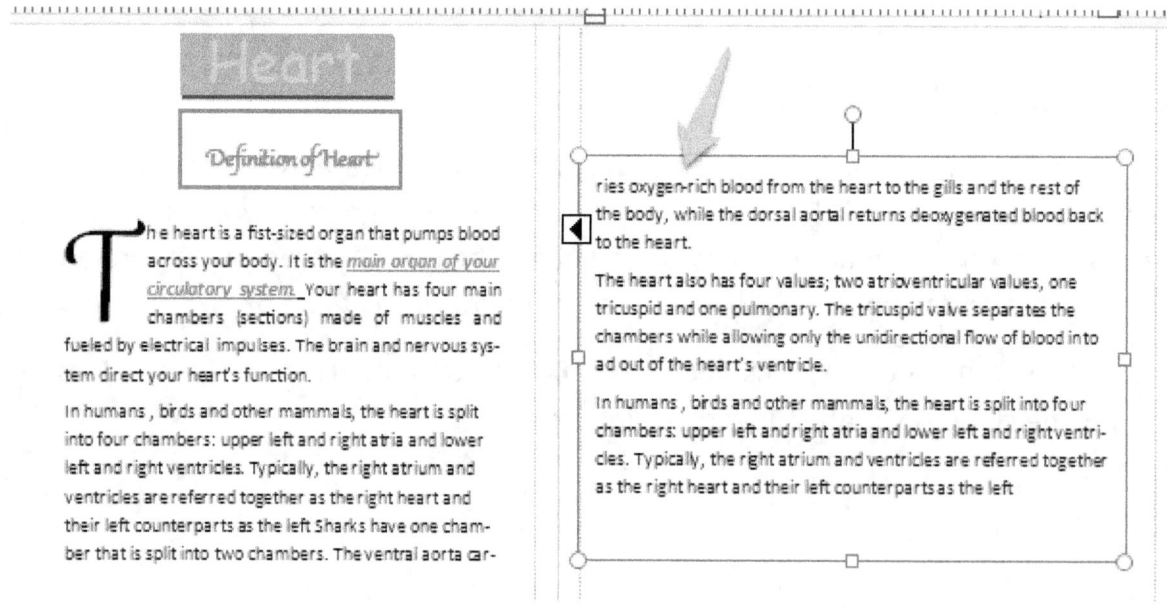

CHAPTER FOUR
INSERTING TABLES

I have added text on "heart function" to this document. Next, I will add a table to explain the text. Follow the steps itemized below to insert the table into your publication.

1) Click the **Insert** tab and click the **Table** menu.
2) Drag over the **number of rows and columns** on the grid that displays to insert a table. I drag over **2 rows and 2 columns** in this case.

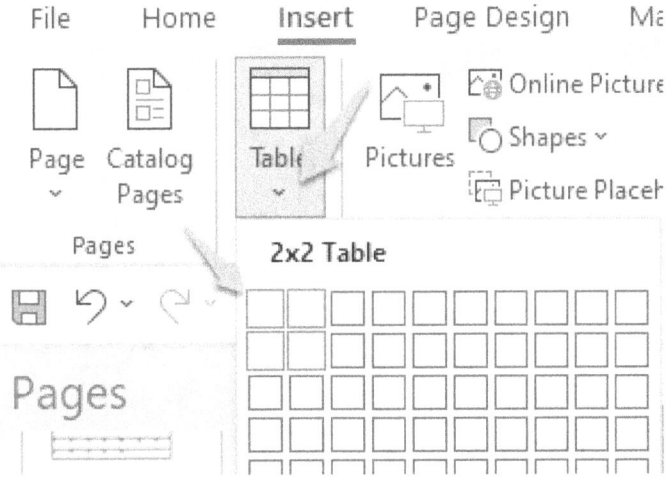

3) This adds **2 rows** and **2 columns** to the document. drag the table to position it and begin typing data into the table.

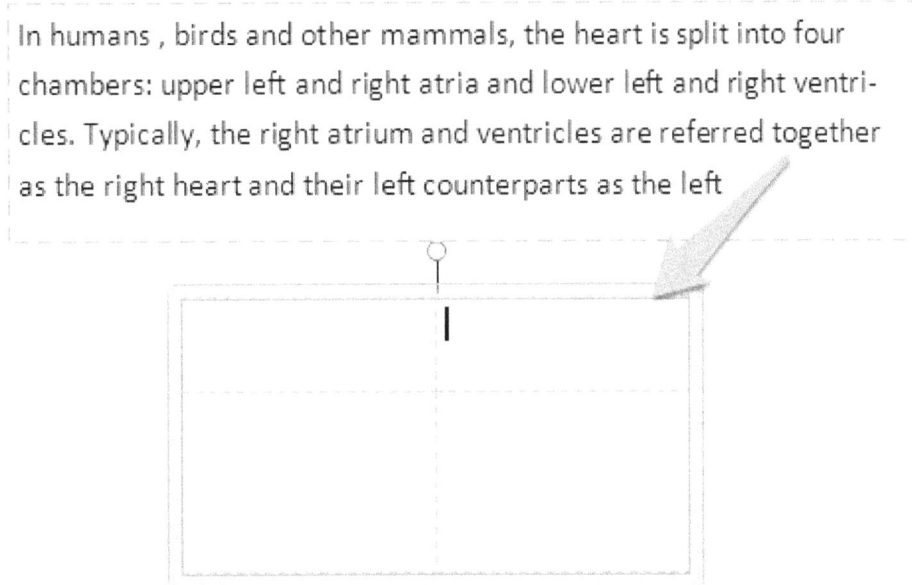

4) Press the **tab** or **arrow keys** to move from cell to cell. When you get to the end of the row, pressing the **tab** key will automatically insert a new row. You can keep on pressing the tab key to continue adding a new row on the last row of the table.

Parts of the Heart	Uses of each part
The right atrium	It receives deoxygenated blood from the body and pumps it to the right ventricle
The right ventricle	It get bloods from the right atrium and pumps it to the lungs to load it with oxygen.
The left atrium	It receives oxygenated blood from the lungs and pumps it to the left ventricle.
The right ventricle	It is the strongest chamber of the heart . It pumps oxygen-rich blood to the rest of the body

RESIZING THE TABLE

- You can resize that table by clicking and dragging one of the **corners of the grey edges**.

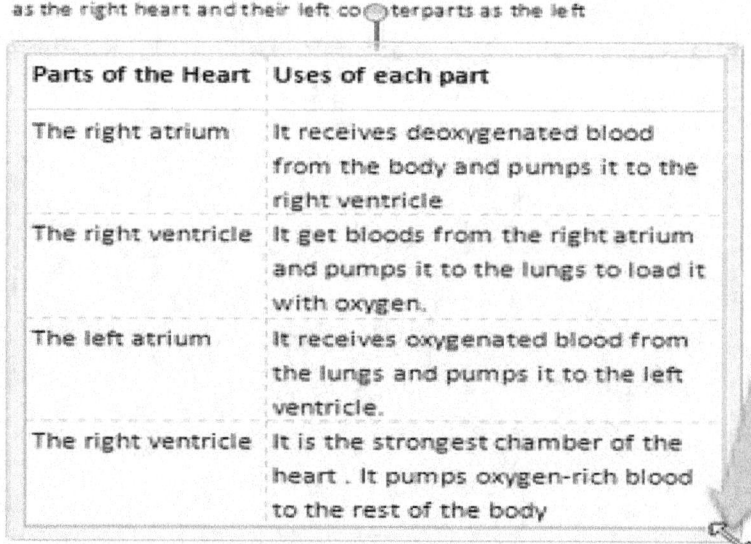

MOVING THE TABLE

- Click anywhere around the table to select it, then click and drag the **grey border** when the four-headed arrow displays to move the table.

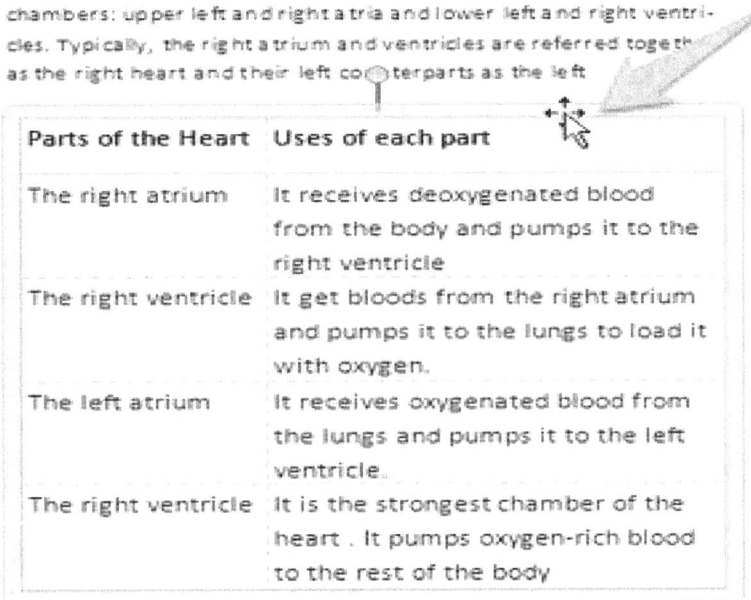

FORMATTING TABLES

Click a table in your document, two tabs will appear which are **the "Table Design" tab,** and the **Layout** tab.

The **Design** tab enables you to select **redefined designs** for your table, such as row and column shading, borders, and colors.

There is a list of designs at the center of the Table design tab. Click the **More** button (**down arrow)** on the lower right of the "Table Formats" panel to access the whole table styles.

In this case, I will select **Brown** headings and **shaded rows** for this table.

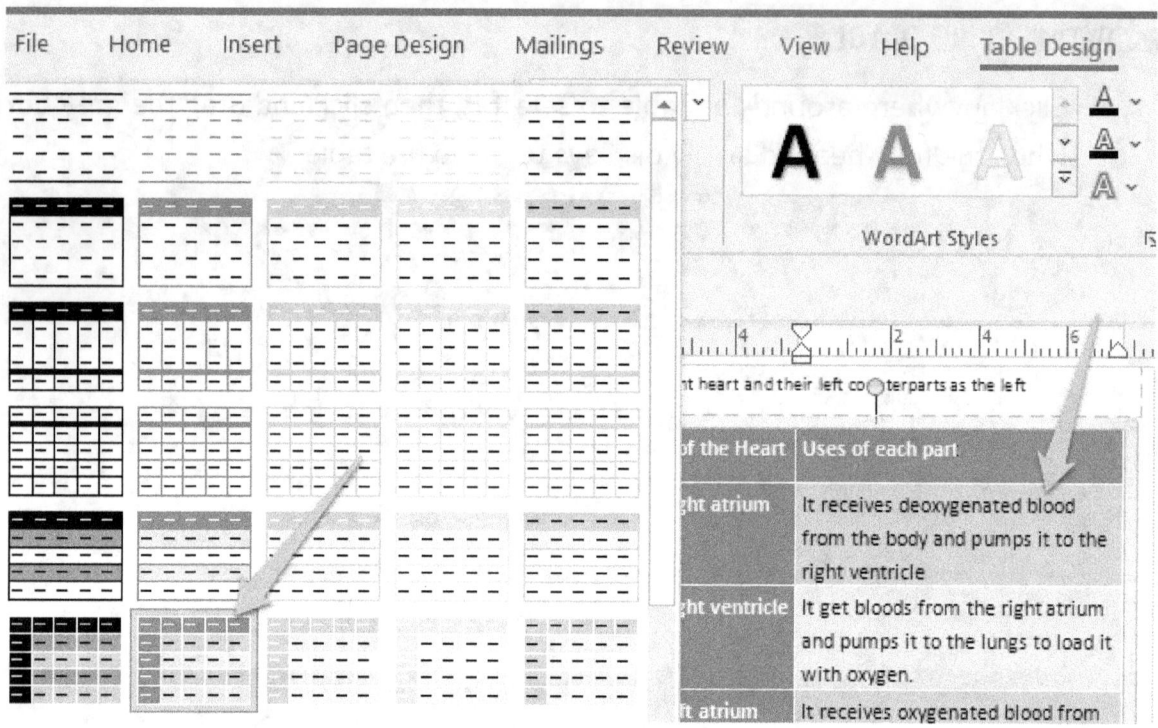

ADDING A COLUMN

A column can be inserted to the left or right side of the table. Follow the steps below to add a column.

1) Click the **column** that will stay on the **left or right side** of the **new column** you want to add.
2) Click the **"Layout"** tab and click the **Insert Left or Insert Right** button.

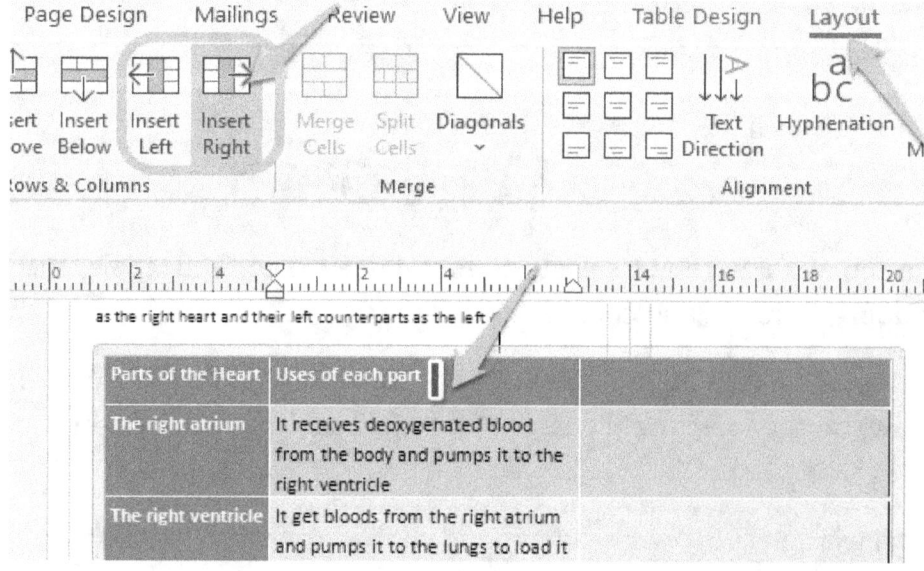

3) A **new column** will be added to your table.

ADDING A ROW

The row can be inserted at the top or below the table. Follow the steps below to add a row.

1) Click the **row** that will stay **above or below** the **new row** you want to add.
2) Click the **"Layout"** tab and click **Insert Above or Insert Below**.

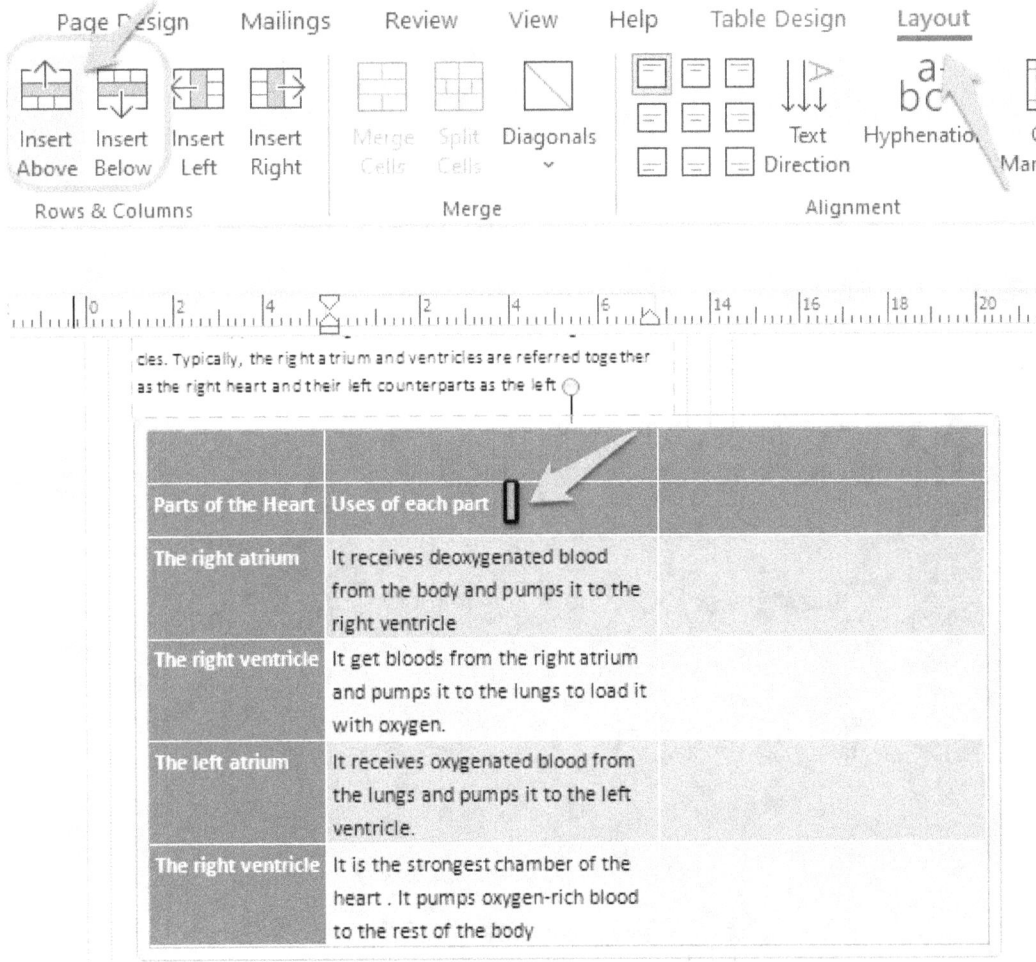

3) A **new row** will be added to your table.

RESIZING ROWS AND COLUMNS

- To resize a row or column, click and drag the **Column or Row** bar **"dividing line"** to resize it.

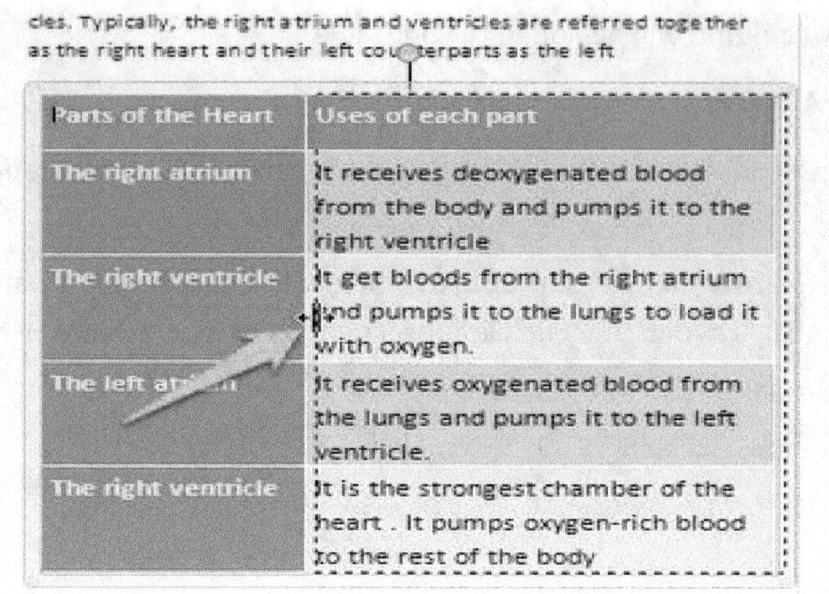

MERGING CELLS

To merge two or more cells, do the following:

1) Select **all the cells** you want to merge.
2) Click the **"Layout"** tab and click **Merge Cells**.

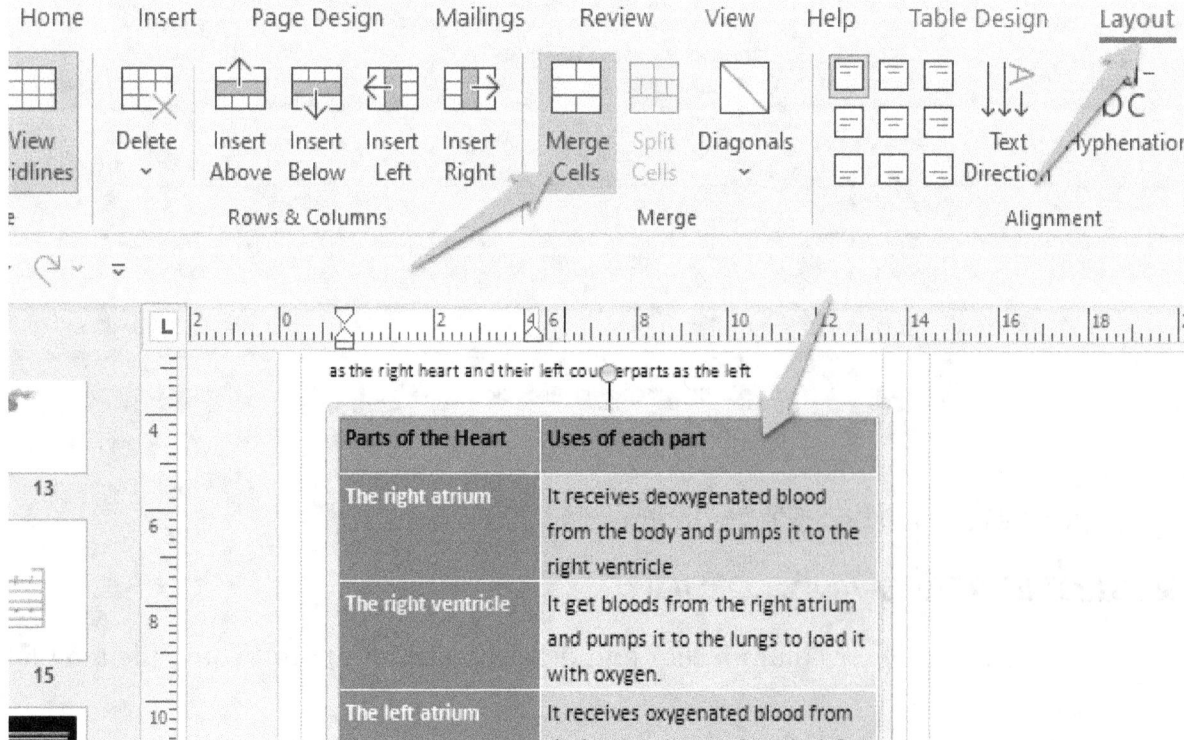

3) The **selected cells** will be merged into a single cell.

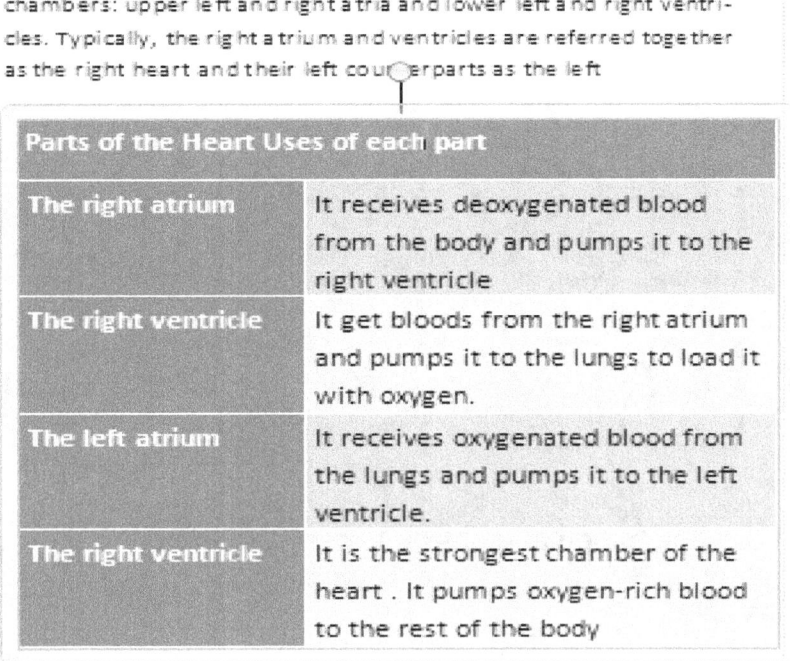

ALIGNING CELL TEXT

You can specify alignment for the text inside the cells of a table. Follow the steps itemized below to specify text alignment within the table's cells.

1) Select the **cells** that have the text you want to align and click the **Layout** tab.

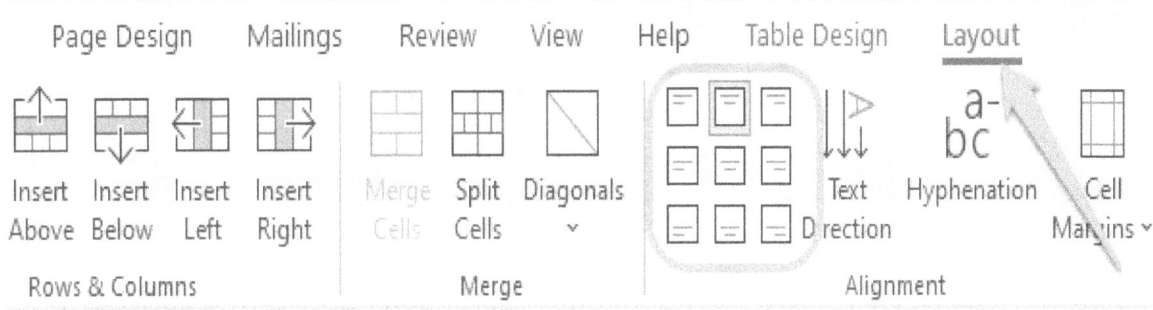

2) Pick any of the **nine boxes** in the **Alignment** group to change the **alignment** for the selected text.
3) Below are **brief tips** on how the **9 alignments** work. Check where each box on the left puts the text in the cells that show on the right side. That is a clue to what each alignment will help you to do.

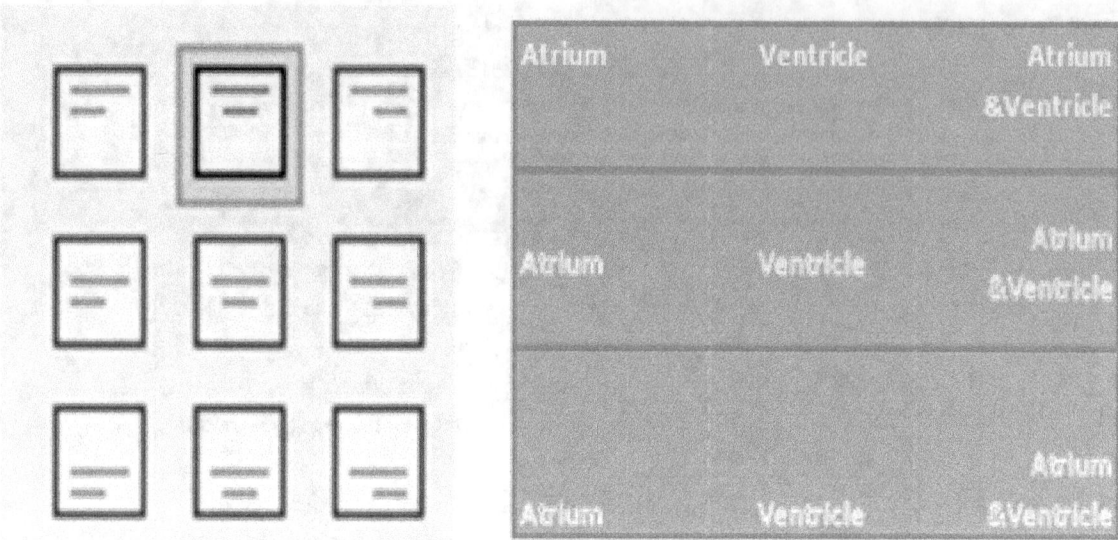

4) You can click the **top middle** button to see its result.

CELL BORDER

1) Select the cells you want to enclose with a **border** and click the **"Table Design"** design tab.
2) Select **thickness** on the Line **Thickness** menu and choose a **Color** on the **Line Color** menu.

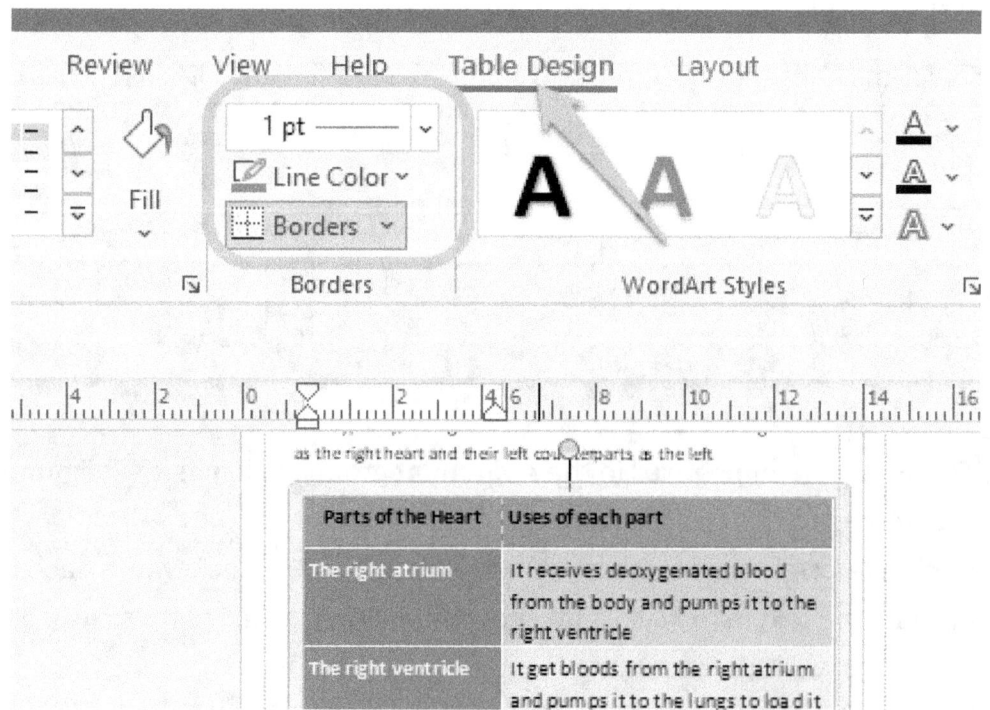

3) Click the **Border** menu and select where you want to place your **border** on the drop-down menu.

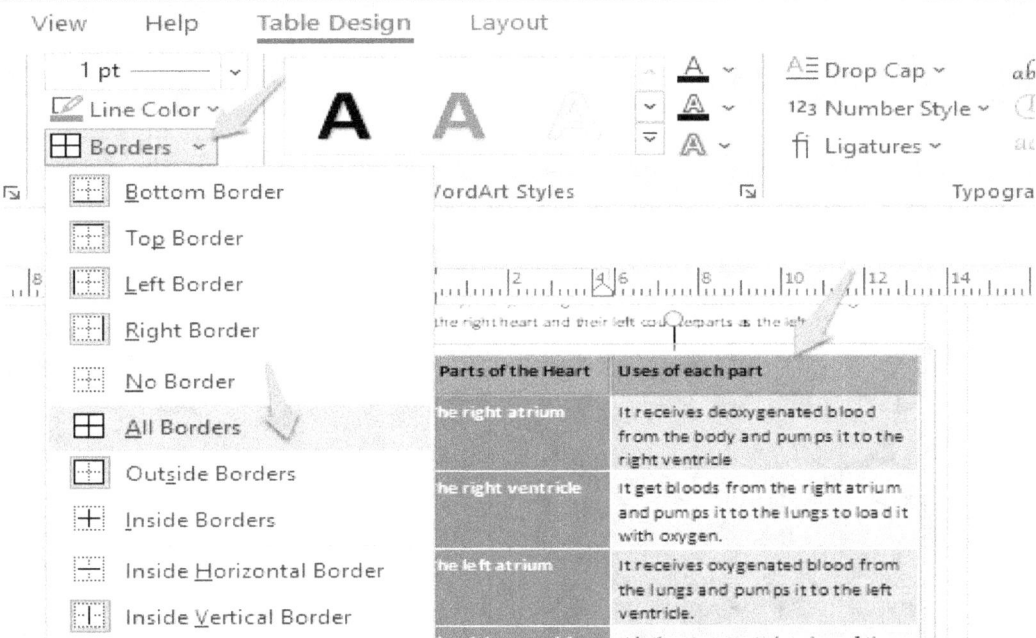

CHANGING CELL COLOR

You can change the cell's color with the following steps:

1) Select the **cell(s)** whose color you want to change.
2) Click the **"Table Design"** tab, click the **Fill** menu, and select a **color** on the fly-out pallet.

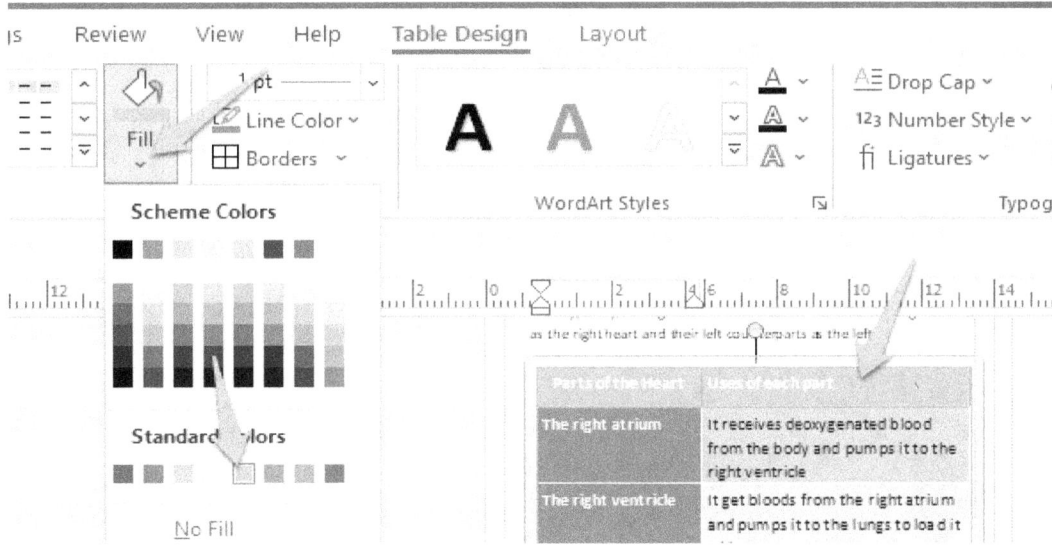

CHANGING TEXT DIRECTION

You can arrange text in your table vertically, you can do this most times for headings.

1) Select the **headings** whose text direction you want to change.
2) Click the **"Layout"** tab and click the **Text Direction** button.

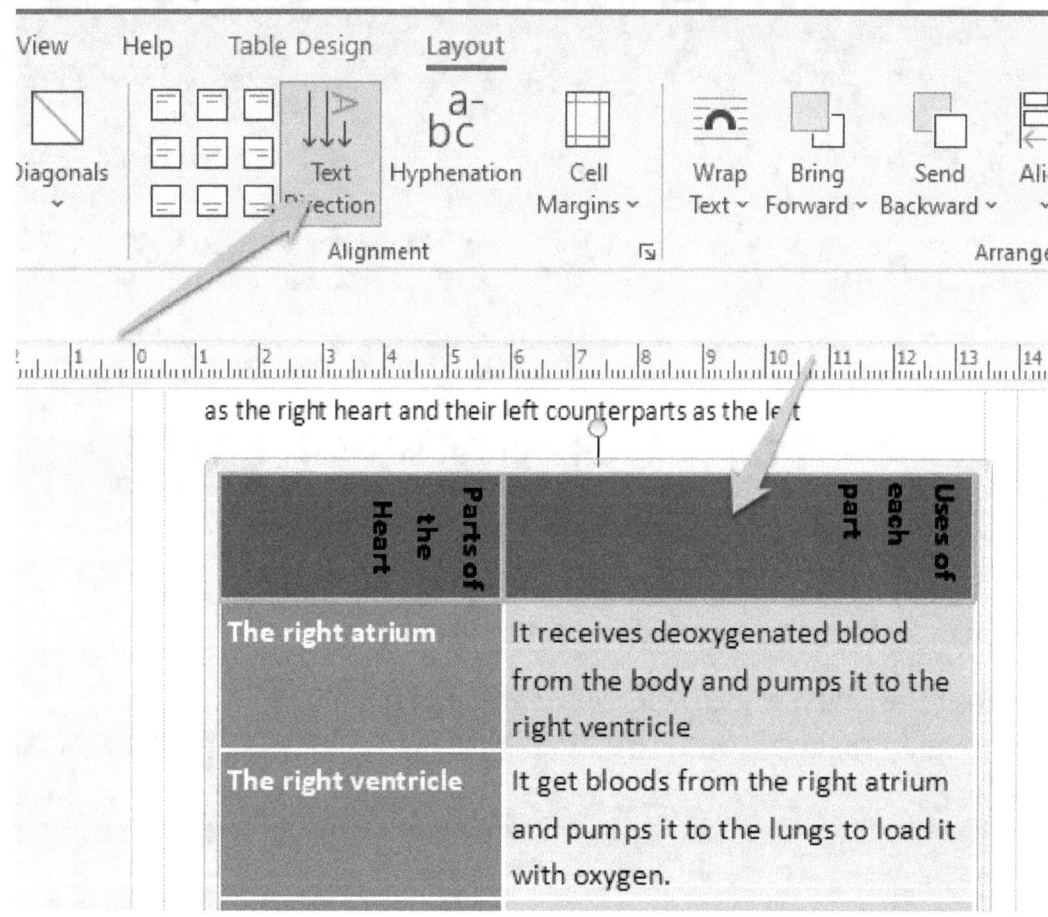

CHAPTER FIVE
GETTING STARTED WITH GRAPHICS

Next, we shall be looking at various ways of adding photos, shapes, and other elements to make your publication colorful.

ADDING PHOTOS

You can add photos to your publication in two ways either by using the photos you stored on your PC or using OneDrive/Internet photos. follow the steps below to add photos from your PC storage to your document.

1) Click the **Insert** tab and click the **Pictures** button.

2) Select the **picture** you want in the **Insert Picture** dialog box and click the **Insert** button.

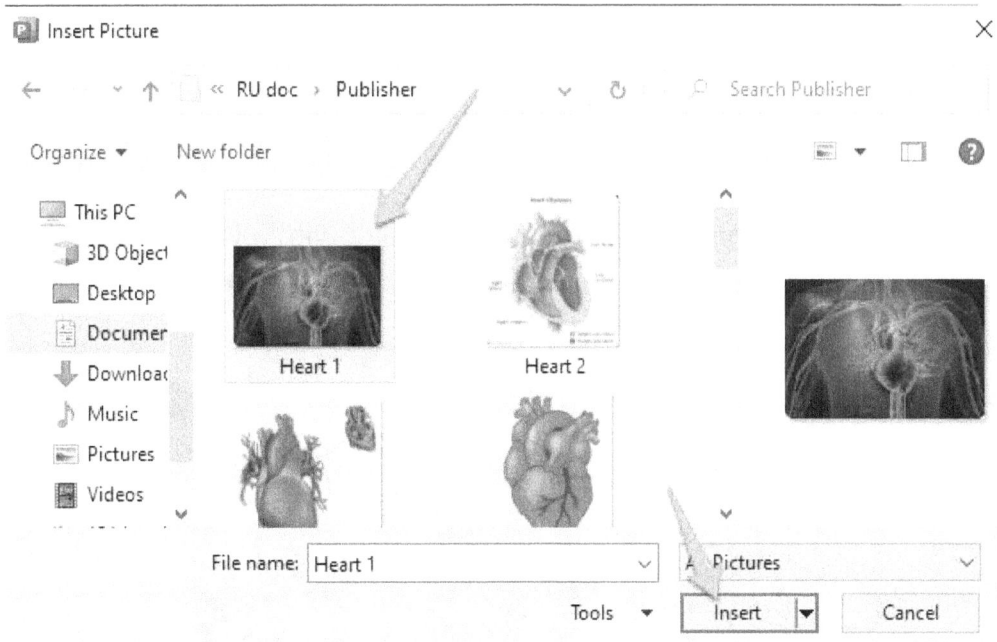

Note: The picture will be placed in your document, most time the picture size may not come in the size you want, you can increase it or reduce it, and next, you will resize your photo.

3) Click the **photo**, **small handles** will display across the photo, the **handles** are called **resizing handles**.

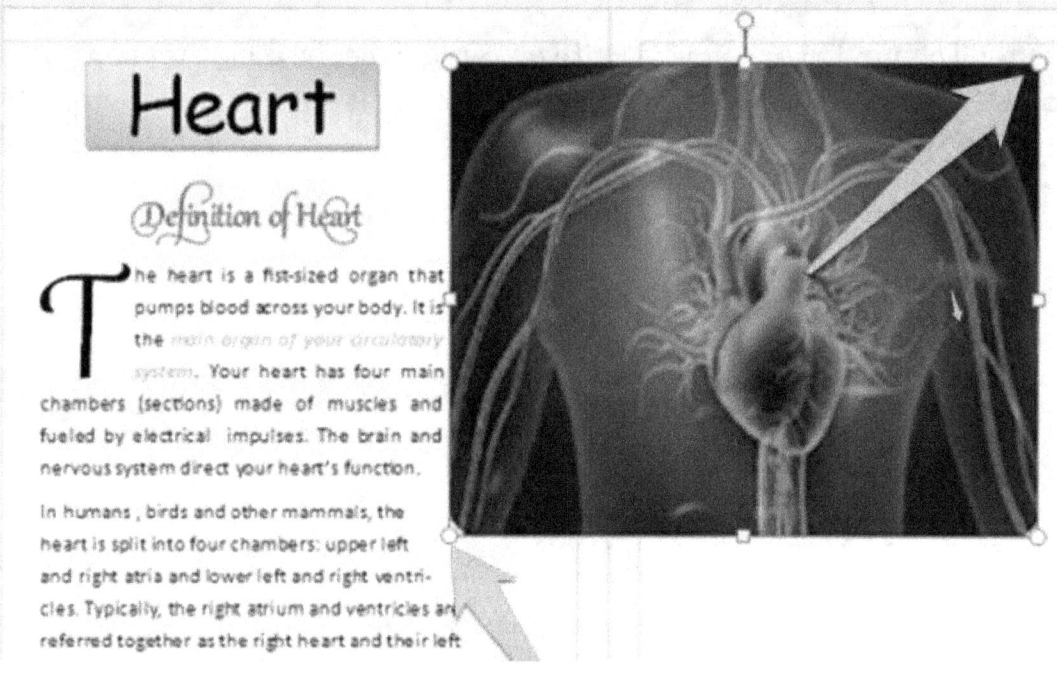

4) Click and drag any of the **resizing handles** to make the photo smaller or bigger as shown below. press down the **Shift** key while resizing to prevent the photo from being distorted.
5) Click and drag the **photo** to place it at any point within your document.

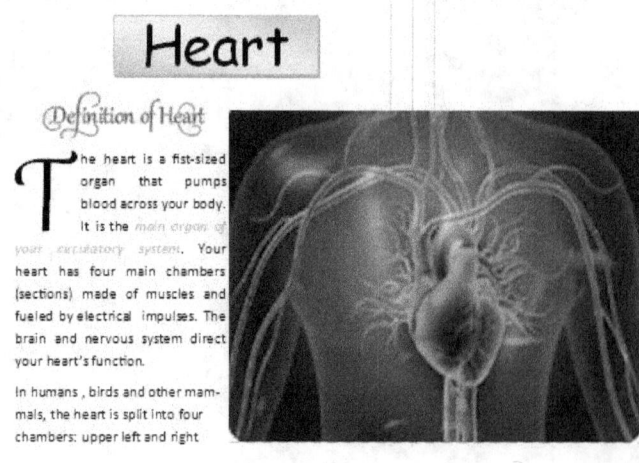

ADDING PHOTOS FROM THE INTERNET

Publisher offers you the privilege to search for images on the internet such as Google, when you get the photos you want, you will download them and store them in your pictures folder. Follow the steps below to add a photo from the internet.

1) Open any **browser** on your PC and type a **keyword** to run a Google search as shown below.
2) Click the **Images** tab and click the **image thumbnail** to view the full size of the image.

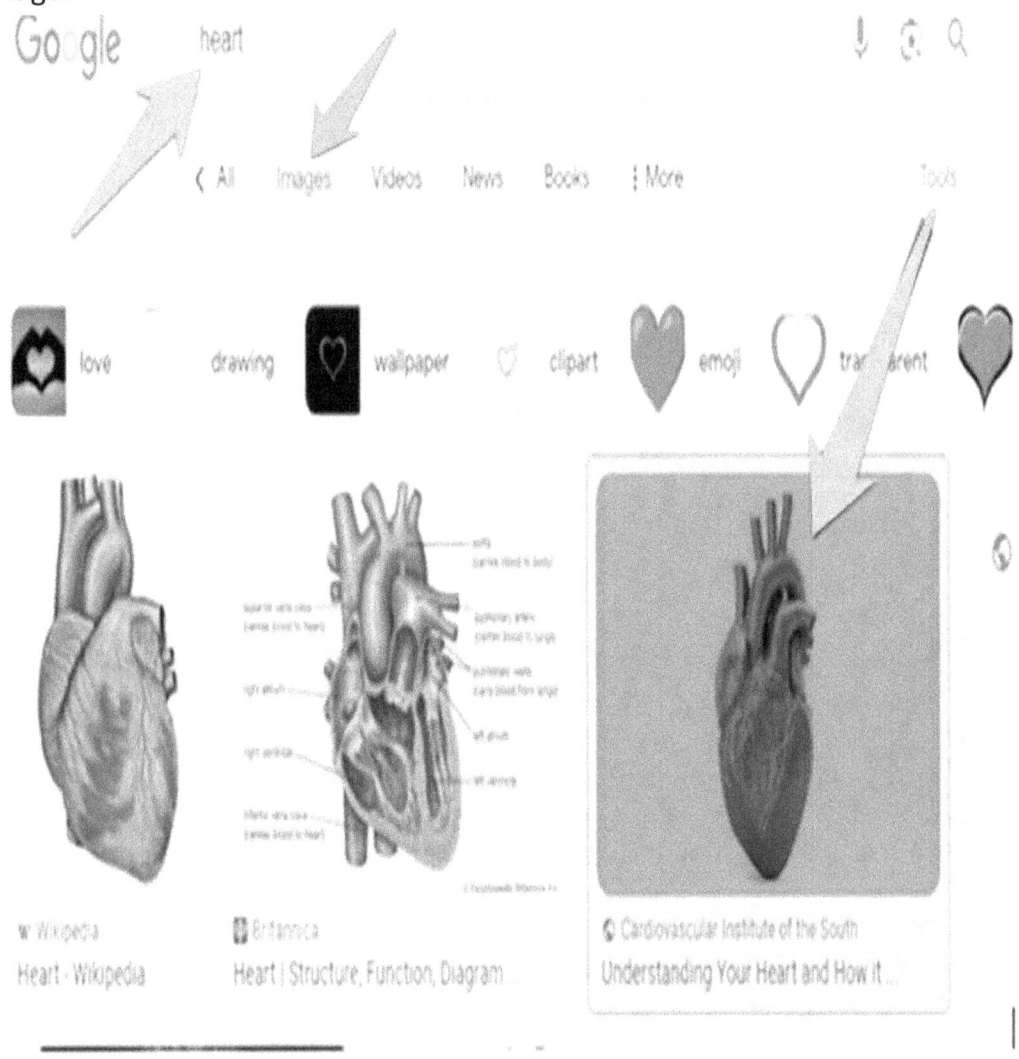

3) Right-click the **image** and choose "**Save Image As**" on the fly-out menu to open the **Save Image** dialog box.

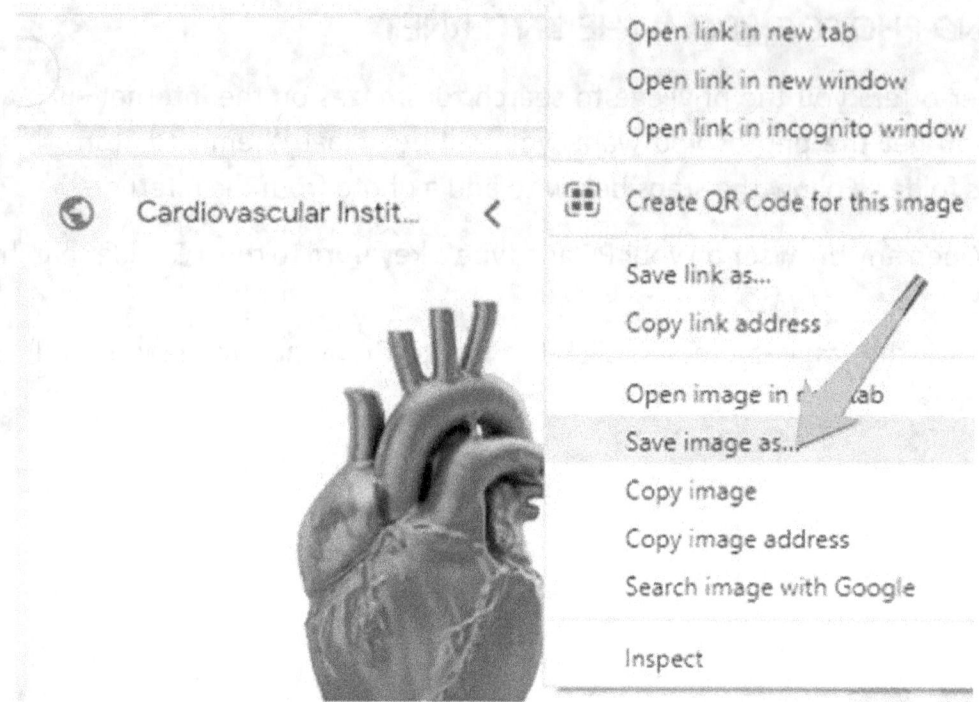

4) Select the **folder** where you want to save your image on your computer or OneDrive folder and click **Save**.

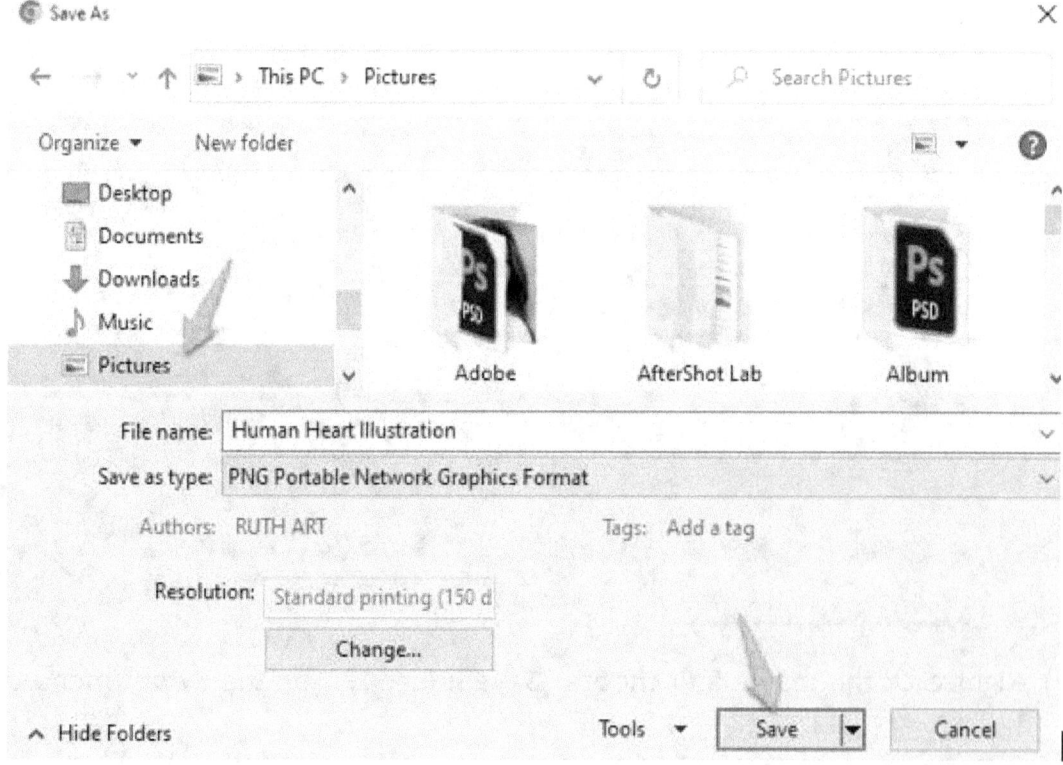

When your photos are stored in your picture folder, you can follow the same process we used in the previous section to add them to your document.

INSERTING CLIPART

In continuation, we shall be adding a new section tagged **"Heart of a Shark"** by using the clipart to demonstrate it. follow the steps below to add a clipart image.

1) Click the **Insert** tab and click the "**Online Pictures**".

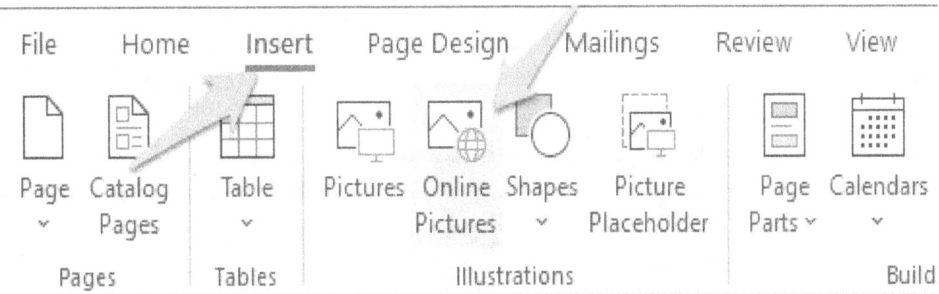

2) Enter the **specific keyword** of what you are finding into the dialog box and click **Enter**.

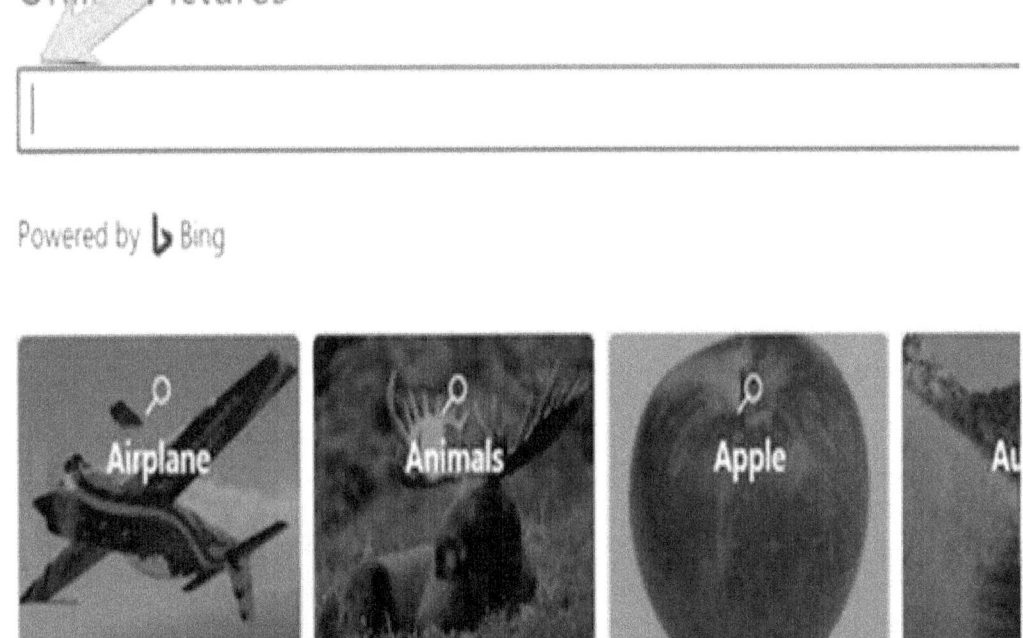

3) Select your preferred **image** on the search result and click **Insert**.

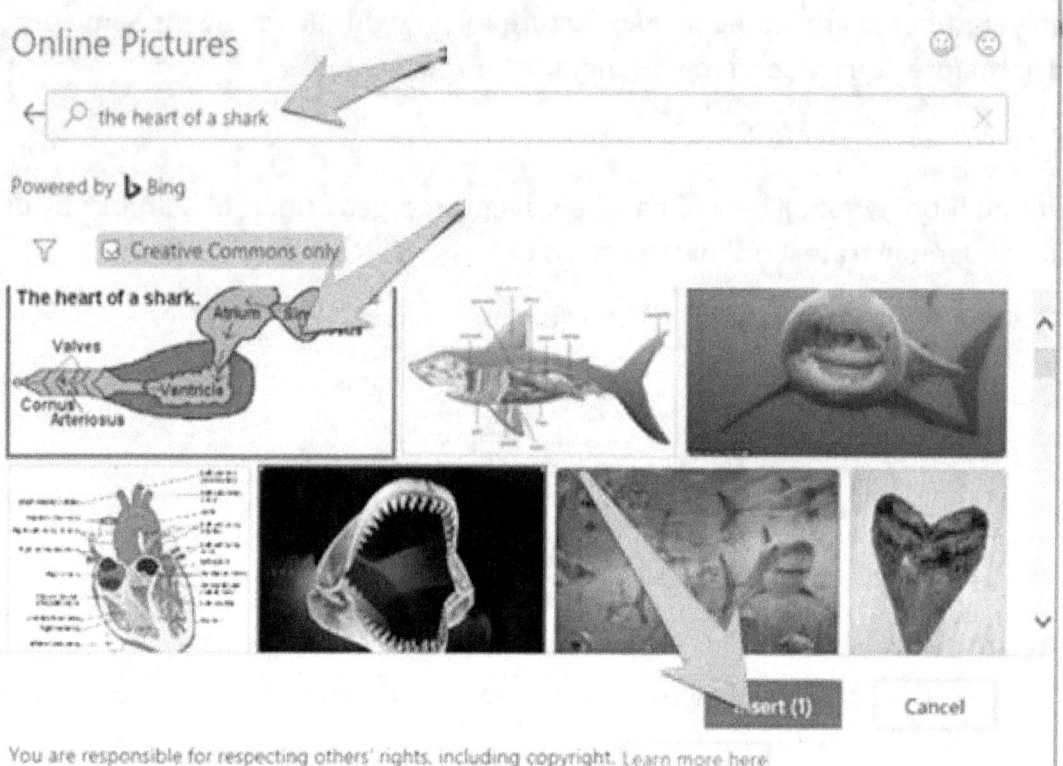

4) Click the **photo**, **small handles** will display across the **photo**, the **handles** are called **resizing handles**.
5) Click and drag any of the **resizing handles** to make the photo smaller or bigger as shown below. press down the **Shift** key while resizing to prevent the photo from being distorted.

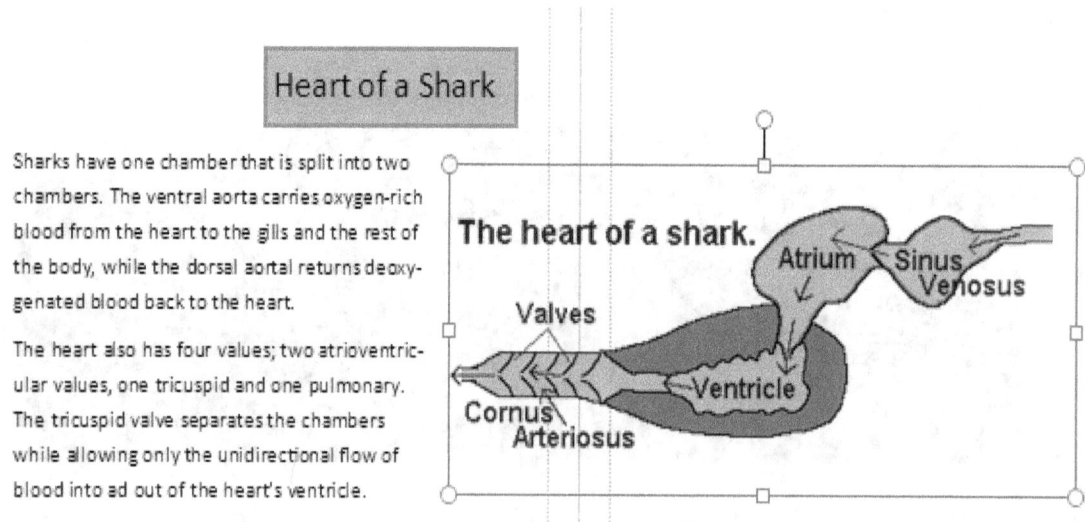

ADDING EFFECTS TO YOUR PICTURES

Follow the steps below to add effects (borders, shadows, reflection, and so on) to your photos.

1) Click your **image** and click the **"Picture Format"** tab.
2) My target is to create a fine glow style for the photo. To achieve this, click the **Picture Effects** menu, click the **"Glow"** menu, and select a **variation** on the fly-out as shown below.

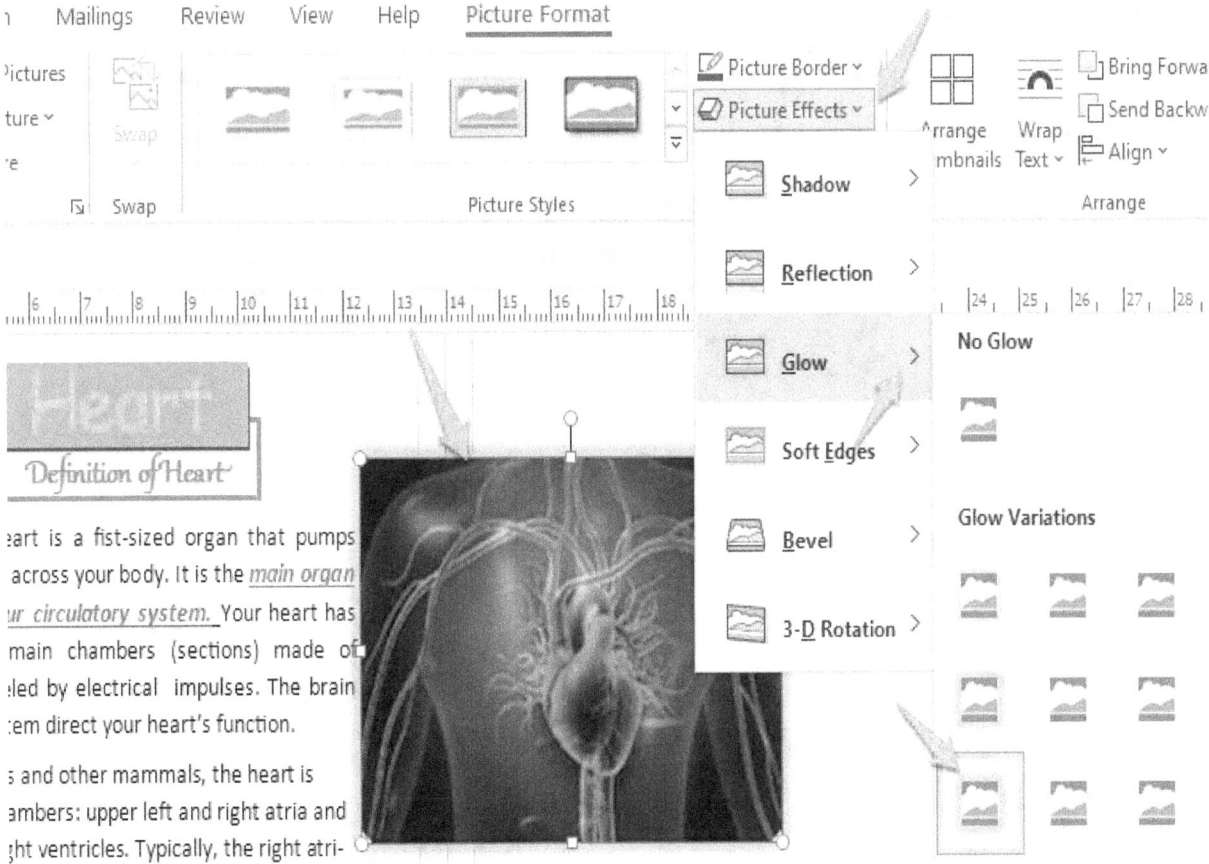

3) You can experiment with other effects like **reflection** or **shadow** to check what they can offer you.

ADDING A CAPTION

1) Click the **picture** you want to caption and click the **"Picture Format"** tab.
2) Click the **Caption** menu and choose the **caption style** you want on the drop-down menu.

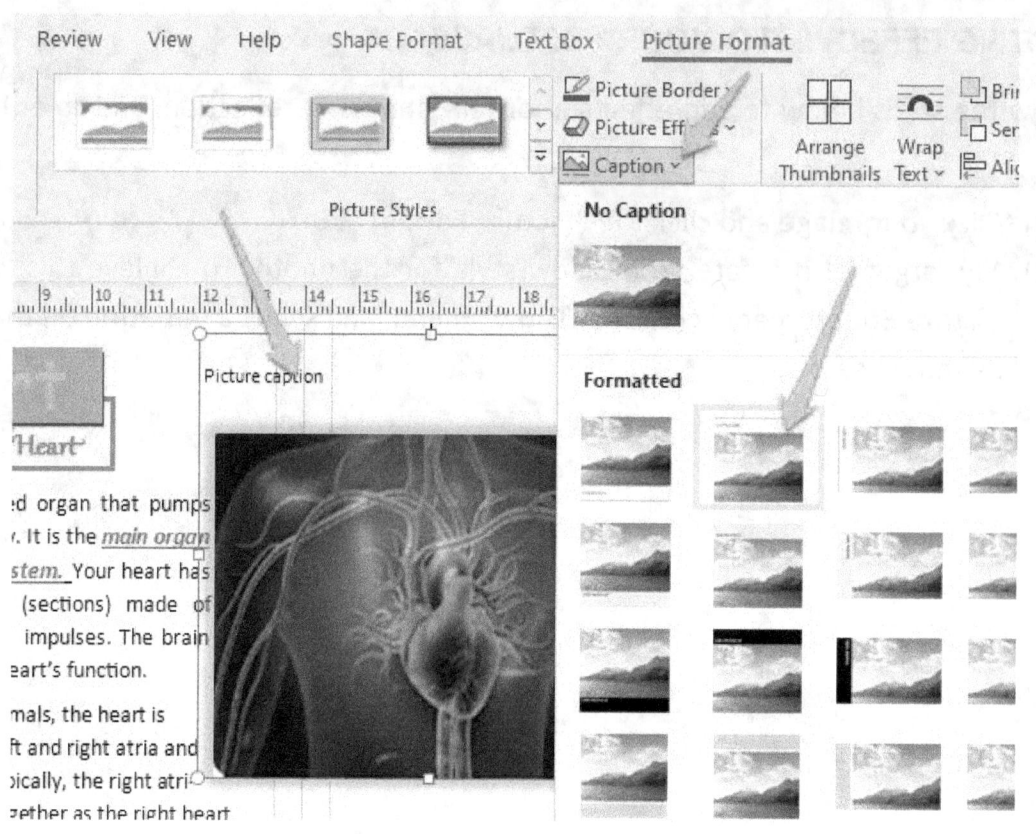

3) Type the **caption** and it will be reflected.

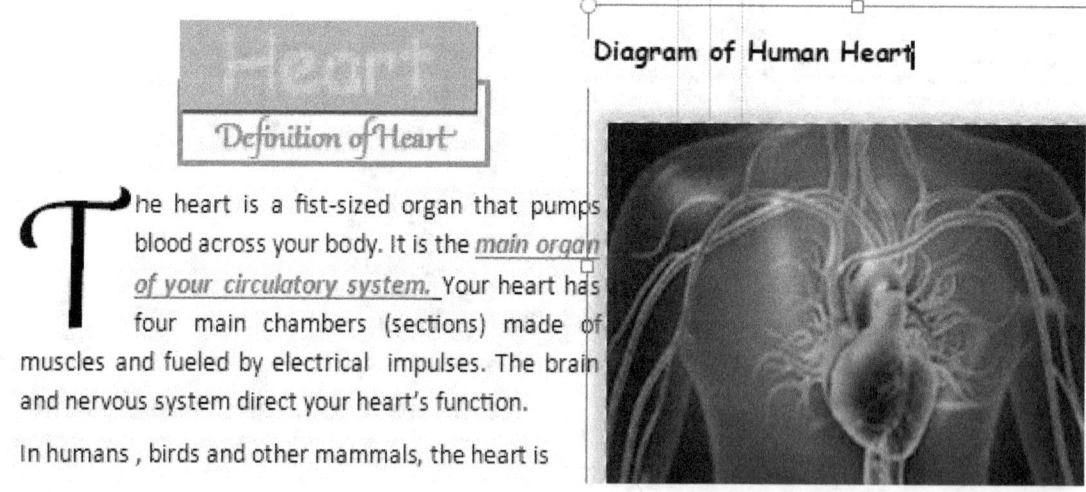

CROPPING PICTURES

Sometimes when you add a photo to your document, you might notice unneeded parts that need to be trimmed out to focus on significant areas of the photo. Follow the steps itemized below to crop your photo.

1) Insert any **picture** from your picture library and click over the **picture** to select.
2) Click the **"Picture Format"** tab and click the **Crop** button. **Crop handles** now appear across the picture border as displayed below.

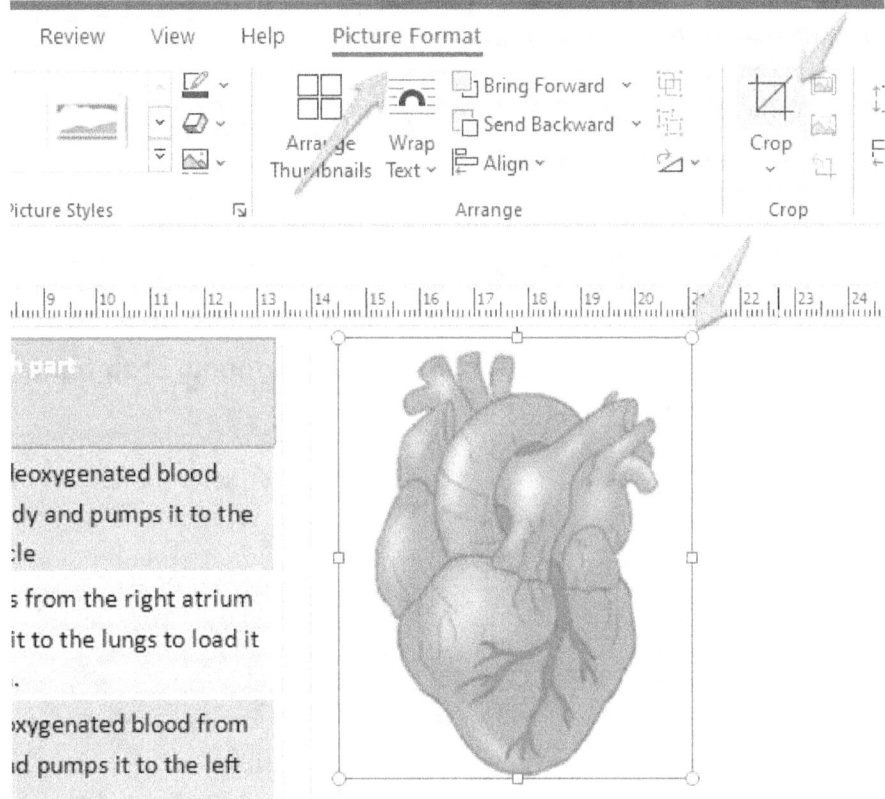

3) Click and drag **crop handles** around the area of the image you want to preserve.

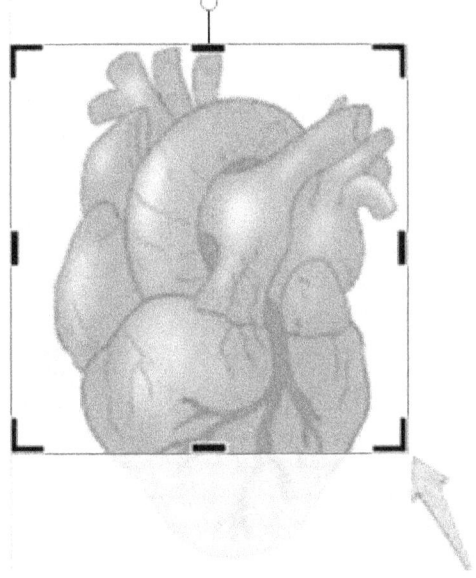

4) The **bright grey portions** are removed to leave the portion of the photo you want to preserve inside the crop square. Click any point on your document to complete the cropping.

CROPPING TO SHAPE

It is so amazing to have a feature that allows you to crop your image to whichever shape you want. To do these, follow these steps.

1) Insert a **photo** from your picture library into the document.
2) To crop to shape, click the **image** and click the **"Picture Format"** tab.
3) Click the **Crop** menu and select **"Crop to Shape"** on the drop-down menu.
4) Choose a **shape** from the **Crop to Shape** fly-out menu. **crop handles** will appear around your photo borders.

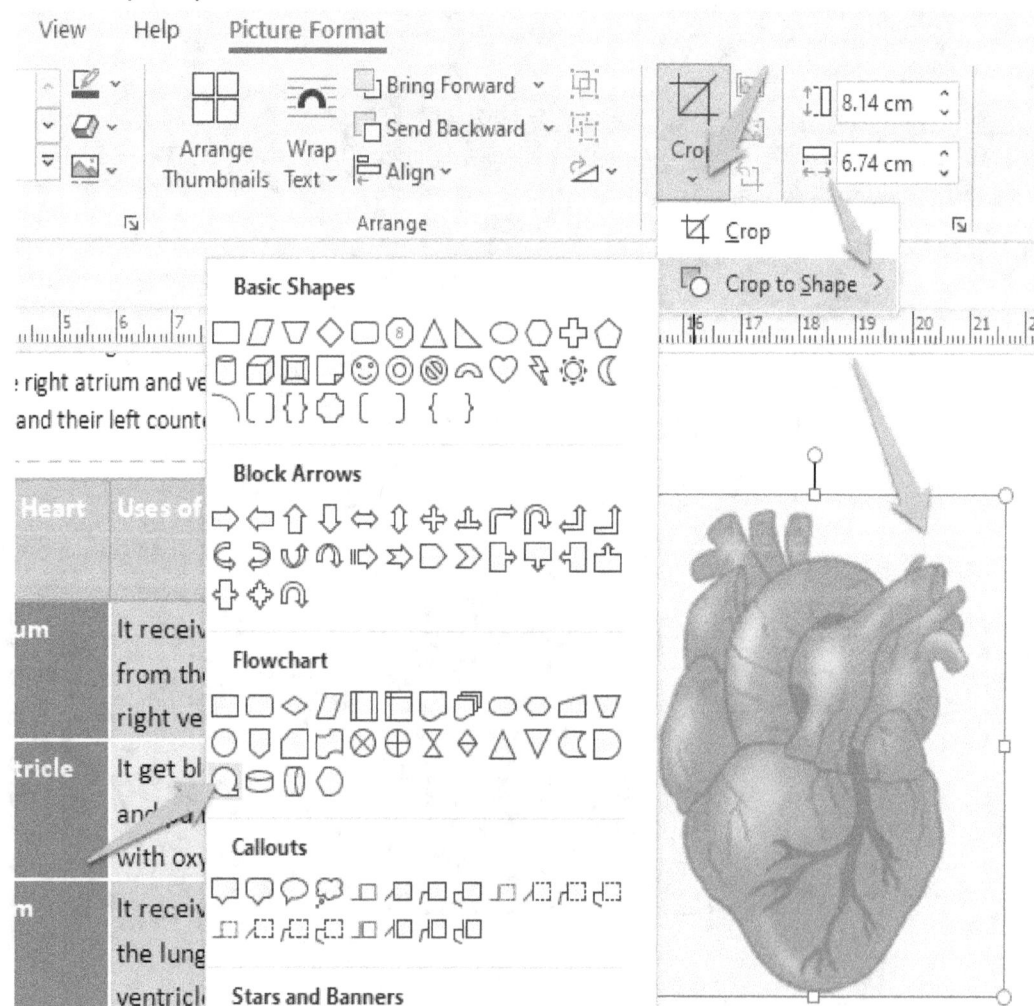

5) Click and drag any of these **handles** around the area of the image you want to preserve.

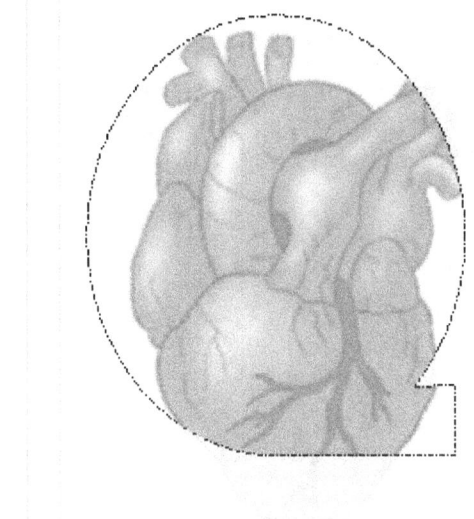

6) The **bright grey portions** are removed to leave the portion of the photo you want to preserve inside the crop square. Click any point on your document to complete the cropping.

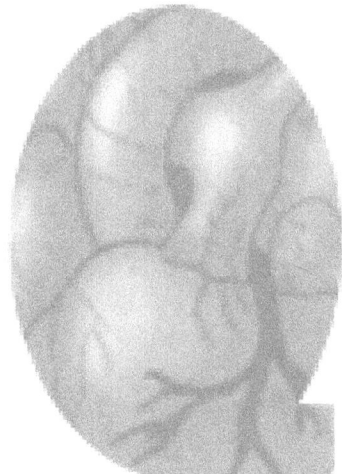

ADJUSTING PICTURES

The brightness and contrast of your photos can be adjusted, you can also recolor them so that the photo can suit your color pattern.

1) Right-click the **photo** and choose **"Format Picture"** on the fly-out.

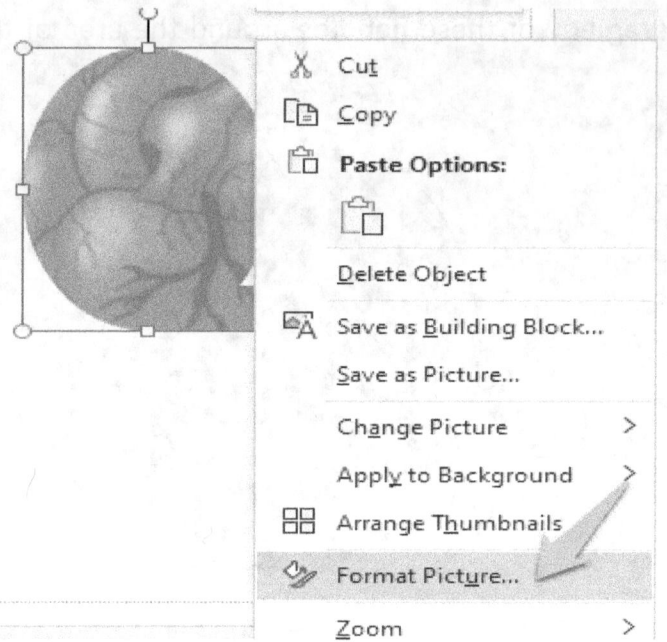

2) Click the **Picture** tab in the **Format Picture** dialog box and drag the **Transparency** slider to adjust photo transparency.

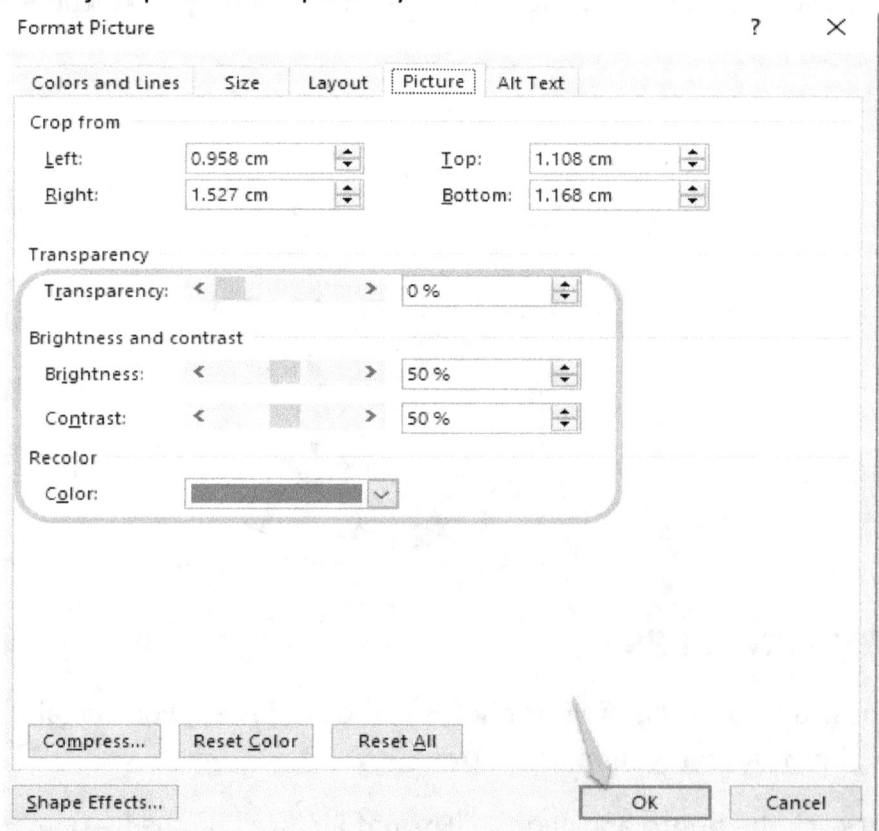

3) Drag the **brightness** and **Contrast** sliders to adjust the brightness and contrast of your picture.
4) Click the **menu** in the **Recolor** heading and select a **color** on the drop-down menu to recolor your photo.
5) Click **OK** to finish the adjustment.

WRAPPING TEXT AROUND PICTURES

By default, the photo is automatically wrapped with text when you insert a photo, it means the text arranges itself around the photo instead of coming above or below it. Follow the steps itemized below to change the text wrap.

1) Click the affected **photo** and click the **"Picture Format"** tab (You can place the image over the text). Then click the **Wrap Text** menu.

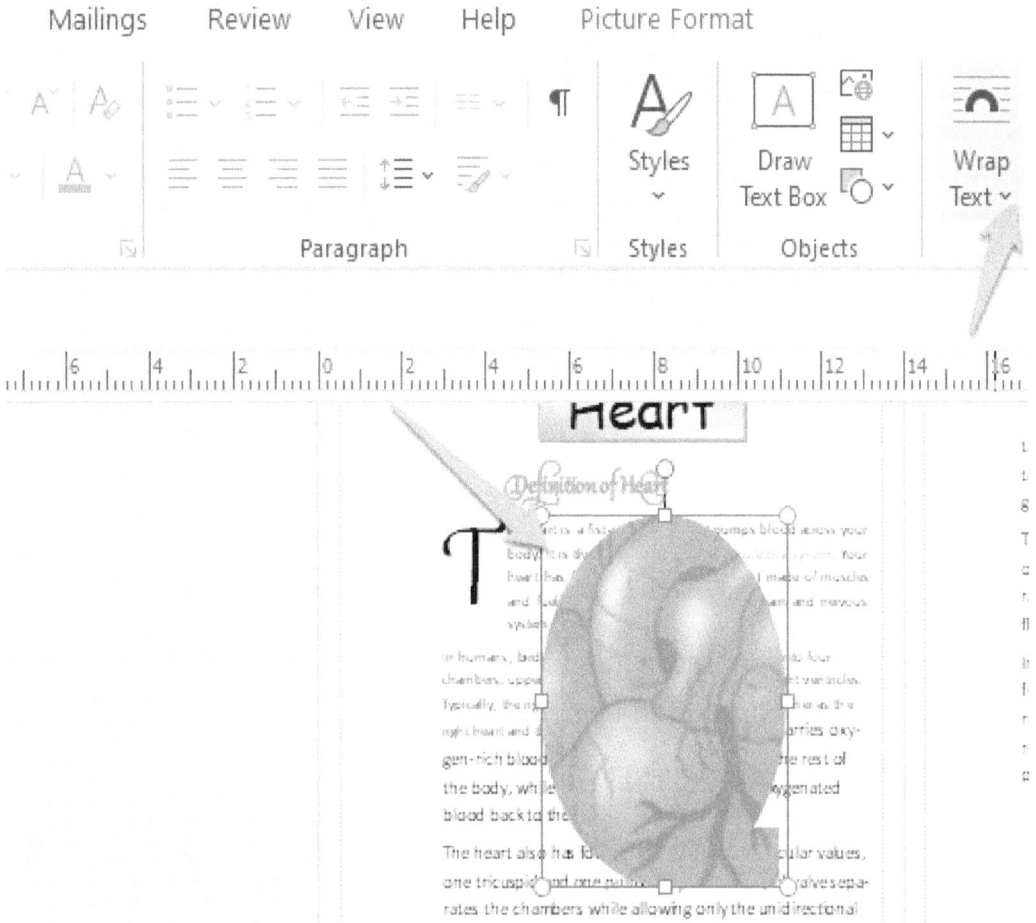

2) Choose **"Tight"** on the drop-down menu to align the text square around the edge of the photo.

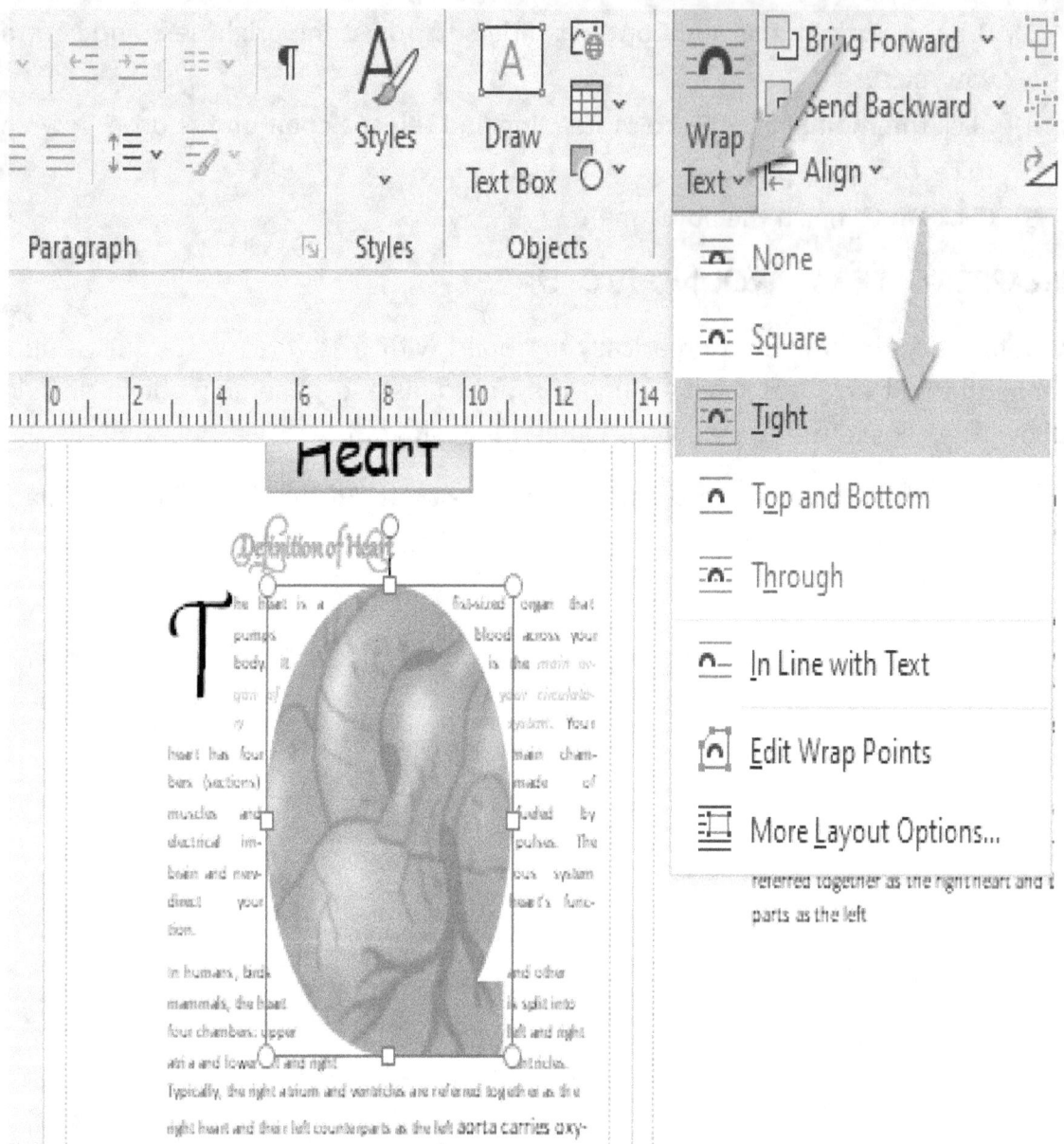

3) Click and drag to reposition if required. As you do this, you will realize that the text will arrange itself around the picture.

CUSTOMIZING WRAP POINTS

Publisher allows you to adjust the points at which the text wraps around the photo. Follow these steps to customize the wrap points.

1) Click the affected **photo** and click the **"Picture Format"** tab.
2) Click the **Wrap Text** menu and choose **Edit Warp points** on the drop-down menu.

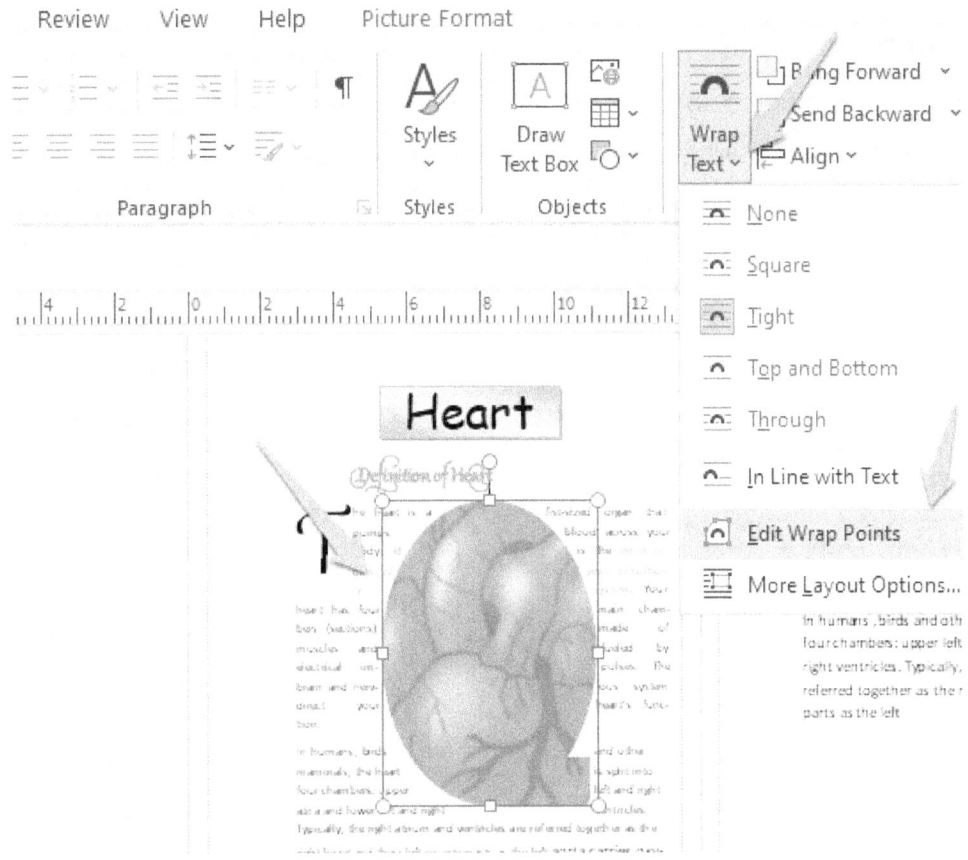

3) A **dotted line** is displayed around the photo, the **dotted line** is known as a **wrap point**. Click and drag the dots to adjust the wrap point.

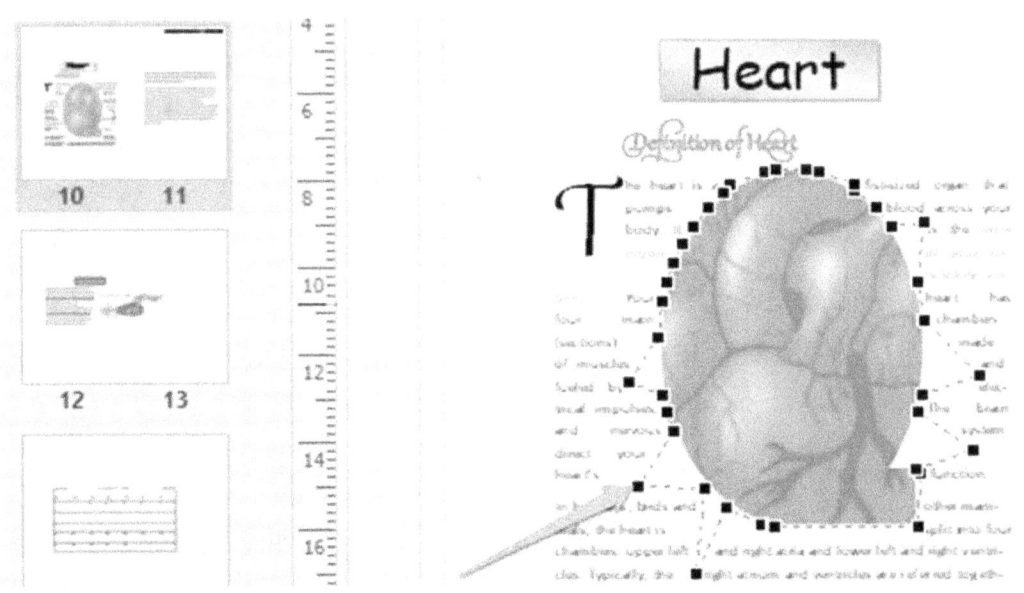

INSERTING SHAPES

The publisher has diverse shapes such as circles, squares, rectangles, lines, and different multiple flow chart symbols. Follow the steps below to add shape to your document.

1) Click the **Insert** tab and click the **Shapes** menu. then choose a **shape** on the drop-down menu.

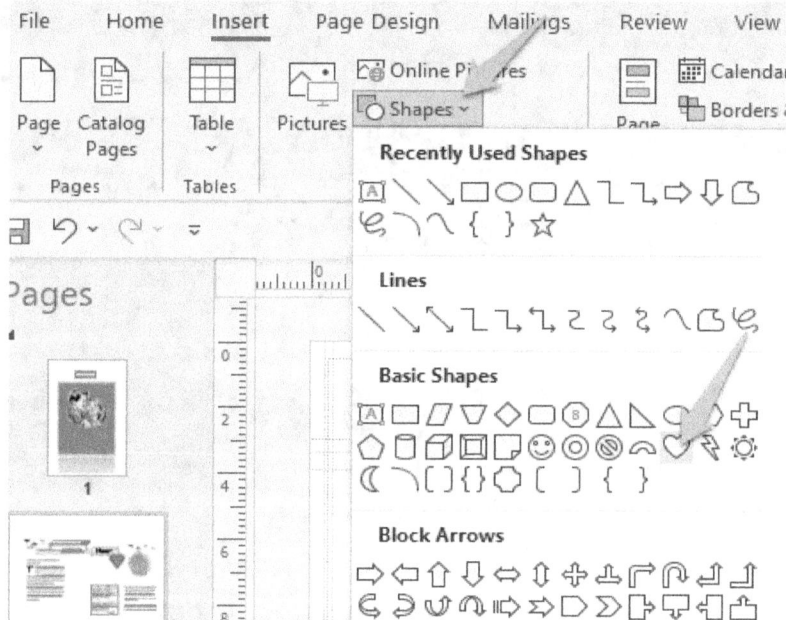

2) Click and drag over the **screen** to create a shape on your document.

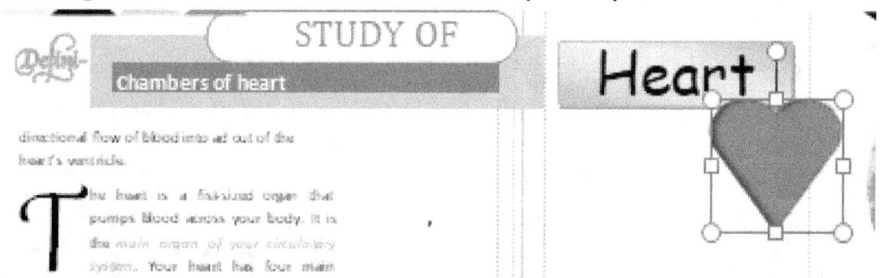

ADJUSTING SHAPES

There are various ways to adjust your shape, you can add shadows, outline the shape, and change the shape color.

CHANGING SHAPE COLOR

1) Click the **shape** whose color you want to change and click the **"Shape Format"** tab.
2) Click the **Shape Fill** menu and choose a **color** on the drop-down menu.

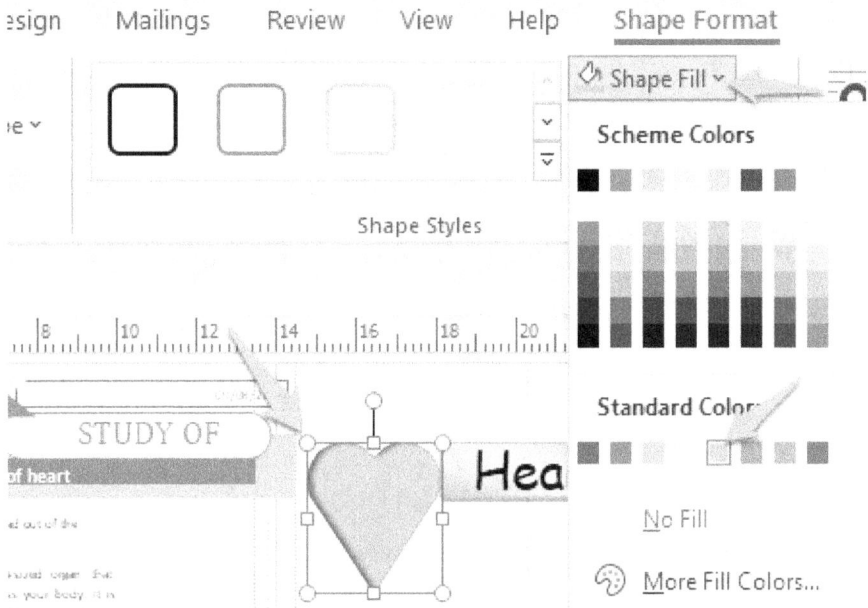

3) If you desire to **add texture** or **gradient,** you can select each of these from their respective drop-down menu.

CHANGING SHAPE BORDER

1) Click the **Shape** whose border you want to change, and click the **"Shape Format"** tab.
2) Click the **Shape Outline** and choose a **color** on the drop-down menu.

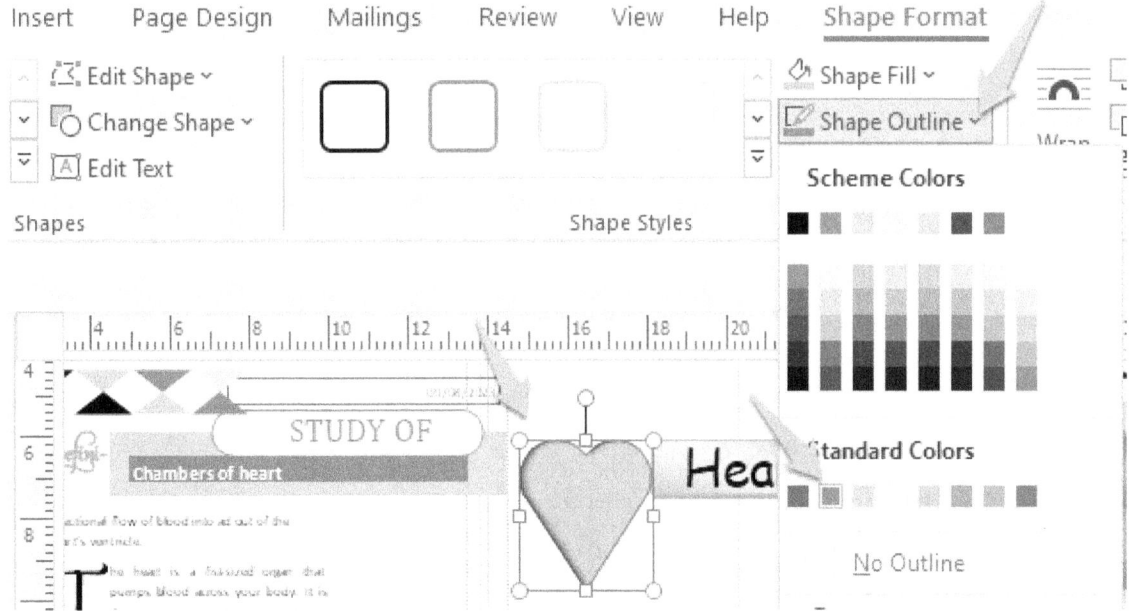

3) To alter the **thickness** of the border, choose the equivalent **weight** on the **Weight** fly-out.

APPLYING SHADOW TO A SHAPE

1) Click the **Shape** and click the **"Shape Format"** tab.
2) Click the **Shape Effects** menu and choose an **effect (shadow, reflection, or glow)** on the drop-down menu.

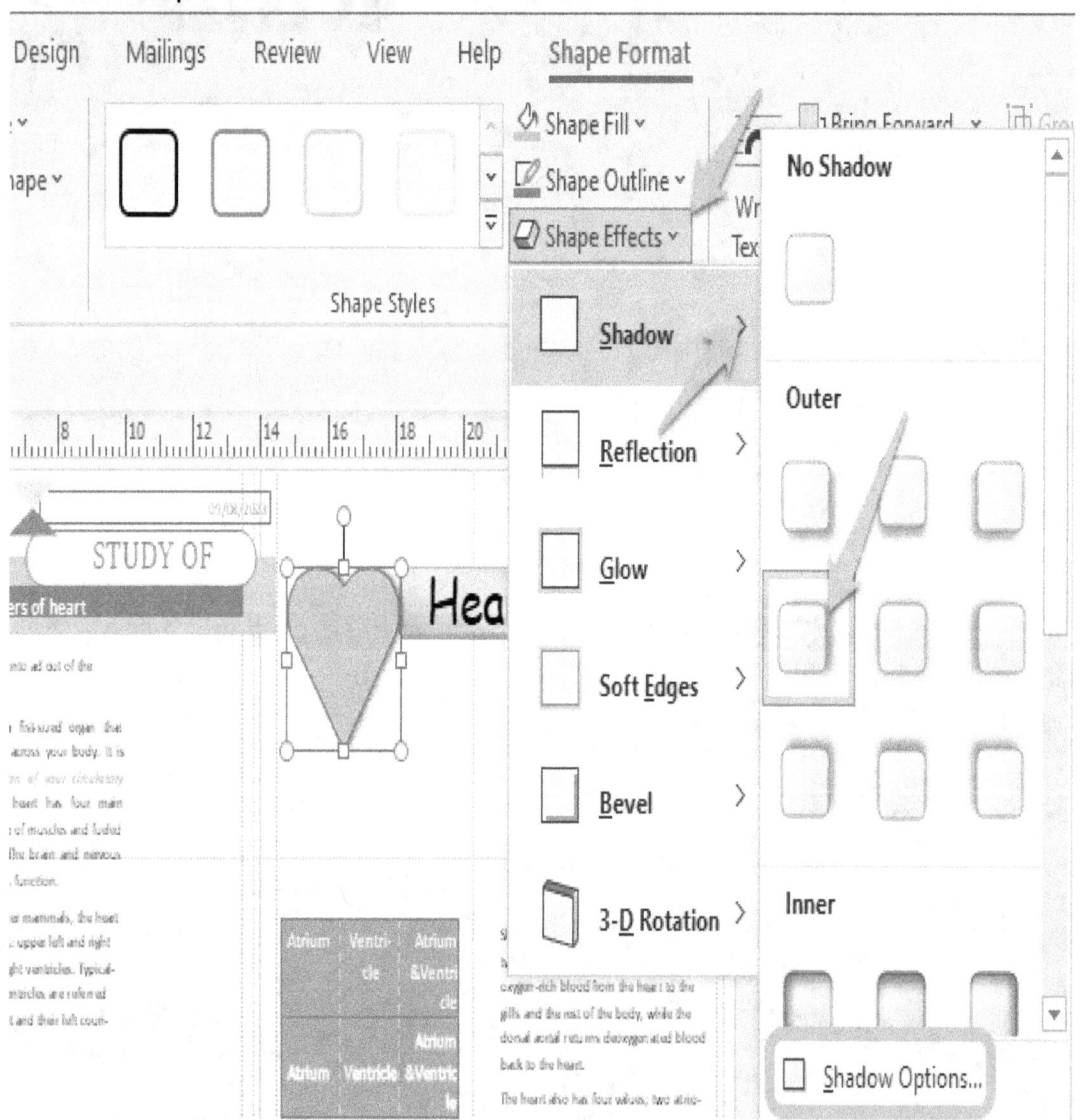

3) To edit the effect, click the respective **Effect options** such as (Shadow or Glow) at the bottom of each effect fly-out menu.
4) The **Format Shape** will appear, adjust the **slider** to customize your effect.

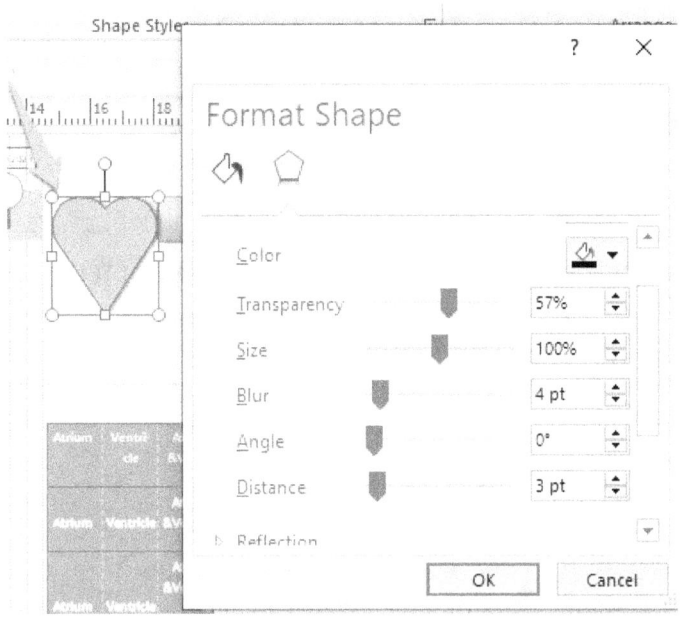

ALIGN OBJECTS ON THE PAGE

You can auto-align elements on your page. Follow these steps to align elements on the page.

1) Select all the **Elements** you want to align, **Ctrl-click** to select **multiple objects**.
2) Click the "**Picture Format**" tab and click the **Align** menu in the **Arrange** group.

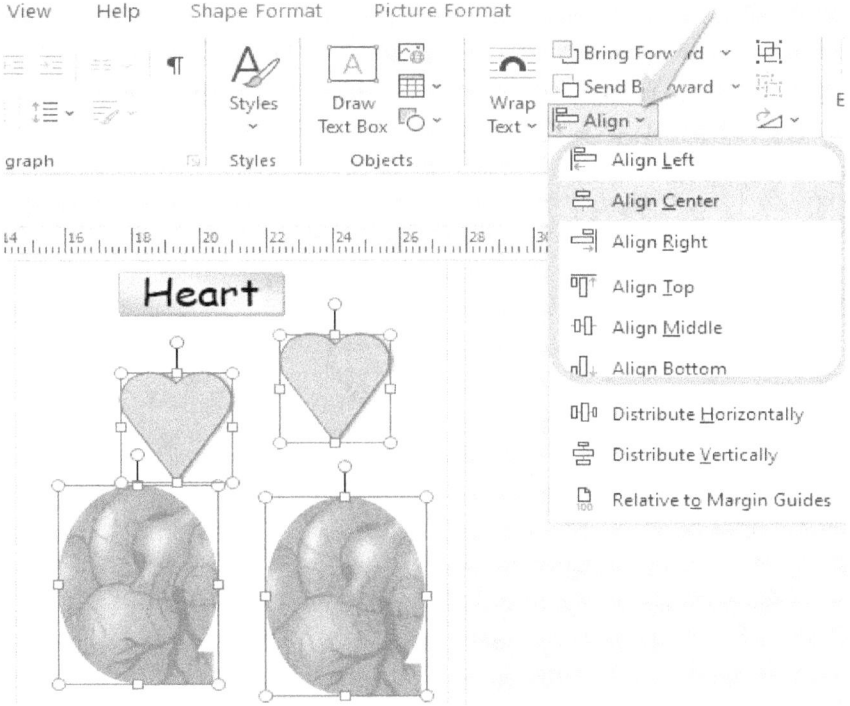

3) Choose an **option** on the **Align** drop-down menu. The alignment options are briefly explained below:
   - **Align Left**: it aligns the left side of the selected objects with the left border of the leftmost selected object.
   - **Align Center**: it aligns the center of the selected objects with the vertical center of the selected object that is in the center.
   - **Align Right**: it aligns the right side of the selected objects with the right border of the rightmost selected object.
   - **Align Top**: it aligns the top side of the selected objects with the top border of the topmost selected object.
   - **Align Middle**: it aligns the selected objects in the horizontal middle with the selected object that is in the middle.
   - **Align Bottom**: it aligns the bottom side of the selected objects with the bottom border of the bottom-most selected object.

DISTRIBUTE OBJECTS ACROSS THE PAGE

You can distribute several objects equally across the page. Follow these steps to do that.

1) Select all the **Objects** you want to distribute by **Ctrl-clicking** to select multiple objects.
2) Click the "**Picture Format**" tab and click the **Align** menu in the **Arrange** group.
3) Choose "**distribute horizontally**" or "**distribute vertically**" on the drop-down menu.

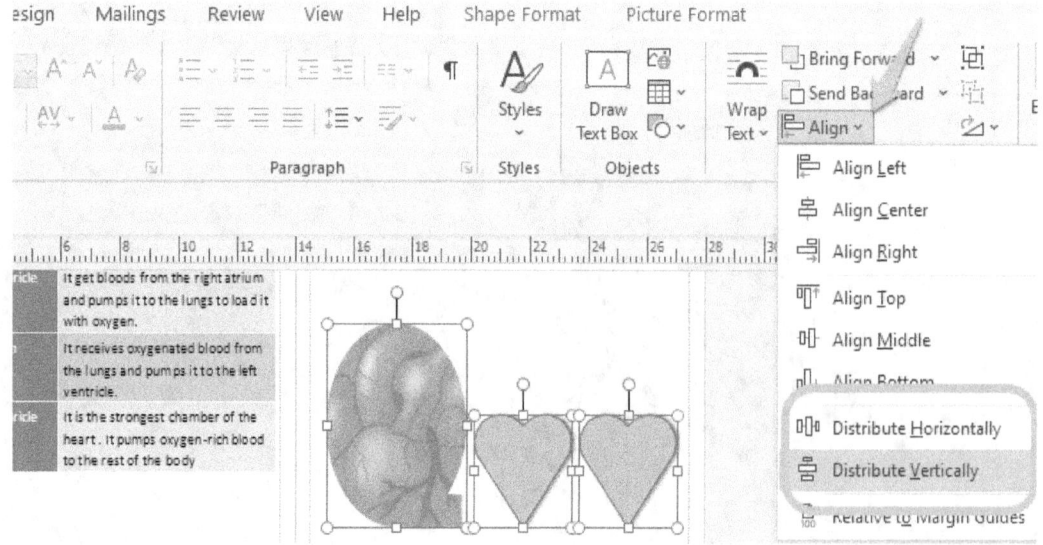

 :

- **Distribute horizontally** moves the selected objects an equal distance apart horizontally throughout your selection.
- **Distribute vertically** moves the selected objects an equal distance apart vertically throughout your selection.

GROUPING AND UNGROUPING OBJECTS

When several objects are grouped, they will be treated as a single entity and you can move the group together. This comes in handy if you make a graphic that has multiple objects and shapes so that you move and resize them without having to adjust them individually. Follow these steps to group multiple objects.

1) Select all the **Objects** you want to group by **Ctrl-clicking** to select **multiple images**.
2) Click the **"Shape Format"** or **"Picture Format"** tab and click the **Group** button.

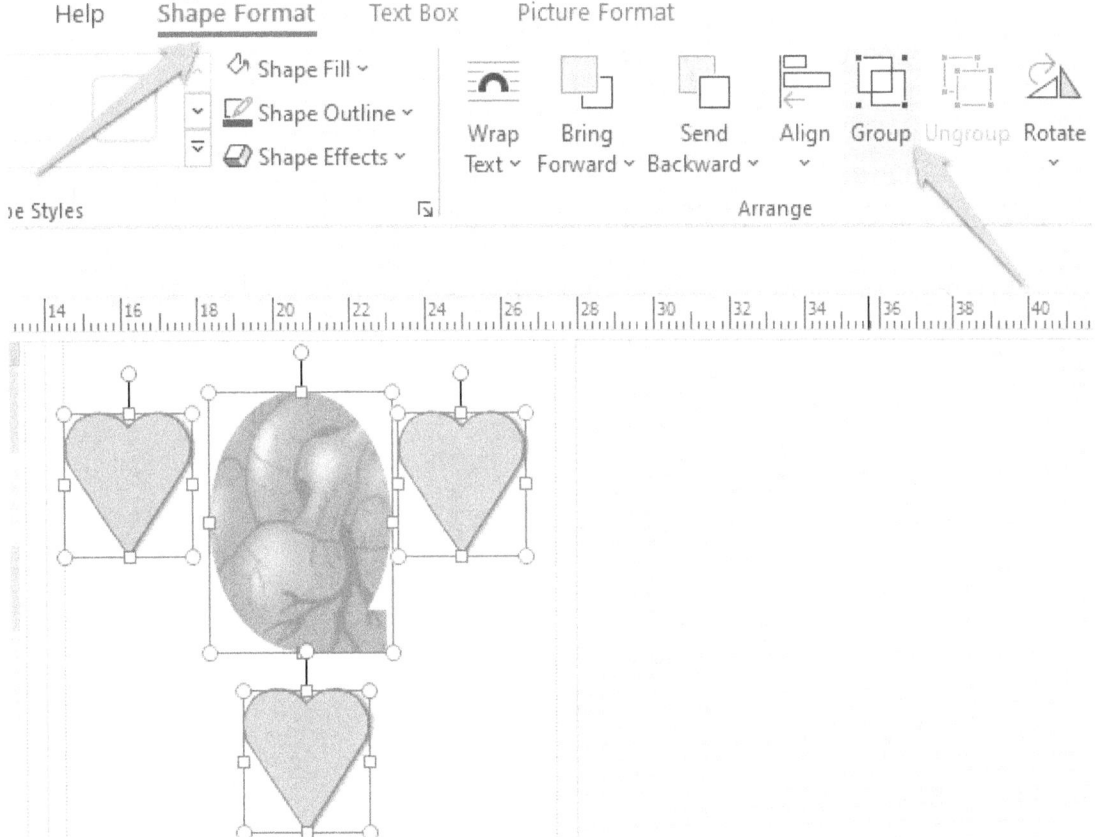

3) Now, you can resize or move the graphic as a single element.

4) To ungroup the object, select the **grouped object**, click the **"Shape Format tab** or **"Picture Format"** tab, and click the **Ungroup** button.

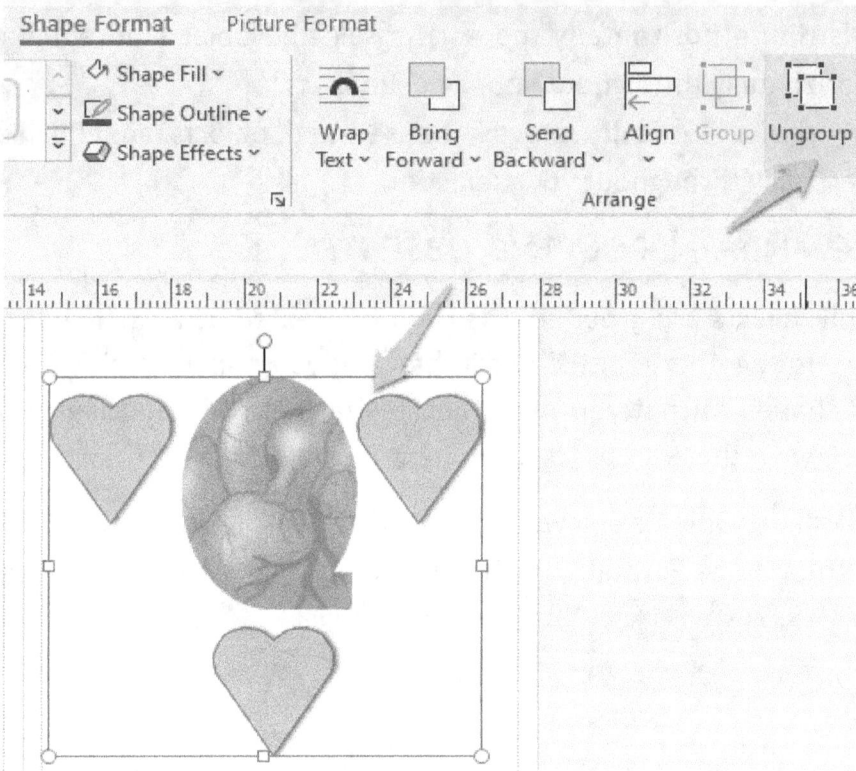

ARRANGING OBJECT LAYERS

Publications are built up with transparent layers. Each time you add an object, shape, text box, or image, you are adding it as a new layer on top. Examine the design that is shown below.

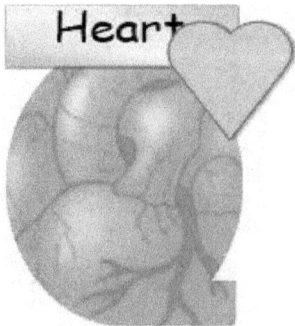

Layers are built up like this:

The Heart icon is on the bottom layer, the text box with "Heart" is above the Heart icon layer and the Love icon is above the Heart icon and text box "Heart".

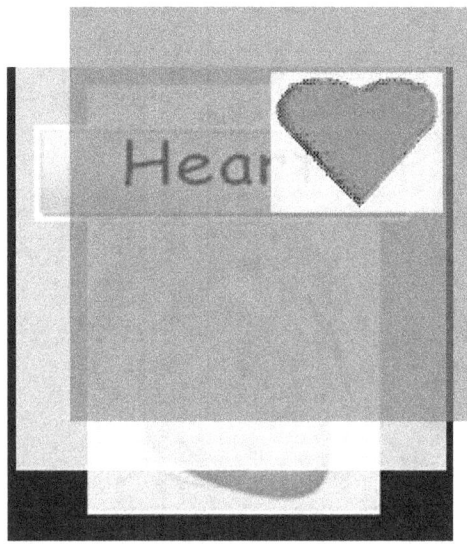

Next, if you want to place the "**Love**" icon, behind the text box **"Heart"**, you simply need to change the layer arrangement.

1) Select the **"Love"** icon click the **"Shape Format"** tab, and click the **Send backward**.

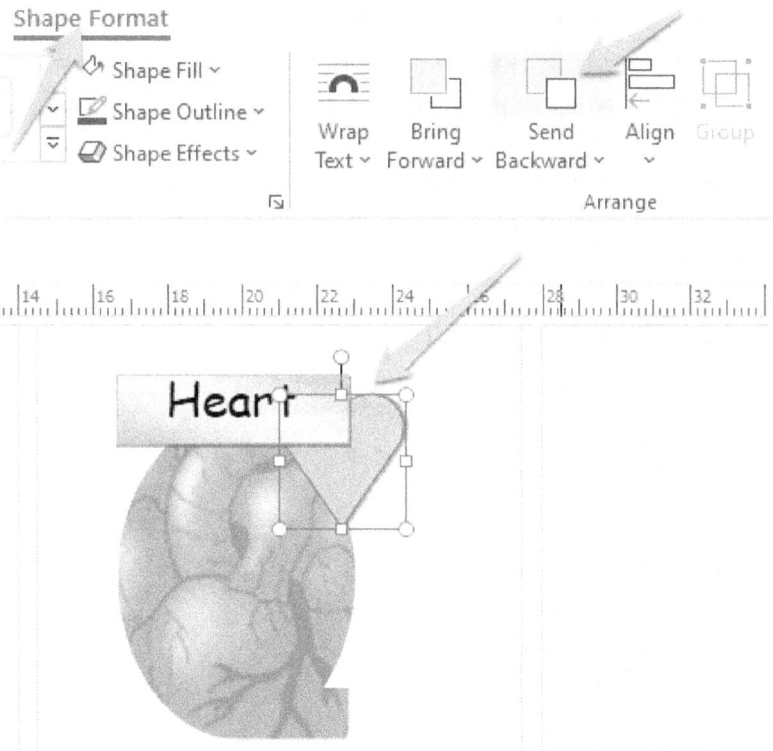

2) You will notice the layer order has been altered. The Love icon is now behind the text box "**Heart**".

USING PUBLISHER PAGE PARTS

Publisher offers pre-designed building blocks that are useful for designing your page. With the page parts, you add titles and sidebars to your page faster, you can also add predefined quotes and stories. Follow the steps below to add a page part.

1) Click the **Insert** tab, click the **Page Parts** menu, and choose a **template** on the drop-down menu.

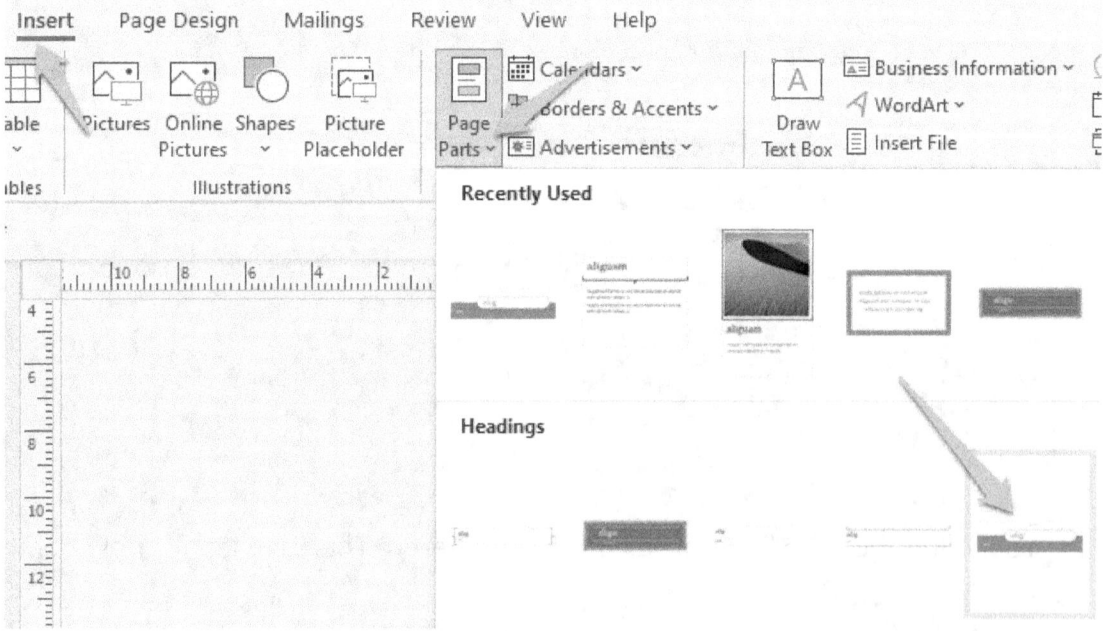

2) Click and drag to reposition the **page part** on your document, you can also resize it if required.

3) Enter your **text** into the **placeholder** to replace the text that comes with the page parts.
4) If the page part has a picture, you can right-click the **photo**, select **Change Picture** on the context menu, and choose **Change Picture** on the submenu.

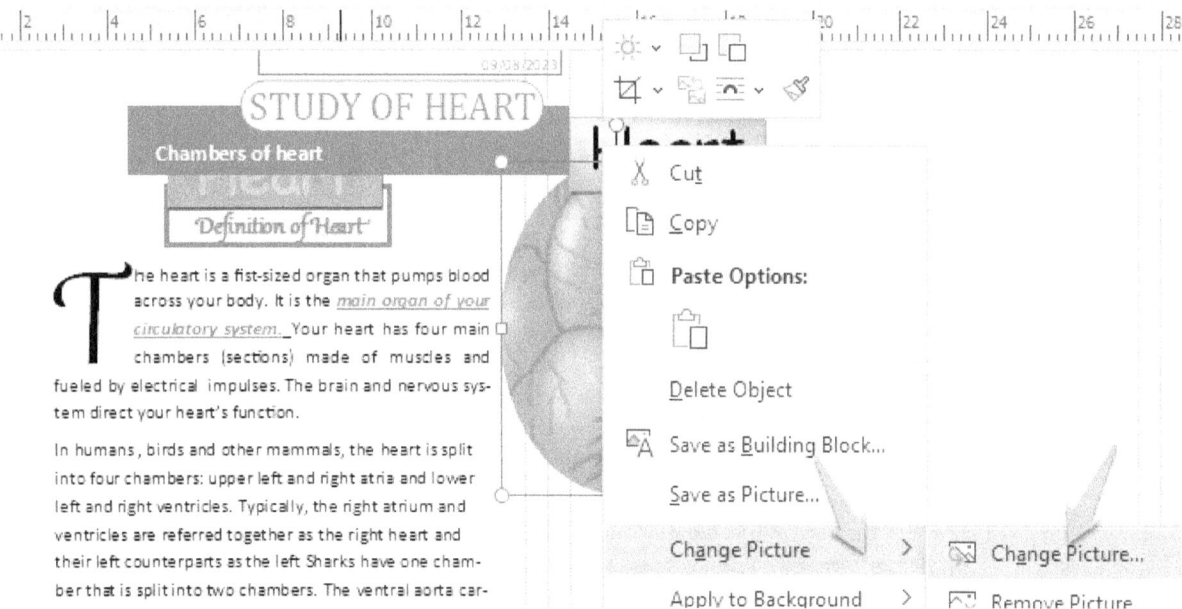

5) Pick the **location (folder)** where you stored the photo you want to use and then choose your **Photo**.

6) If you wish to change the color. Click the **page part** and click the **"Shape Format"** tab.
7) You can then use the **Shape Fill** menu to change the fill color, the **Shape Outline** menu to change the border color, and the **Shape Effects** menu to apply shadow, glow, or reflection to the page part. If the page part has multiple parts, you can apportion different fill colors to each of the parts.

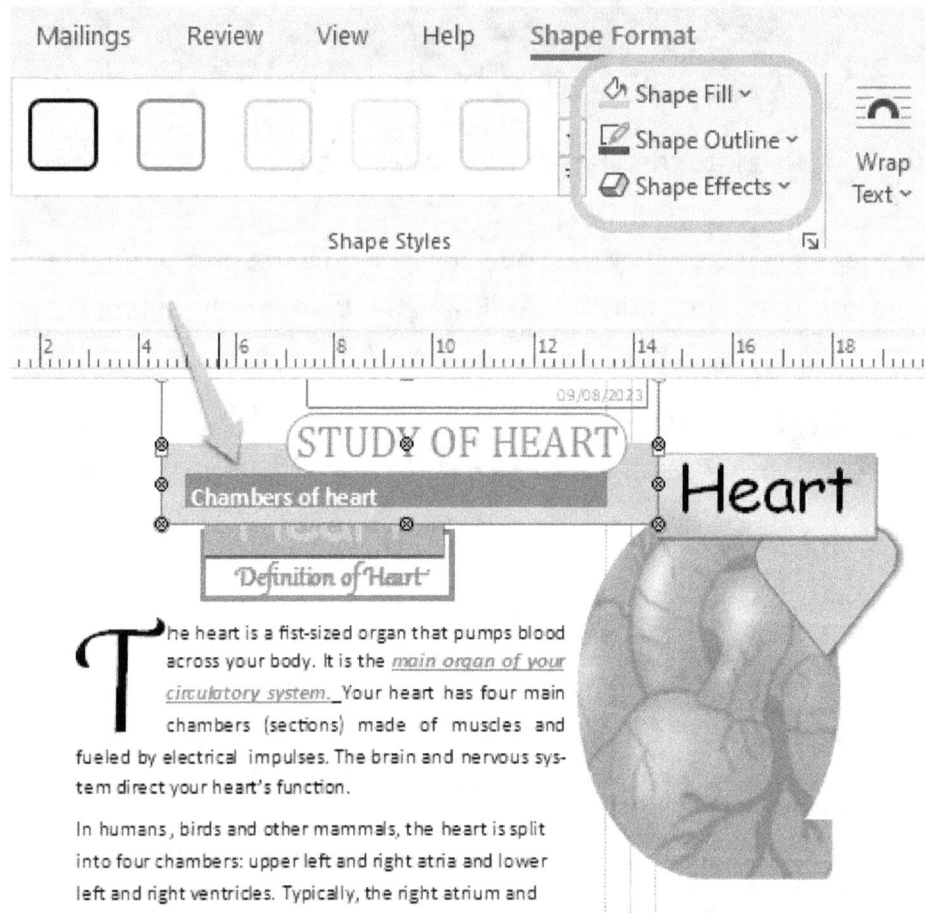

8) You can also use the **Shape Style Presets** that are available on the **"Shape Format"** tab.

INSERTING BORDERS AND ACCENTS

You can place a border on your page, text box, or image. you can also add accents which are little ornaments that can be used to highlight other objects. Follow the steps itemized below to add borders and accents.

1) Click the **Insert** tab and click **"Borders and Accents"**.

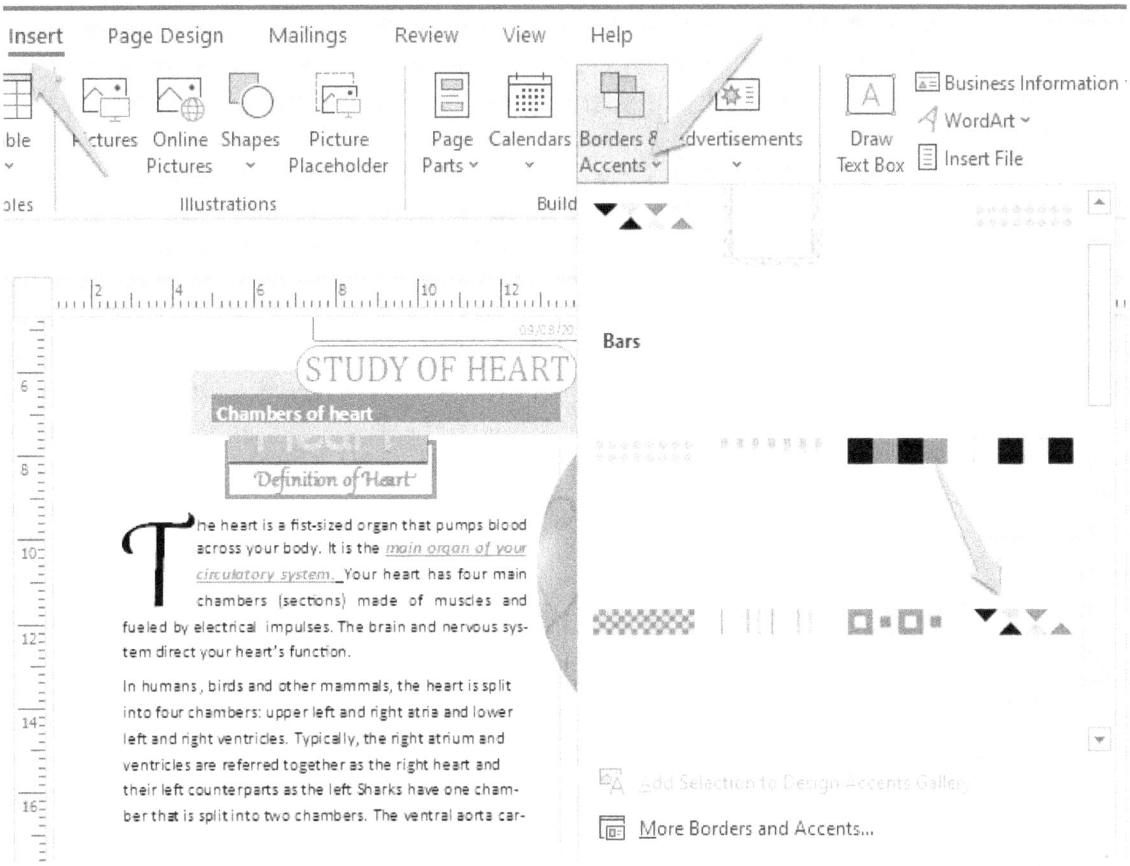

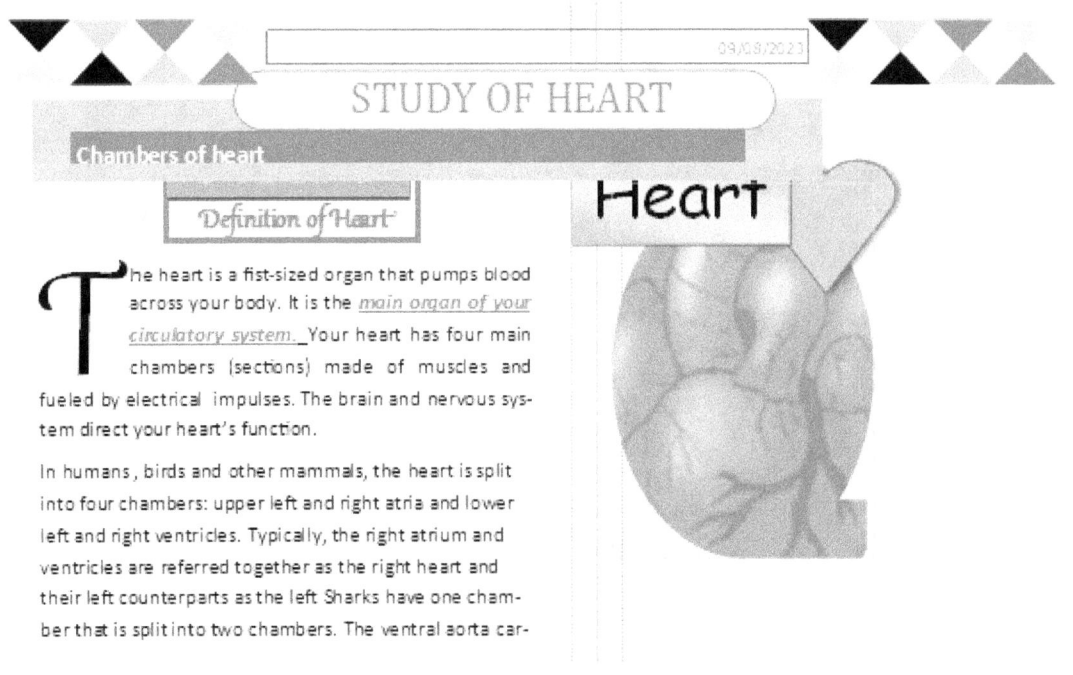

2) You can reposition and resize the accent within the page.

INSERTING CALENDARS

1) Click the **Insert** tab, click the **Calendar** menu, and choose a **template** on the **Calendar** drop-down menu.

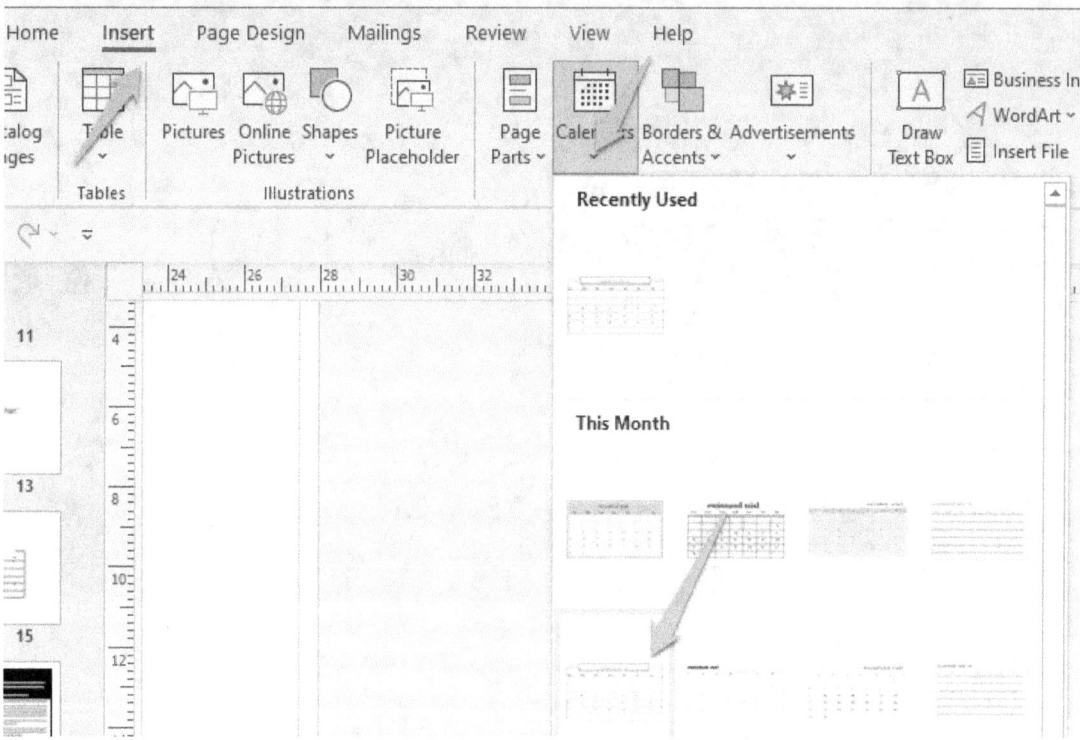

2) You can reposition and resize your calendar within the page.

APRIL 2024						
Sun	Mon	Tue	Wed	Thu	Fri	Sat
	1	2	3	4	5	6
7	8	9	10	11	12	13
14	15	16	17	18	19	20
21	22	23	24	25	26	27
28	29	30				

3) If you want to add a calendar with a specific month, click **More Calendars** on the **Calendar** drop-down menu to access the **Building Block Library** dialog box.

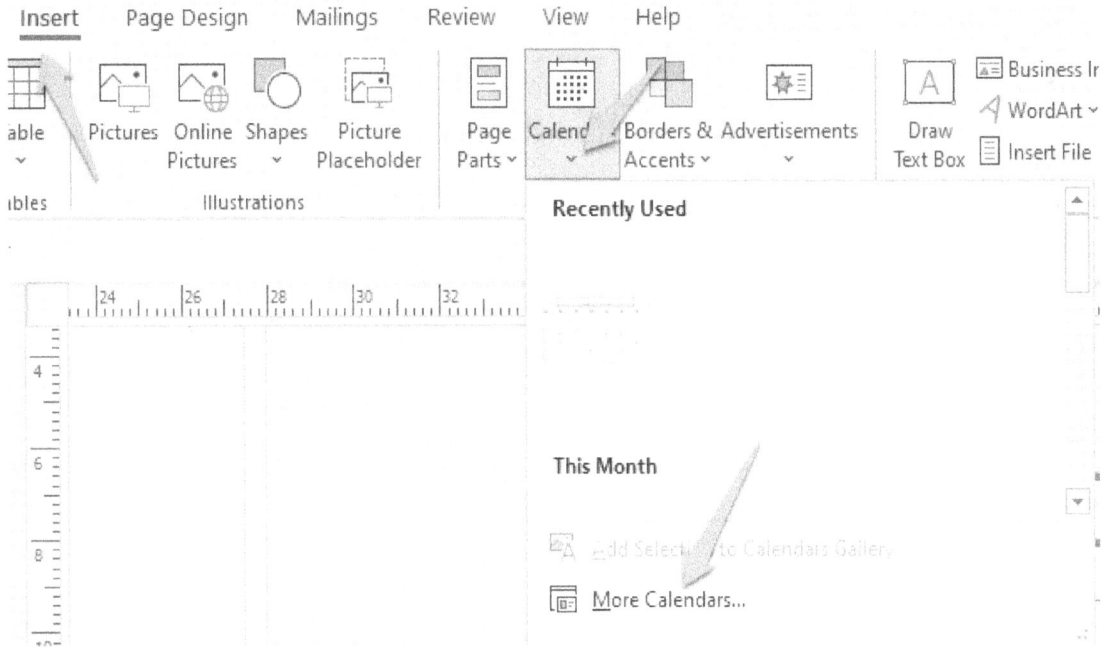

4) Choose a **template**, and specify the month and year on the right side of the dialog box. Then click the **Insert** button to complete the insertion.

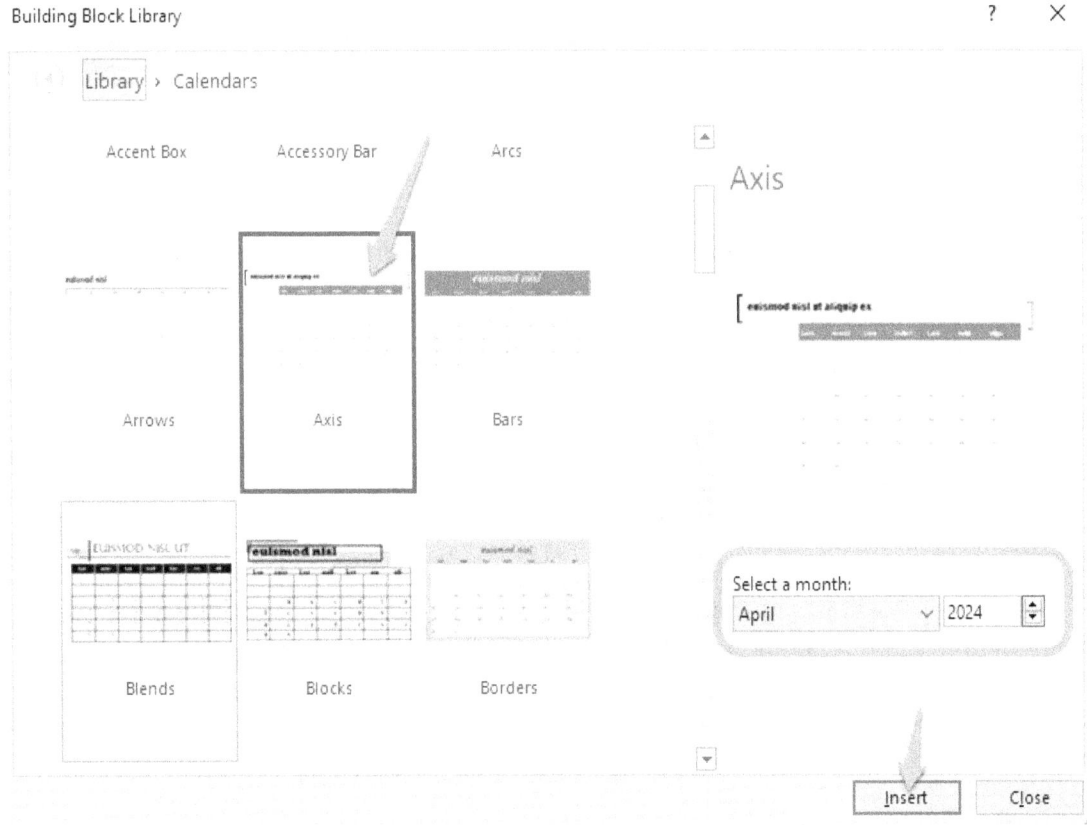

ADDING ADVERTISEMENTS

Advertisements come in different types such as attention grabbers, ads, free offers, and so on. Follow these steps to insert an Advertisement.

1) Click the **Insert** tab and click the **Advertisement** menu.
2) Choose a **template** on the **Advertisement** drop-down menu.

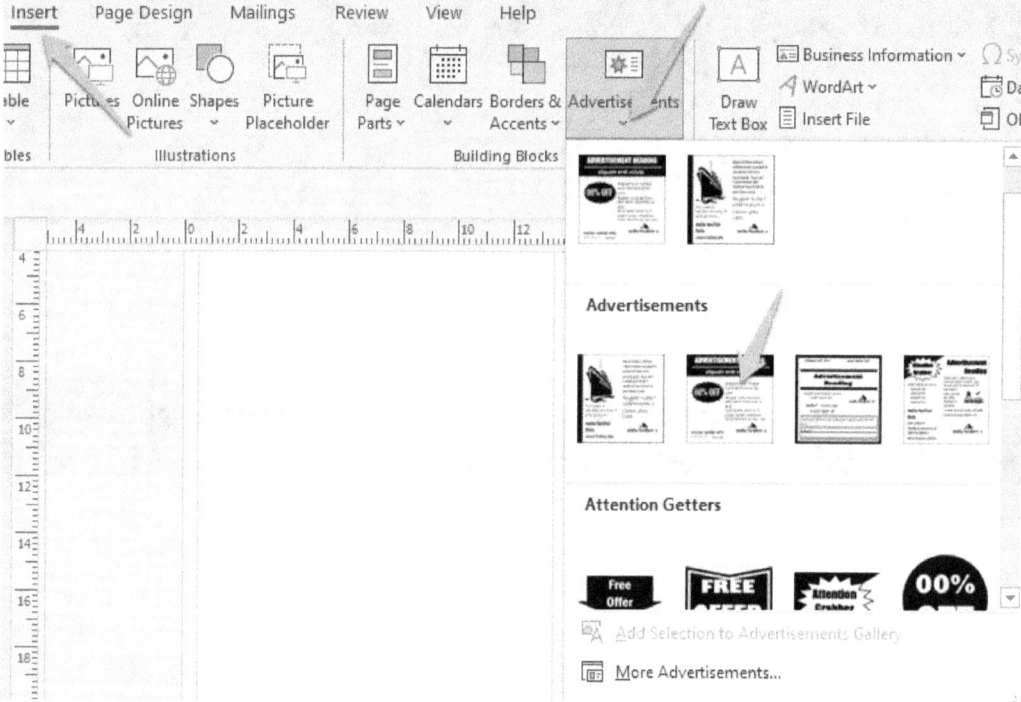

3) You can click **"More Advertisements"** at the lower part of the drop-down menu to access all the ad templates.
4) You can reposition and resize the ad on the page.

5) Enter the **text** you want to add into the **text boxes**.
6) To change an image, right-click the **image**, select **Change Image** on the context menu, and choose **Change Image** on the submenu.
7) Pick the **location** where you stored the photo you want to use and then choose your photo.

INSERTING WORDART

WordArt comes in handy for creating headings and eye-catching text. Follow the steps below to insert WordArt.

1) Click the **Insert** tab and click the **WordArt** menu.
2) Choose a **style** on the drop-down menu, and the **Edit WordArt Text** dialog box appears.

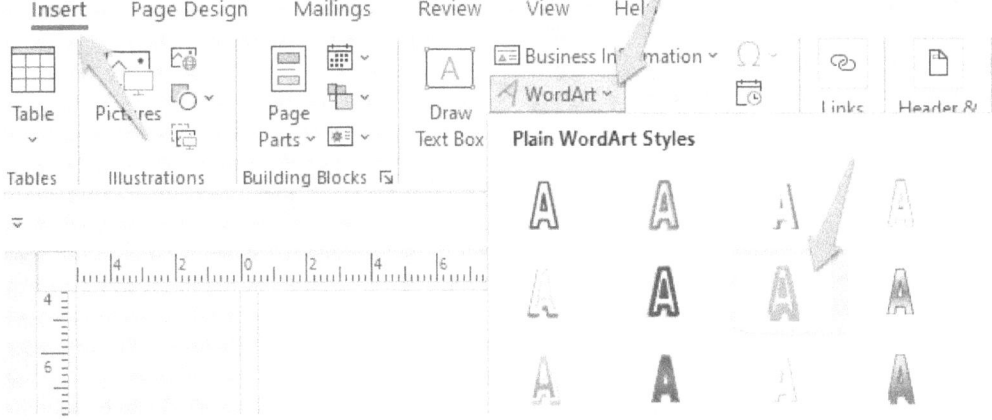

3) Set the **font** and **font size** and then type your **WordArt text**.
4) Then click **OK**.

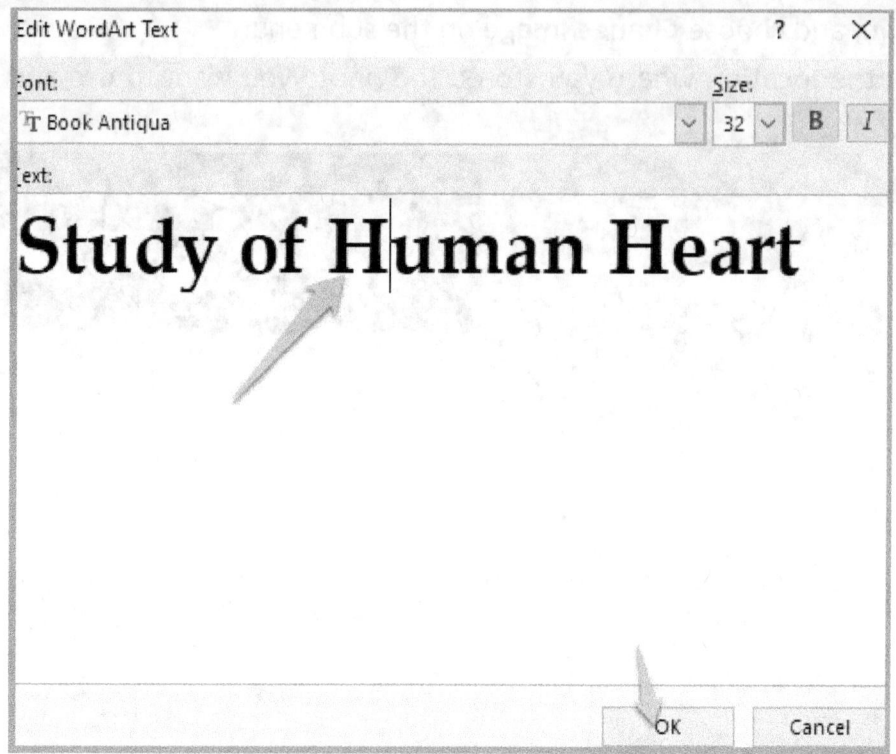

5) You can change the style of the text using the **preset** on the **WordArt Tools Format** tab.

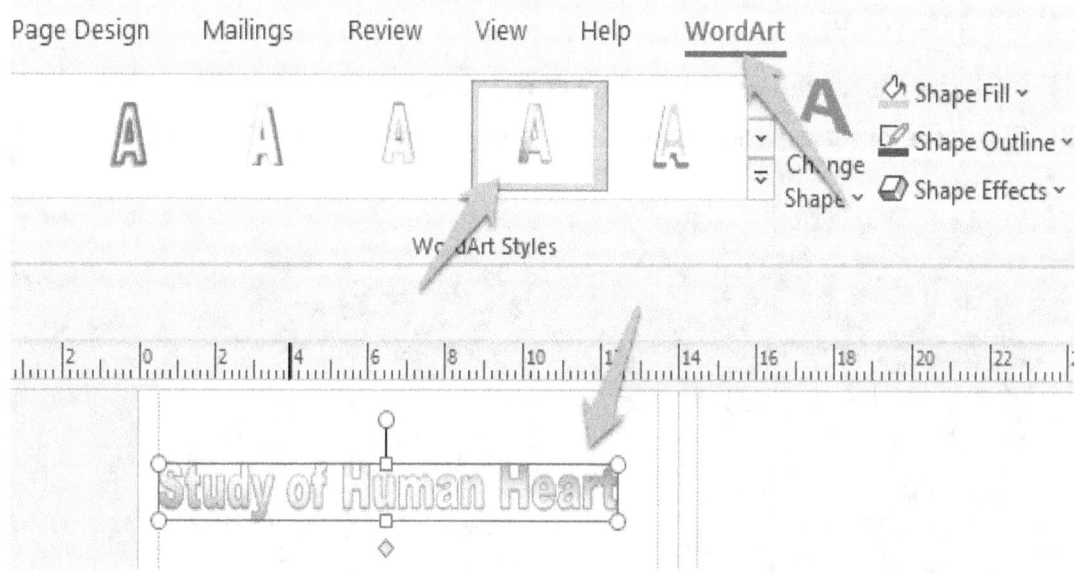

6) You can add a **shadow**, **reflection**, or **glow** effect using the "**Shape Effects**" menu.

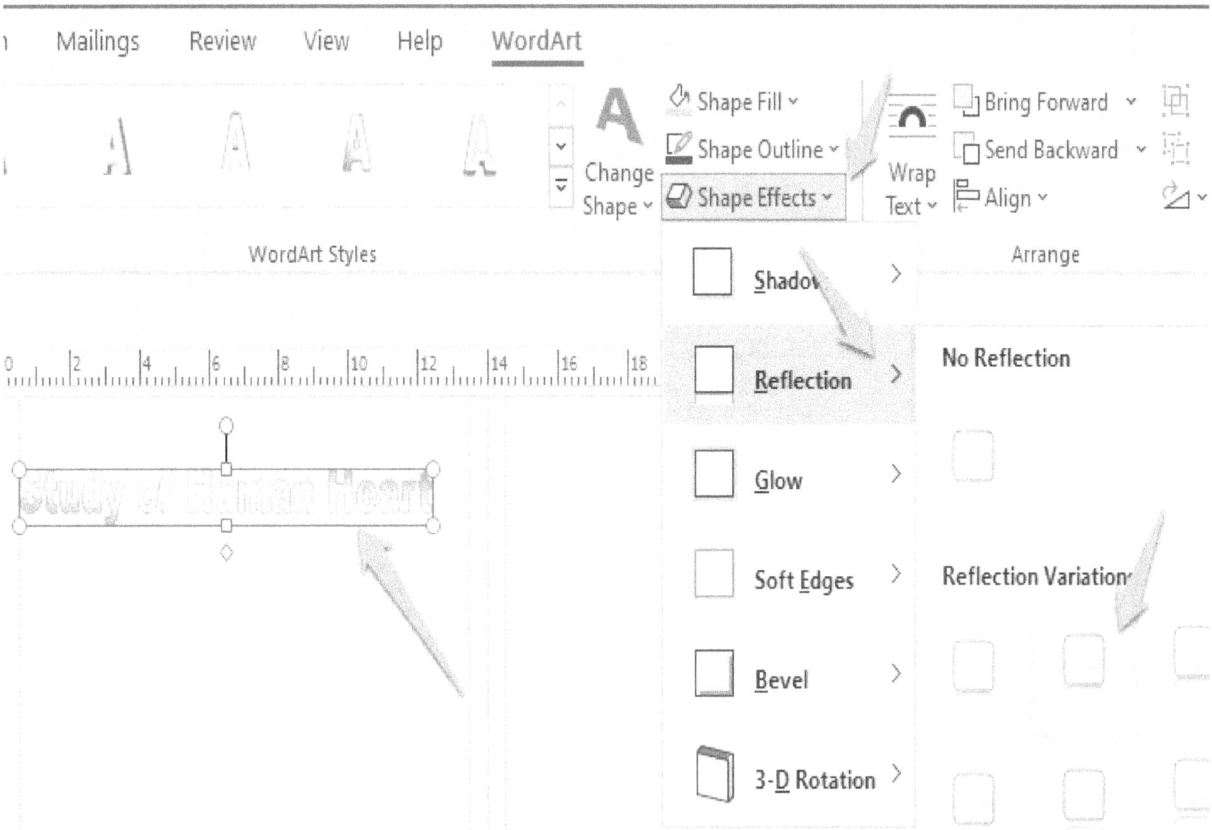

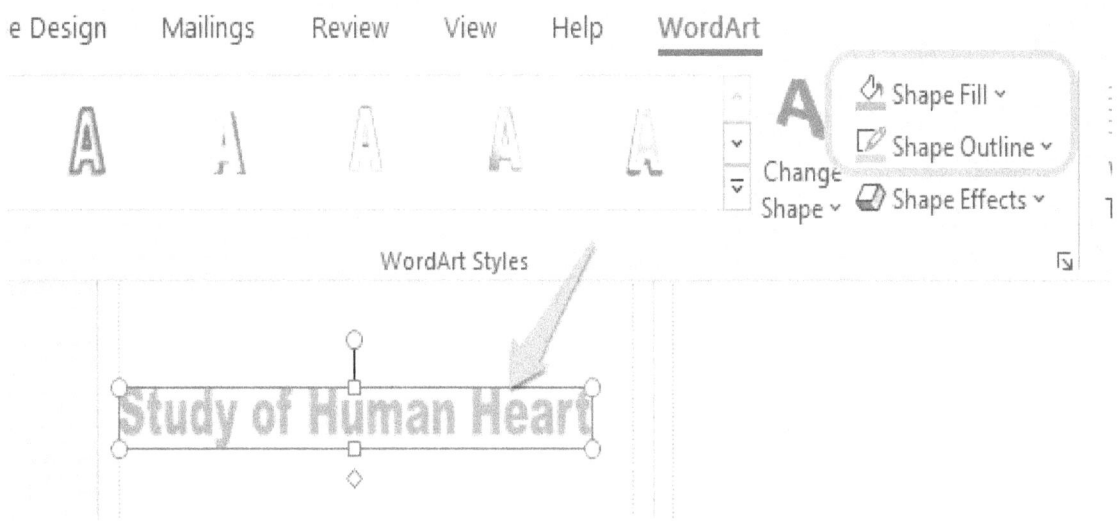

7) You change the **color** using the **"Shape Fill"** menu and the border using the "Shape Outline" menu.

8) You can change the shape of the text. To change the shape of the text, click the Change Shape menu and choose a shape on the drop-down menu.

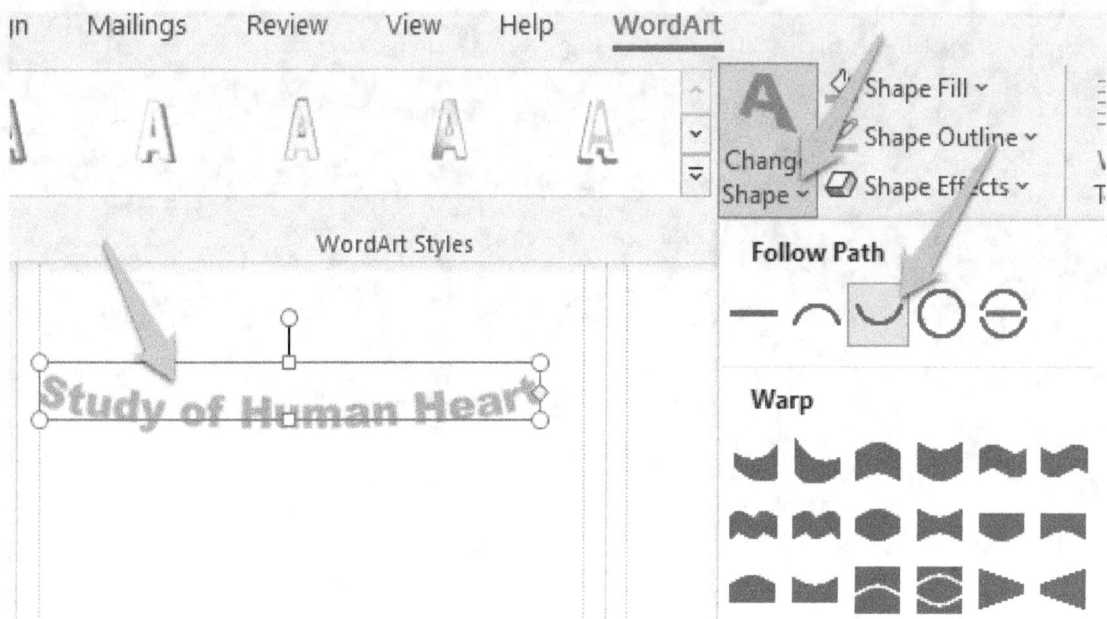

9) To alter the **shape**, click and drag the **small yellow handle** on the WordArt.
10) You can **resize** the **WordArt** with the resize handles, or **rotate** the **WordArt** with the rotation handle.

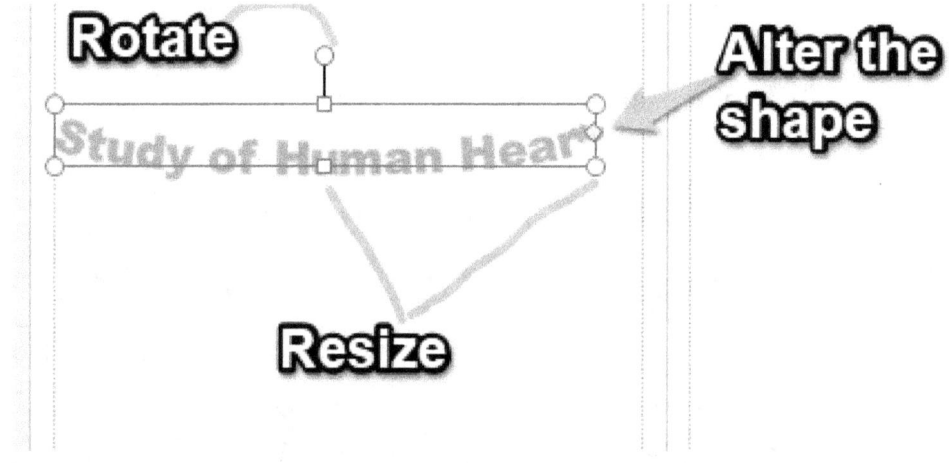

CHAPTER SIX
GETTING STARTED WITH MAIL MERGE

With Publisher, you can create envelopes and invite people using the Mail Merge.

MAIL MERGE ENVELOPES

Mail merge is useful for creating an envelope for many recipients at once rather than creating it for each individual which is laborious and time-consuming. Follow the steps itemized below to create mail merge envelopes.

1) Click the **File** tab and select **New** on the File Backstage.
2) Scroll down on the right pane, click the **Built-in** tab, and then select **Envelopes**.

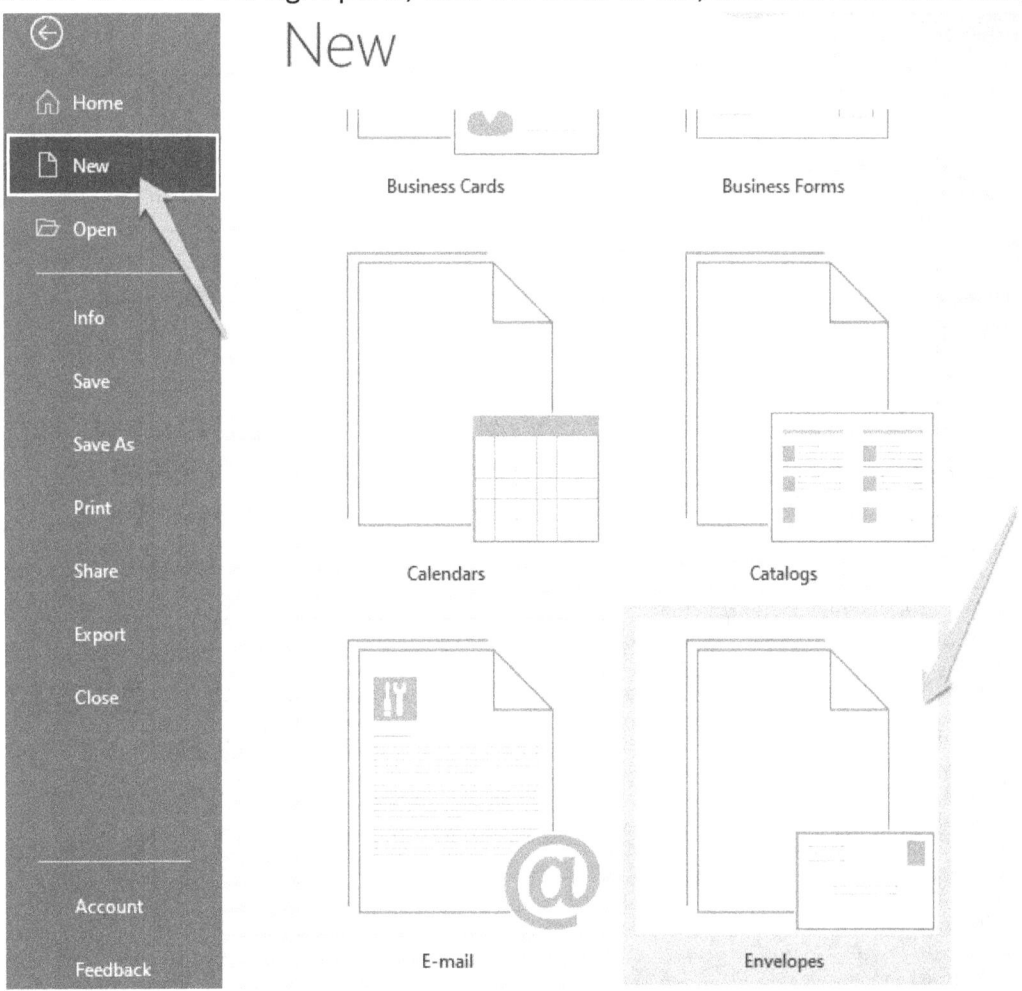

3) Scroll down to where "**blank sizes**" are located and choose the size of envelope you want to use. Then click **Create**.

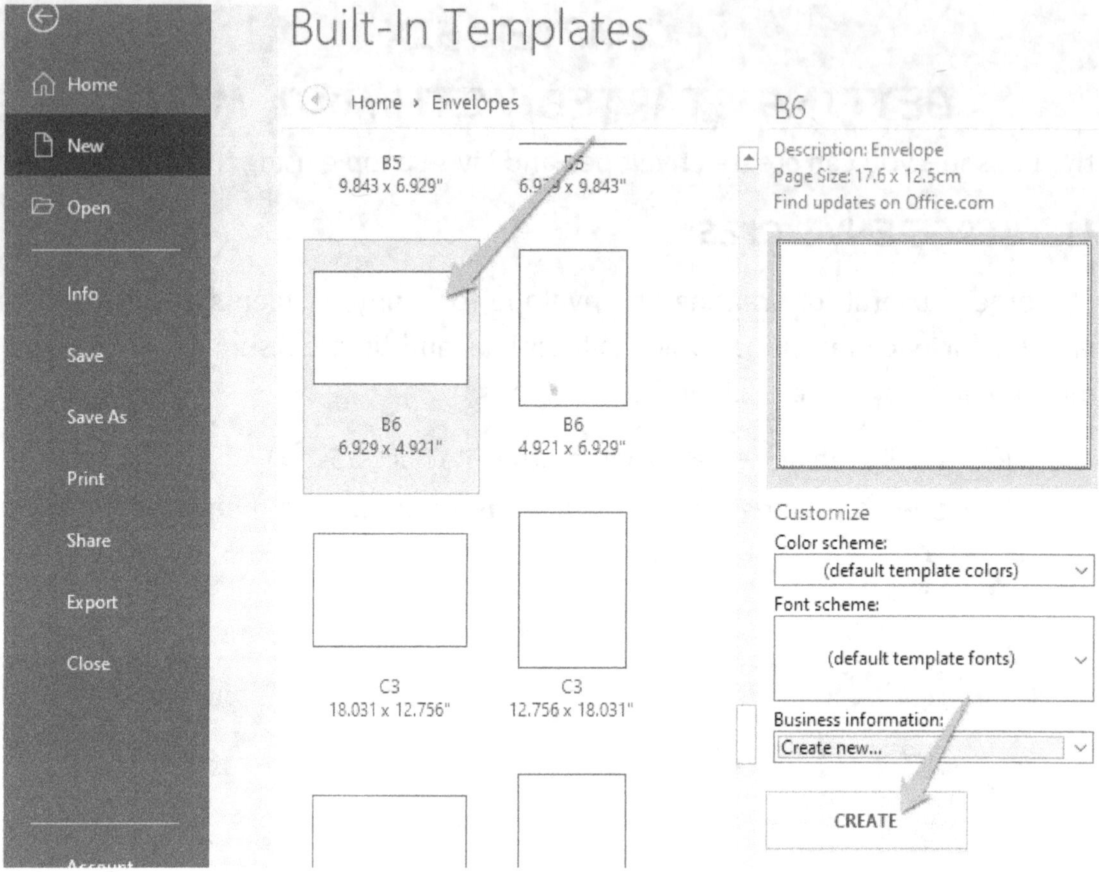

Note: Next, we will need to add a data source. This is typically a list of names and addresses. A perfect place to store names and addresses is an **Excel worksheet**. You can also import the addresses in your Outlook Contact list.

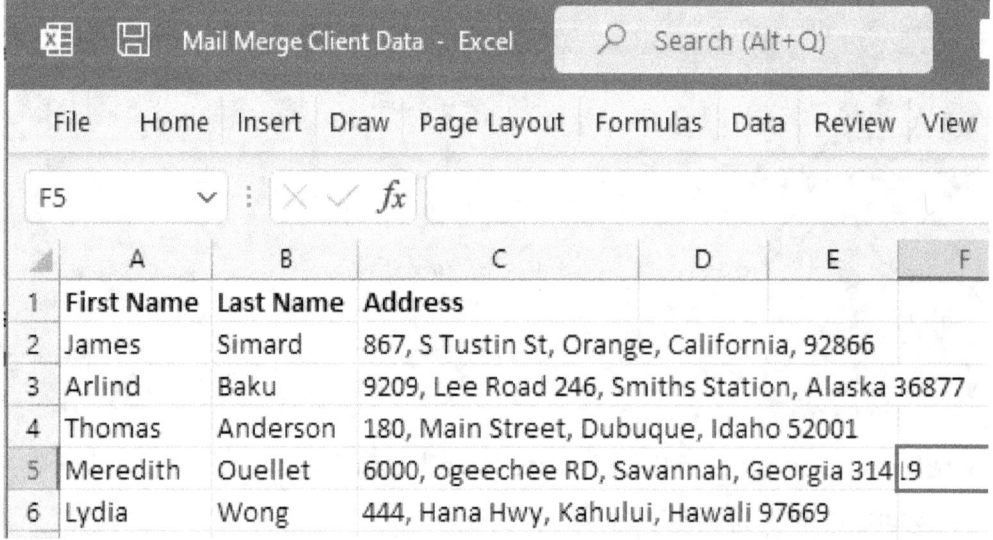

I have my client list saved to an Excel worksheet as shown above. So I will be using it in this case. The process is the same if you have your contact saved on Outlook.

4) To choose a data source, click the **Mailing** tab and click the **"Select Recipients"** menu.
5) Choose "**Use an Existing List**" on the drop-down menu to access the Select Data Source dialog box.

Note: if you don't have a data source saved, you can choose Type a New List to manually type your recipients list.

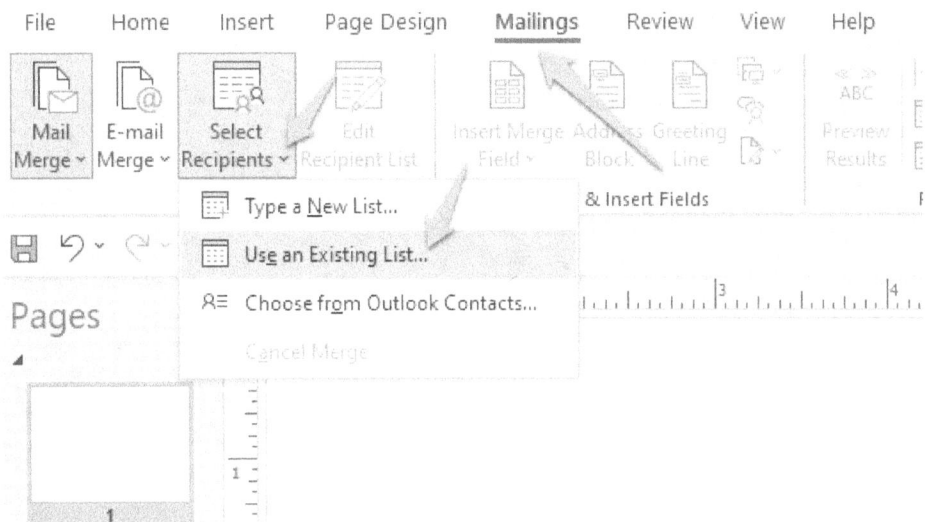

6) Locate and click your data source. I will select **Mail Merge Client Data.xlsx** in this case and click **Open**.

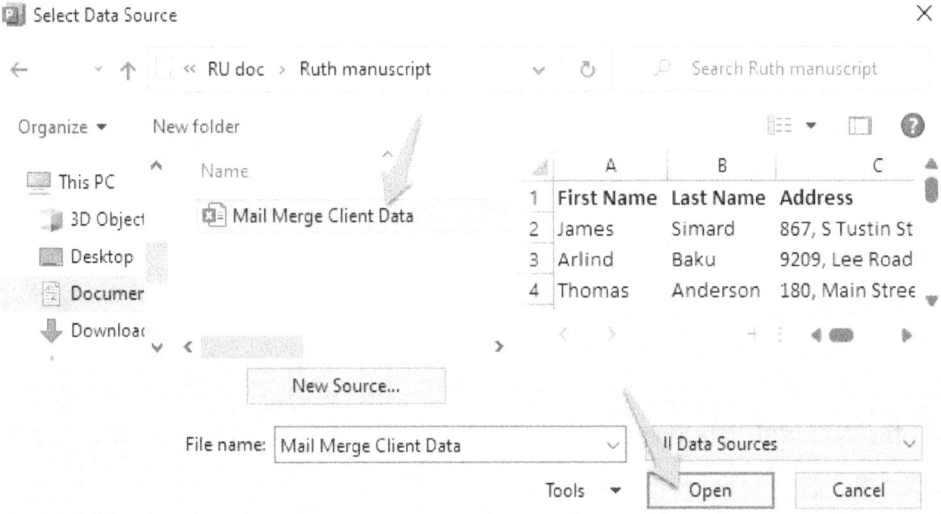

7) Click **OK** on the subsequent two dialog boxes that appear. Now, it is time to create your envelopes.

8) Click the **Mailing** tab and click the **"Address Block"** to add the addresses from your contact data source (**Mail Merge Client Data.xlsx**). Then click **OK** in the **Insert Address Block** dialog box.

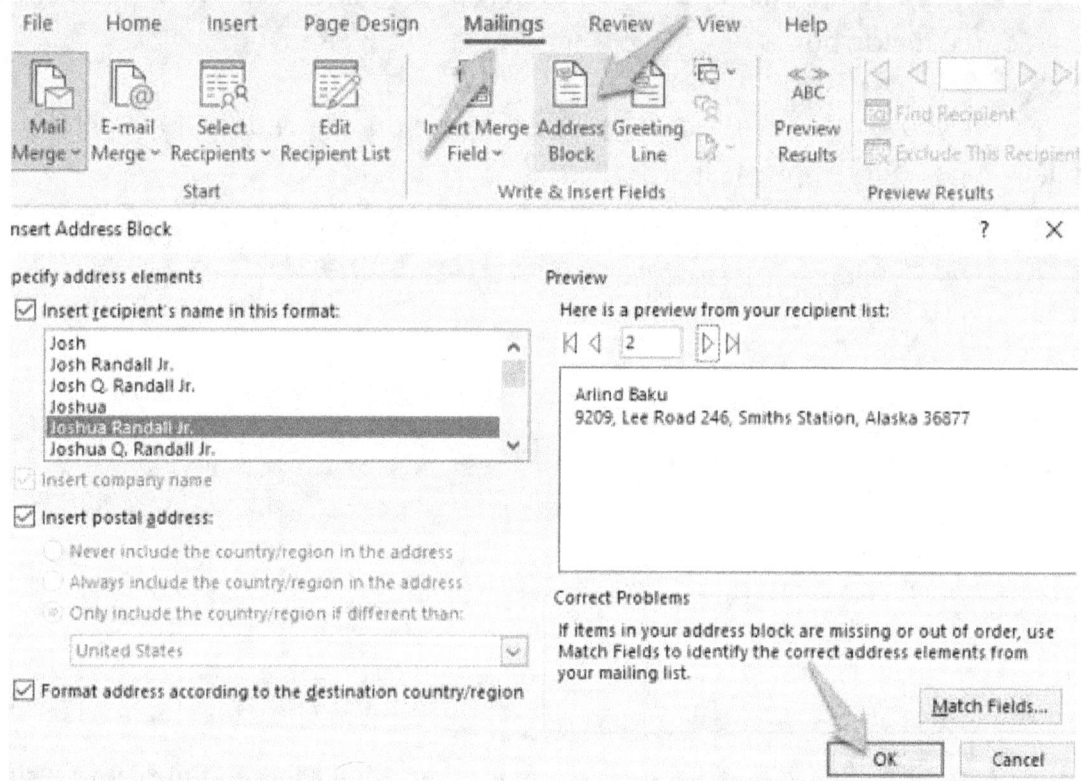

9) Your **Address Block** will now be visible on the work area, you can resize it to your preference.

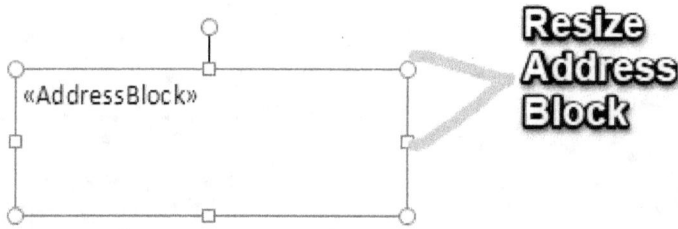

10) To preview the envelopes, click the **Mailing** tab and click **"Preview Results"**. You can flip through the envelopes using the **next/previous record** buttons.

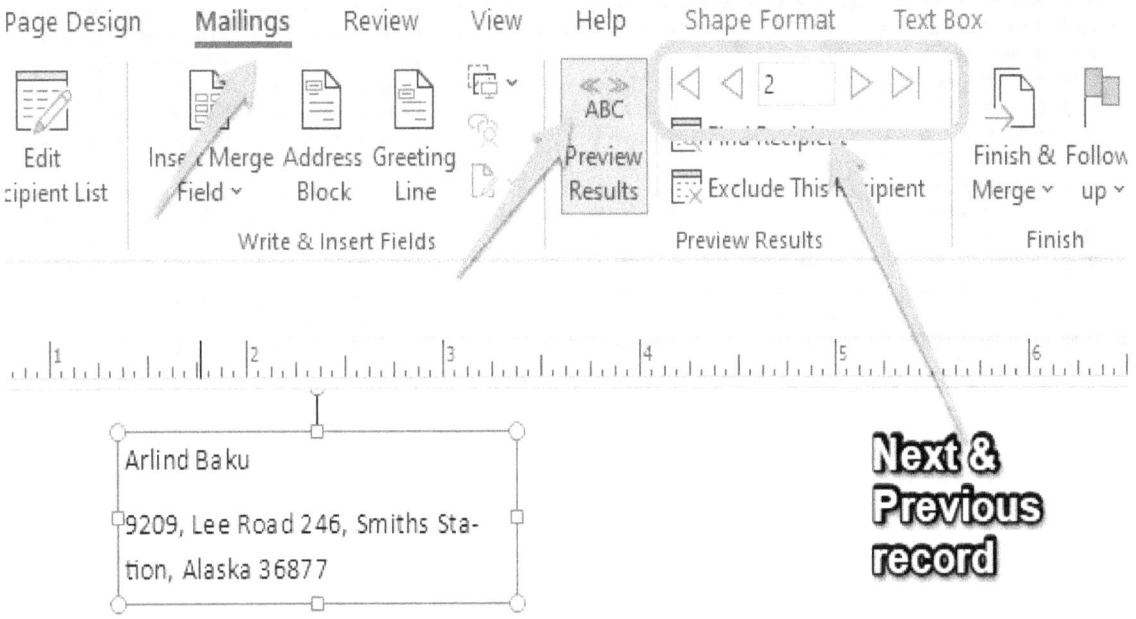

11) To complete the process, click the **Mailing** tab and click the "**Finish & Merge**" menu.

12) Select "**Merge to Printer**" on the drop-down menu to forward all to the printer, and confirm to load envelopes to the printer's paper tray.

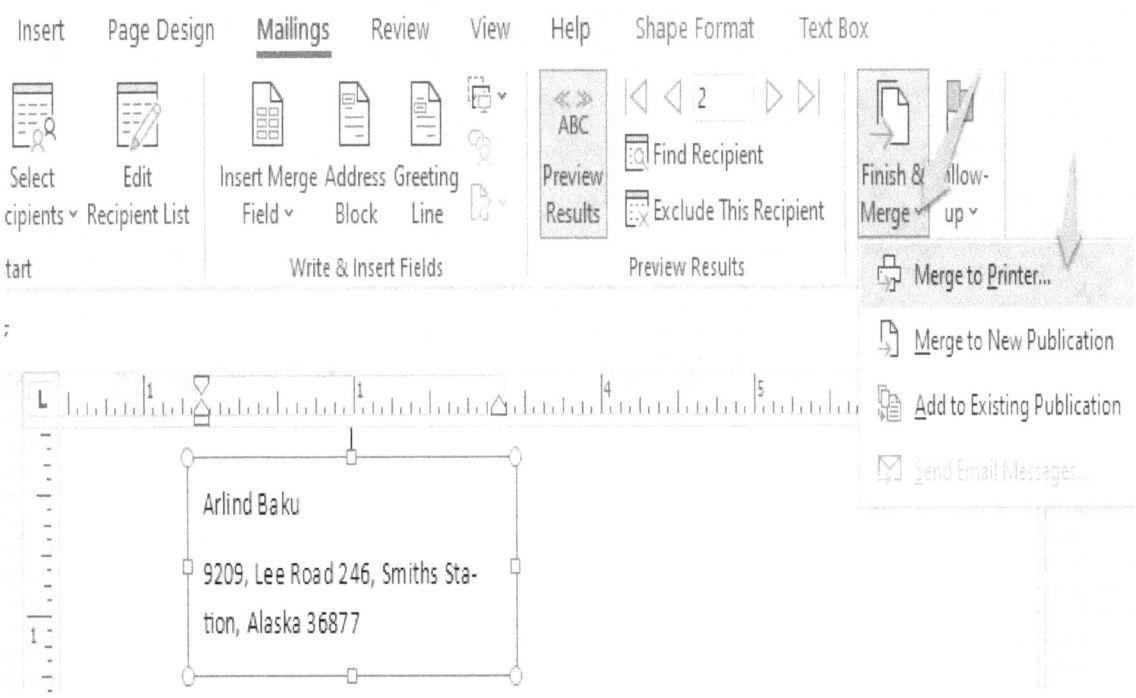

13) Choose "Print All Records" on the Print dialog box and then click the Print button.

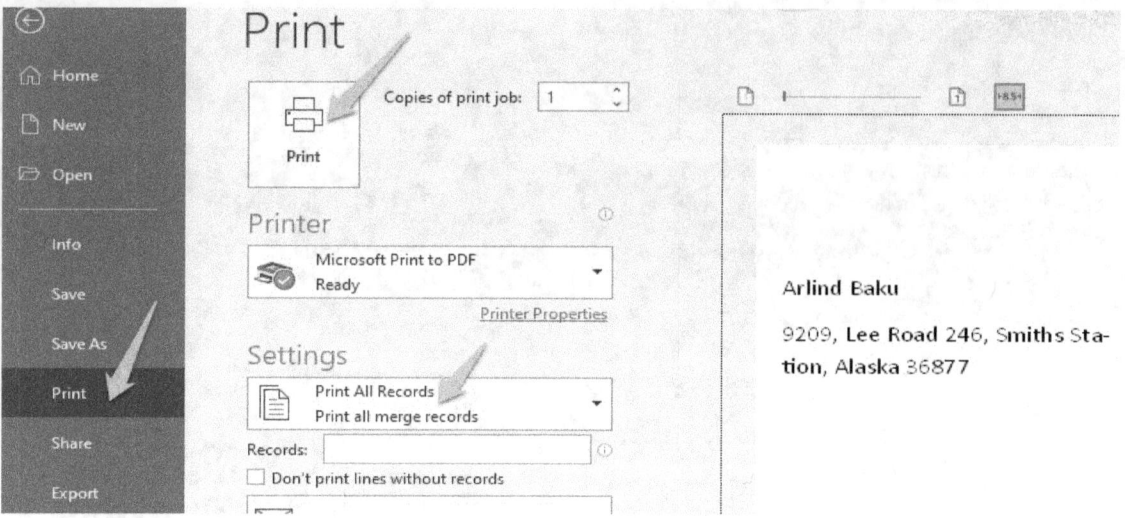

MAIL MERGE AN INVITATION

We have done printing our envelopes, Next, we will create the invitation card. Follow the steps itemized below to create your invitation:

1) Click the **File** tab and click the **New** on the File Backstage. You will type the publication template you want to use. In this case, I am creating an invitation card, so I am going to type **"Invitation"**.

2) Double-click the **template** you prefer. Next, you will have to add your data source.

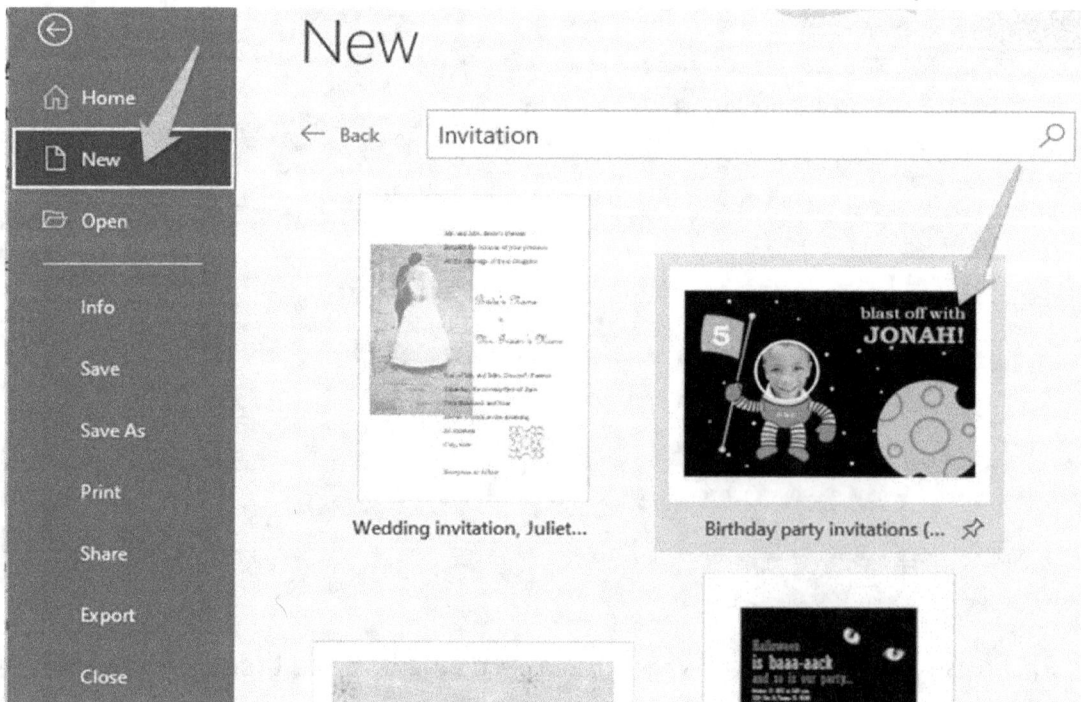

3) To add a data source, click the **Mailing** tab and click the "**Select Recipients**" menu. Choose "**Use an Existing List**" on the drop-down menu to access the Select Data Source dialog box.

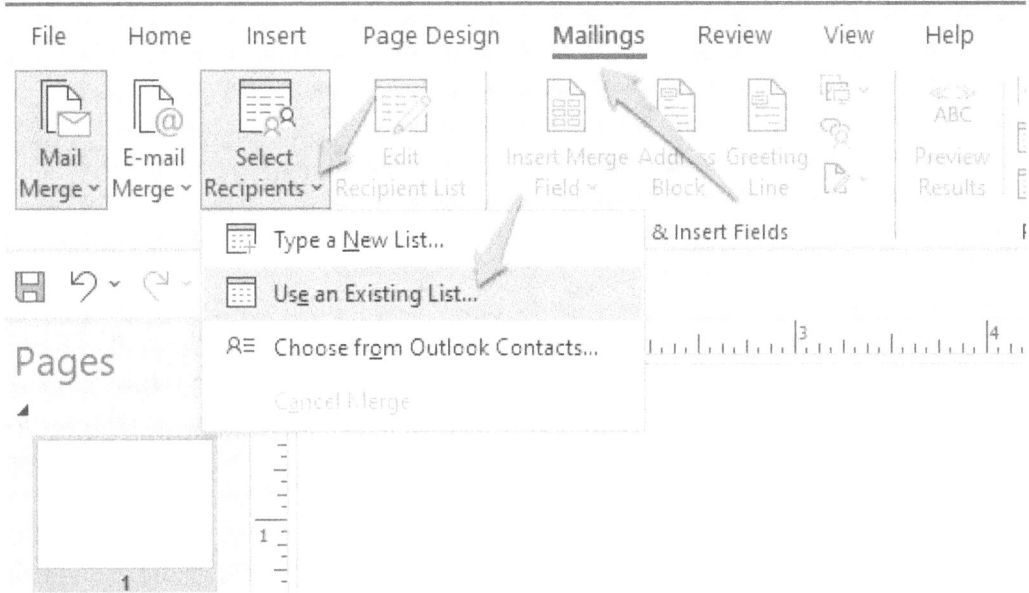

4) Locate and click your data source. I will select Mail Merge Client Data.xlsx in this case and click **Open**. Next, we will start to add our names from the Mailing tab.

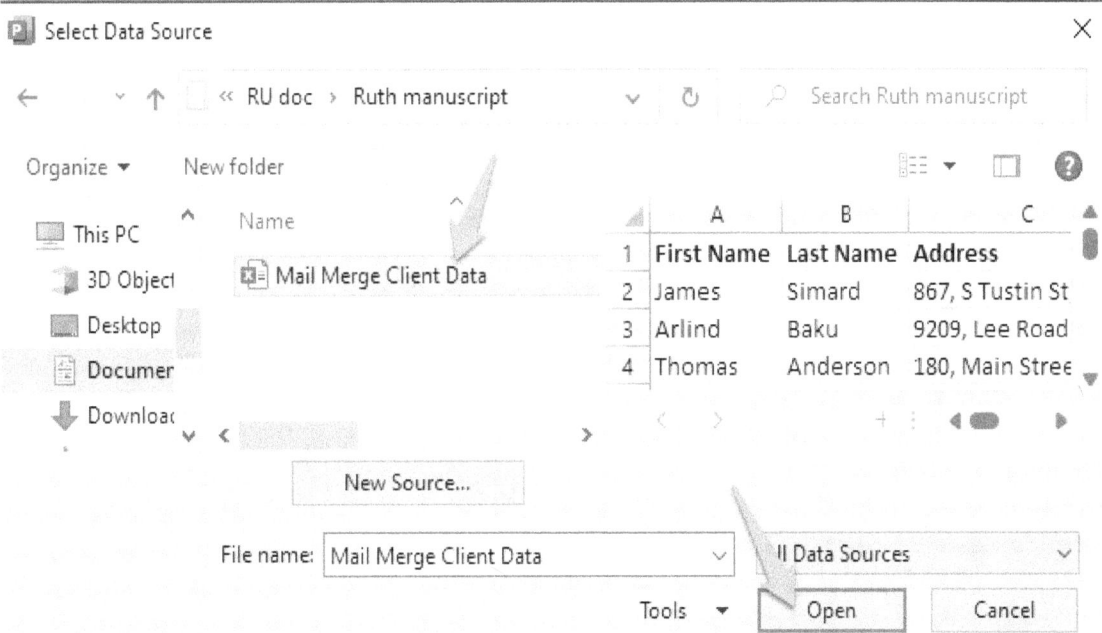

5) Click the "**Mailing** tab, click the **Insert Field** button, and choose **First Name** on the list. Click the "**Insert Merge** Field" button and select **Last Name.**

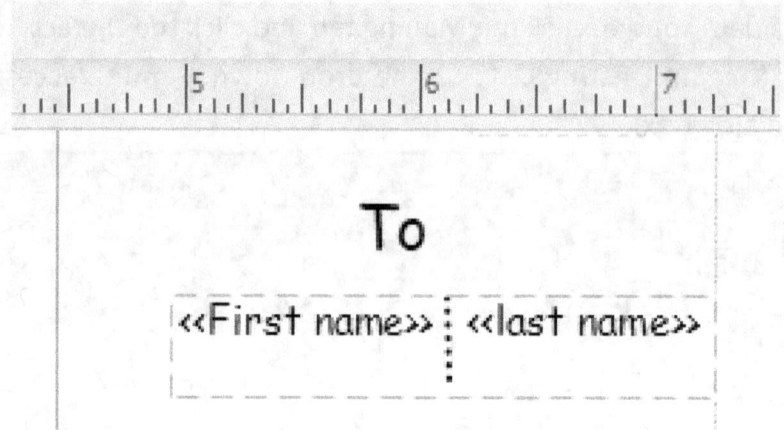

6) Reposition the text box and change the font type if you wish. When you are done adding all the fields with the Merge Fields of the Mailing tab, click **"Preview Results"**. You will have a design that looks like this (a customized invitation for each name). you can customize it in any form you want.

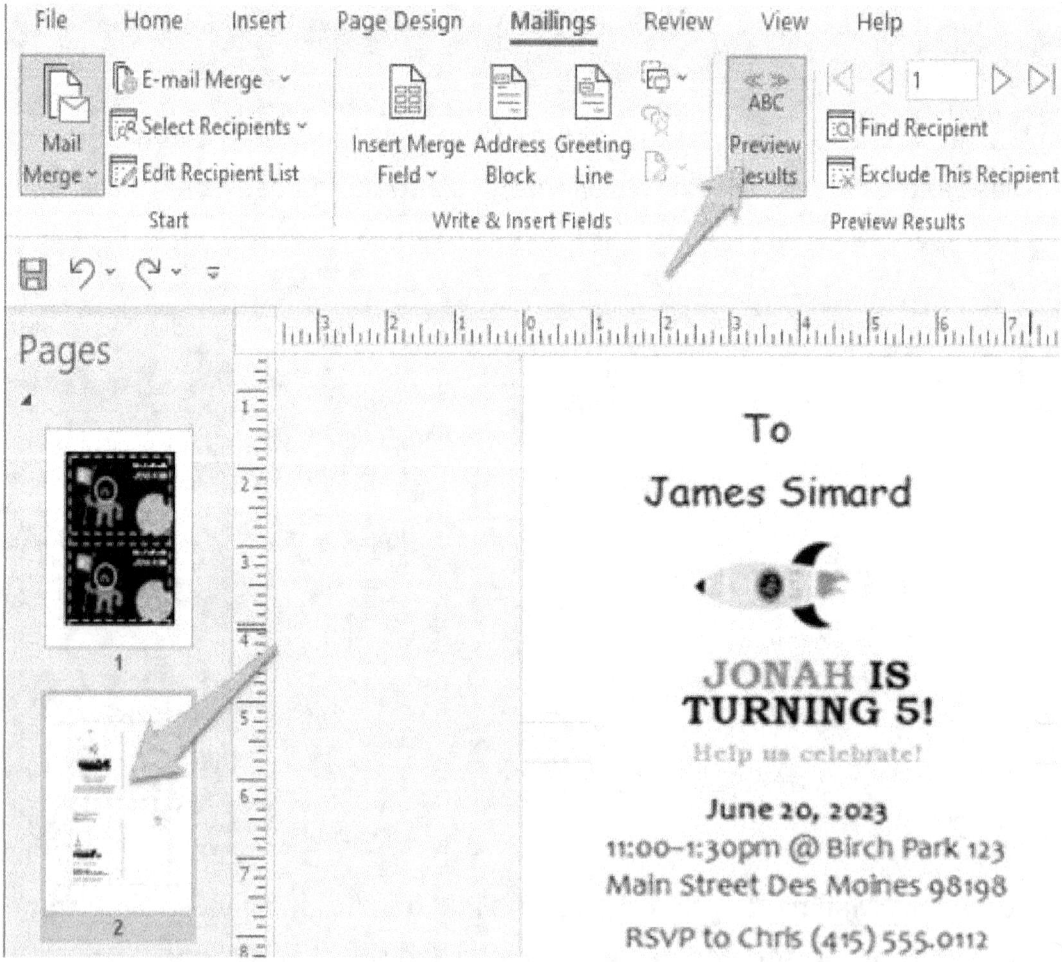

7) To complete the process, click the **Mailing** tab and click the "**Finish & Merge**" menu.

8) Select "**Merge to Printer**" on the drop-down menu to forward all to the printer, and confirm to load envelopes to the printer's paper tray.

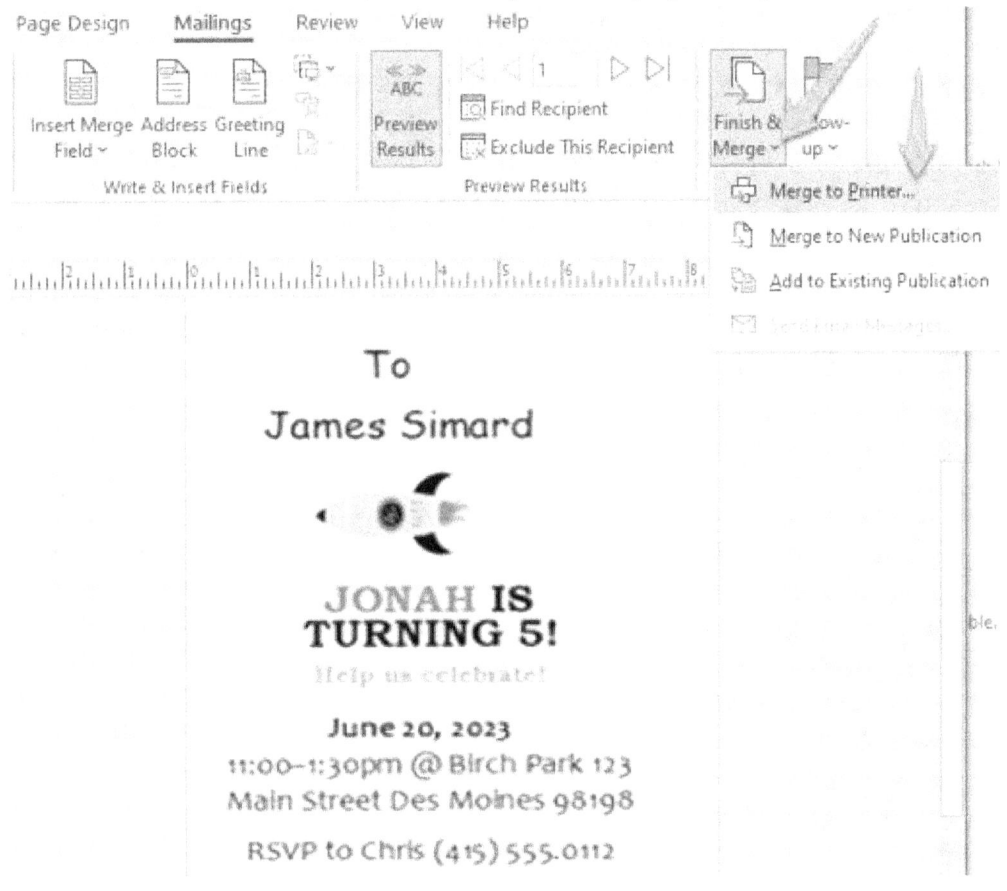

CHAPTER SEVEN
GETTING STARTED WITH PUBLISHER TEMPLATES

This chapter will train you how to use the load of preformatted templates that are available and how to create a template from scratch.

LOCATING AND USING AN IN-BUILT TEMPLATE

When you launch Publisher, a home screen will appear with thumbnails of diverse templates that you can use for publication. Follow these steps to locate and use a template for your design.

1) The ideal way to locate a template is to search for it with the search box. Click **New** on the Left pane of the **Home screen** or **File Backstage.**
2) Type the type of template, you want to find in the search box. I will enter a **Greeting Card** in the case.

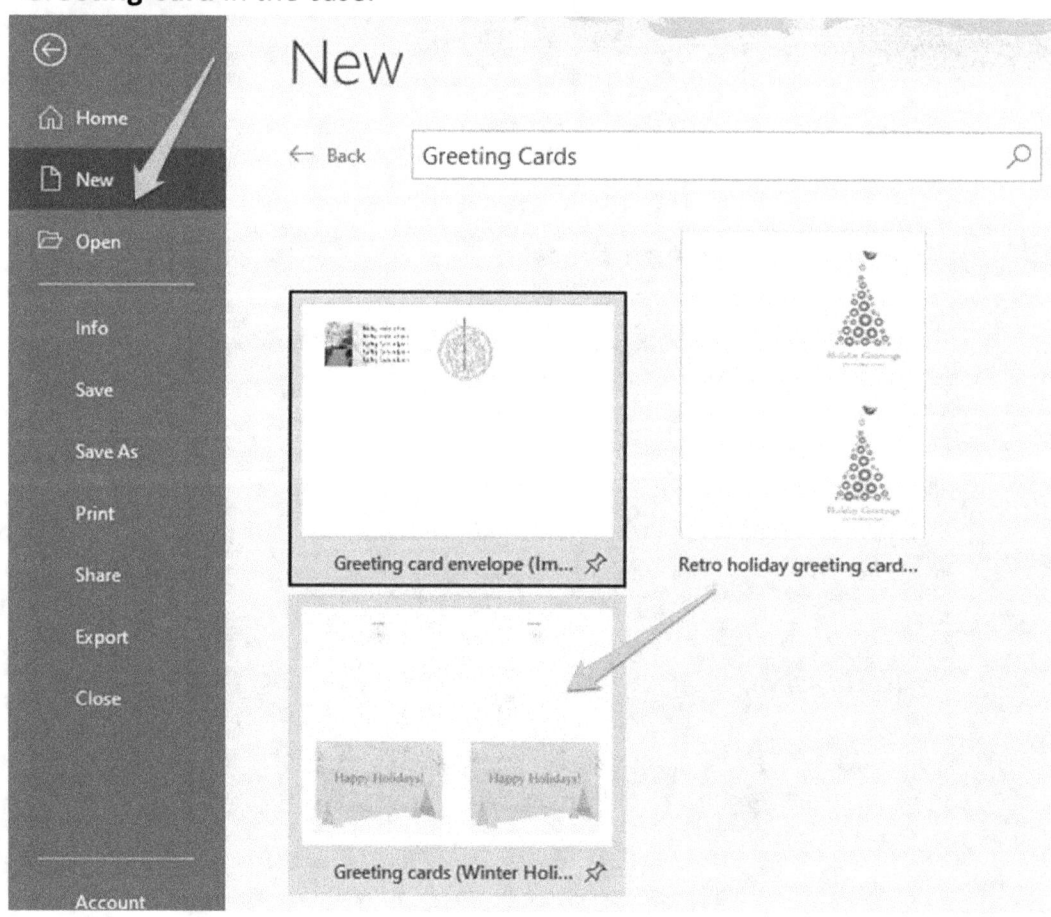

3) Choose the template you want to use from the search result by double-clicking the template thumbnail.

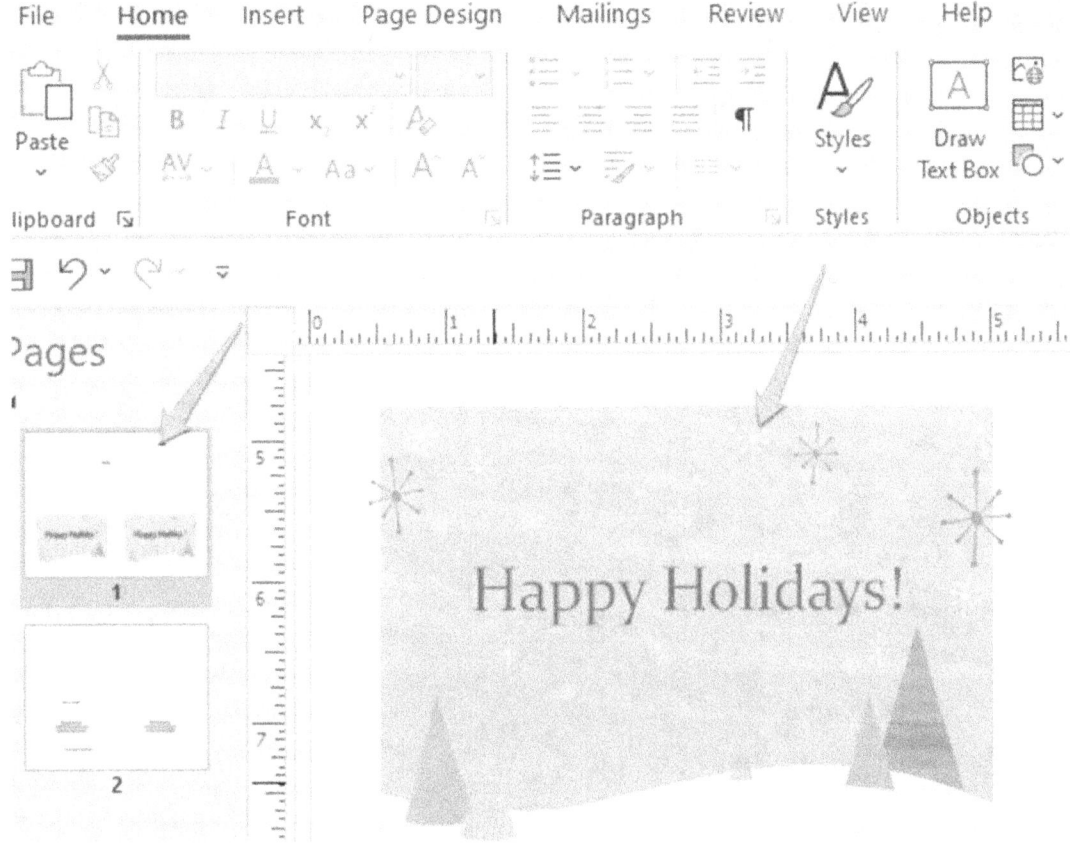

4) You can change the image and text of the template. To change the **text**, click on the **text** and type your **new text**. To change the image **right-click** and select **Change Picture** on the fly-out menu.

CREATING YOUR OWN TEMPLATE

You can build up your own style and save it as a template that you can use to create new documents using the same style. For instance, fonts, heading sizes and layout.

After you have designed a publication, follow the steps below to save a publication design as a template.

1) Click the **File** tab and select **Save As** on the File Backstage.

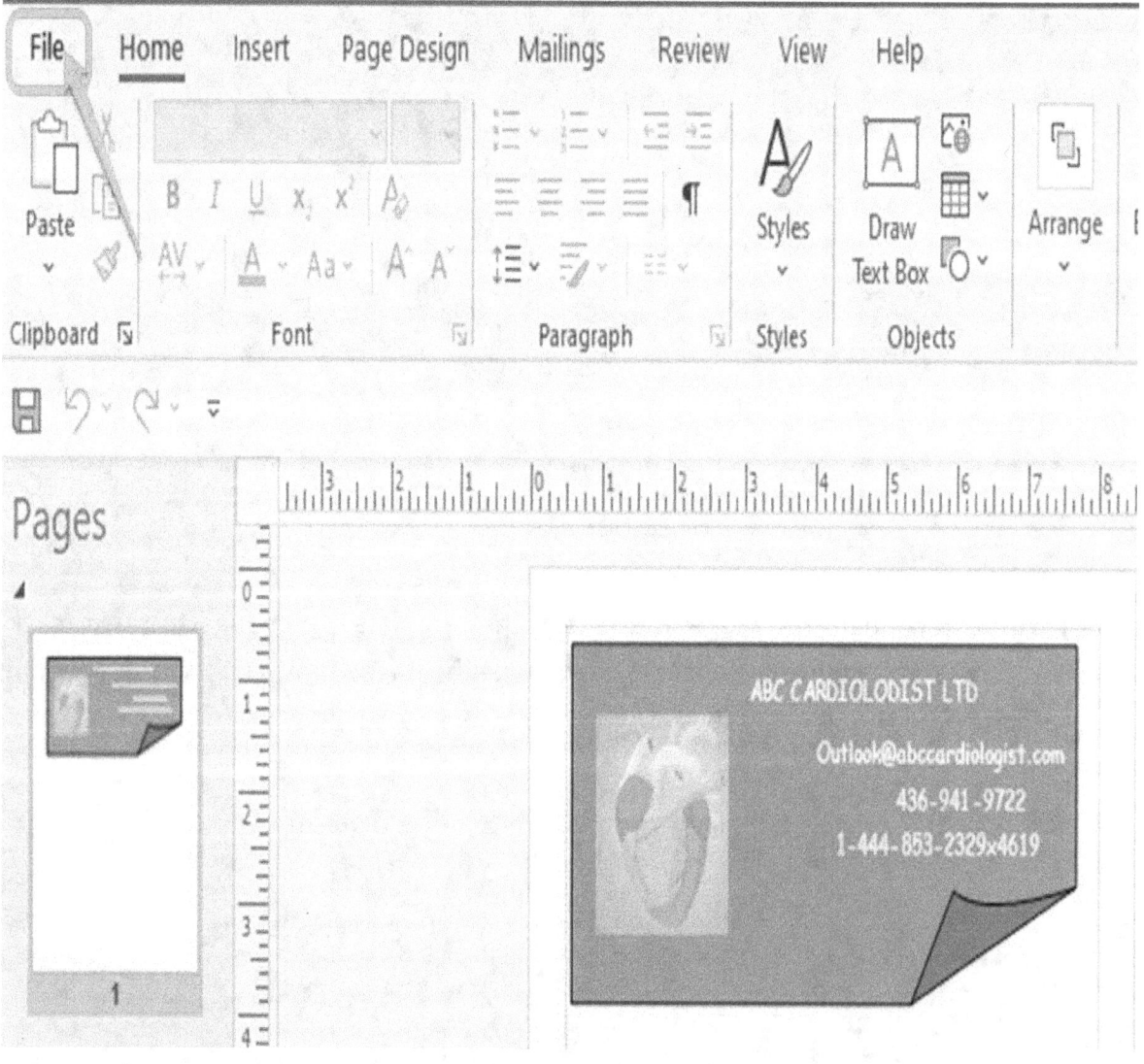

2) You can save it on "**OneDrive**" or any other **folder**.
3) Click the "**Save as type**" menu and choose "**Publisher template**". Then click **Save**.

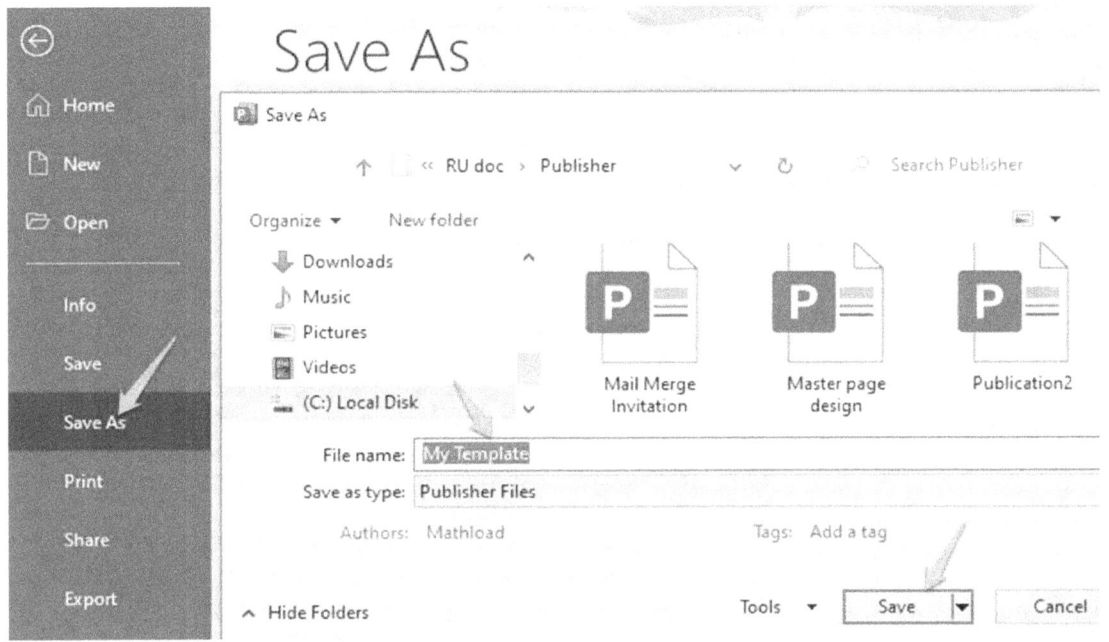

4) To create a new file using the template, click the **New** button on the **Home screen** or **File Backstage**.
5) Click the **Personal** tab on the right pane, you might need to scroll down to see the "**Personal**" tab.

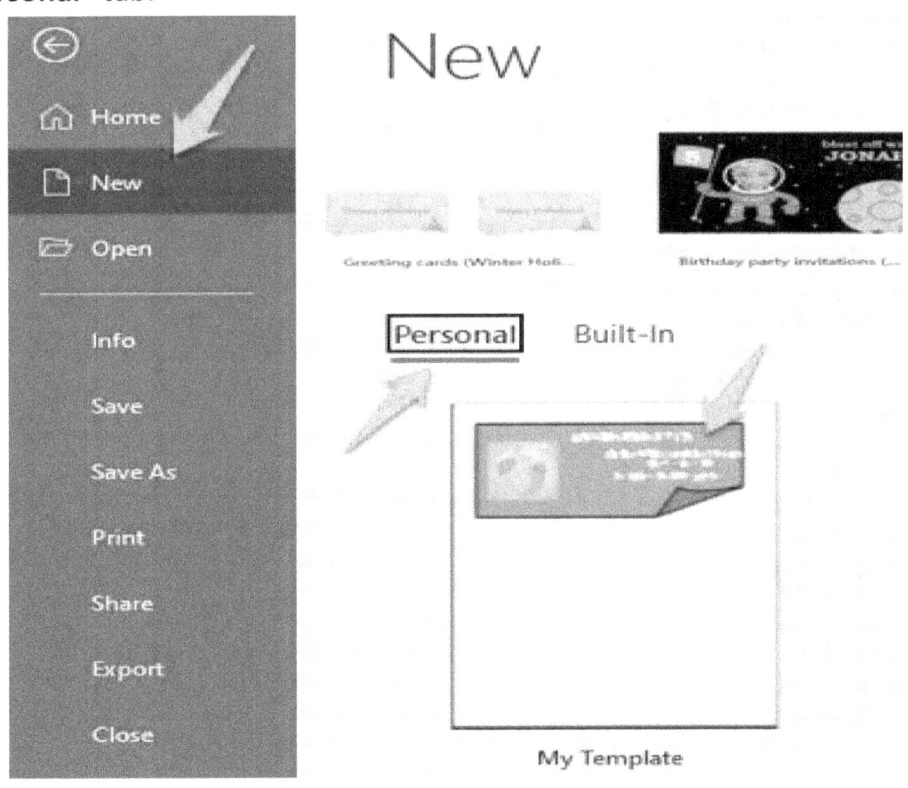

6) Double-click the **template** and begin to enter **new text.**

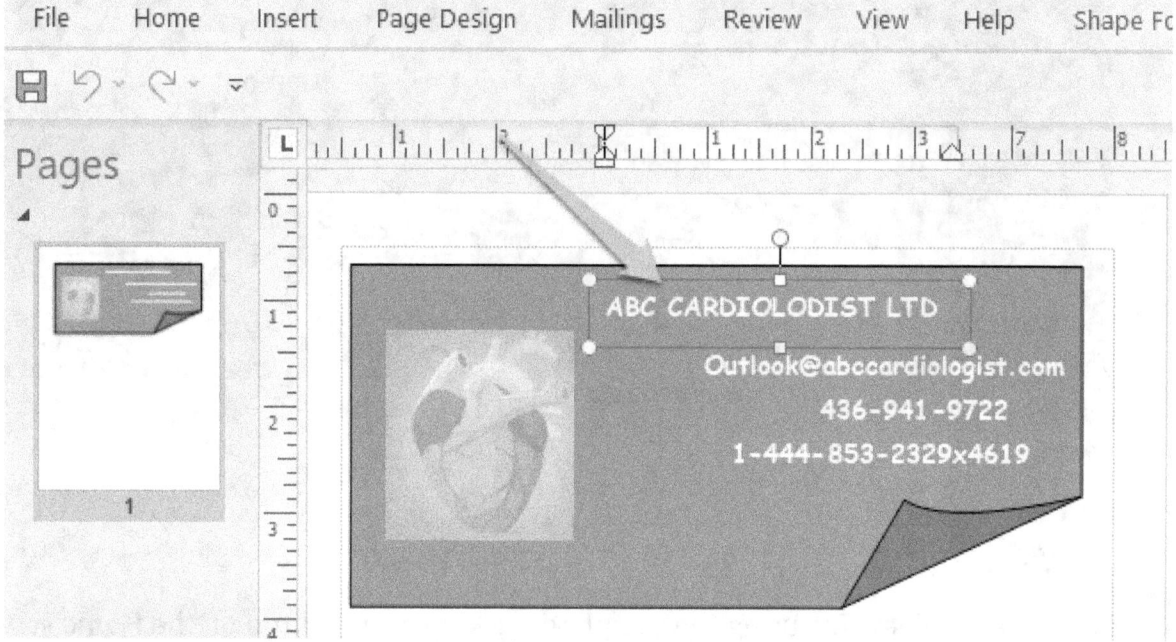

7) Then save it as a new publication by right-clicking the **File** tab and choosing **Save As** on the File Backstage.

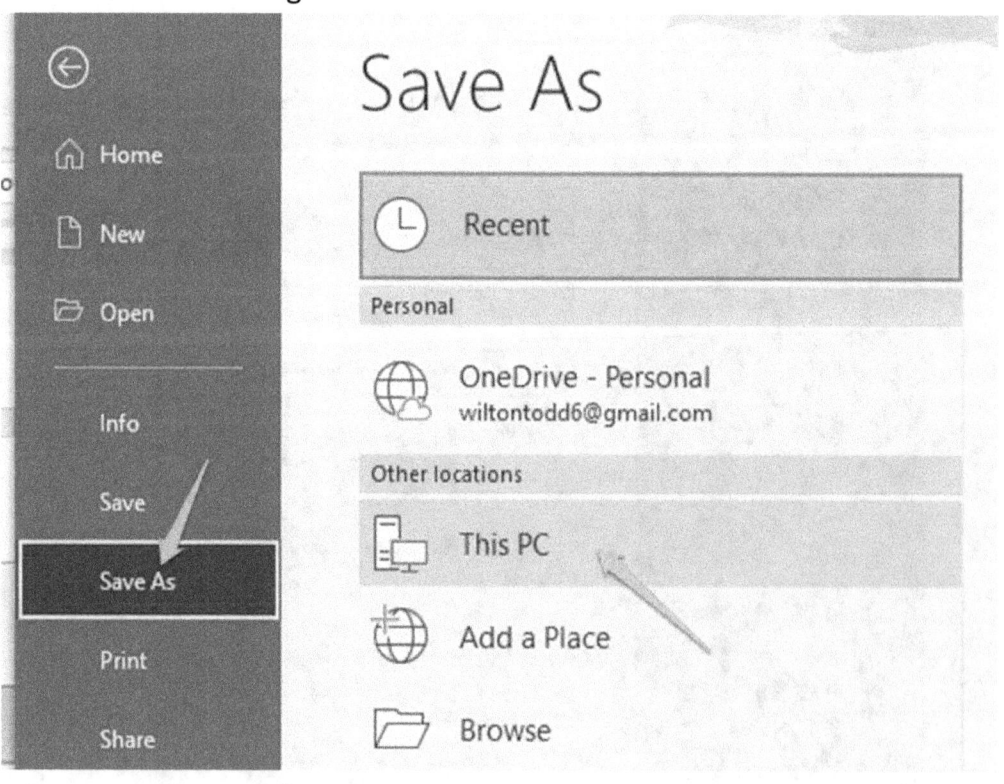

8) Specify the **folder** where you want to save your document and provide a concise **name** for it.

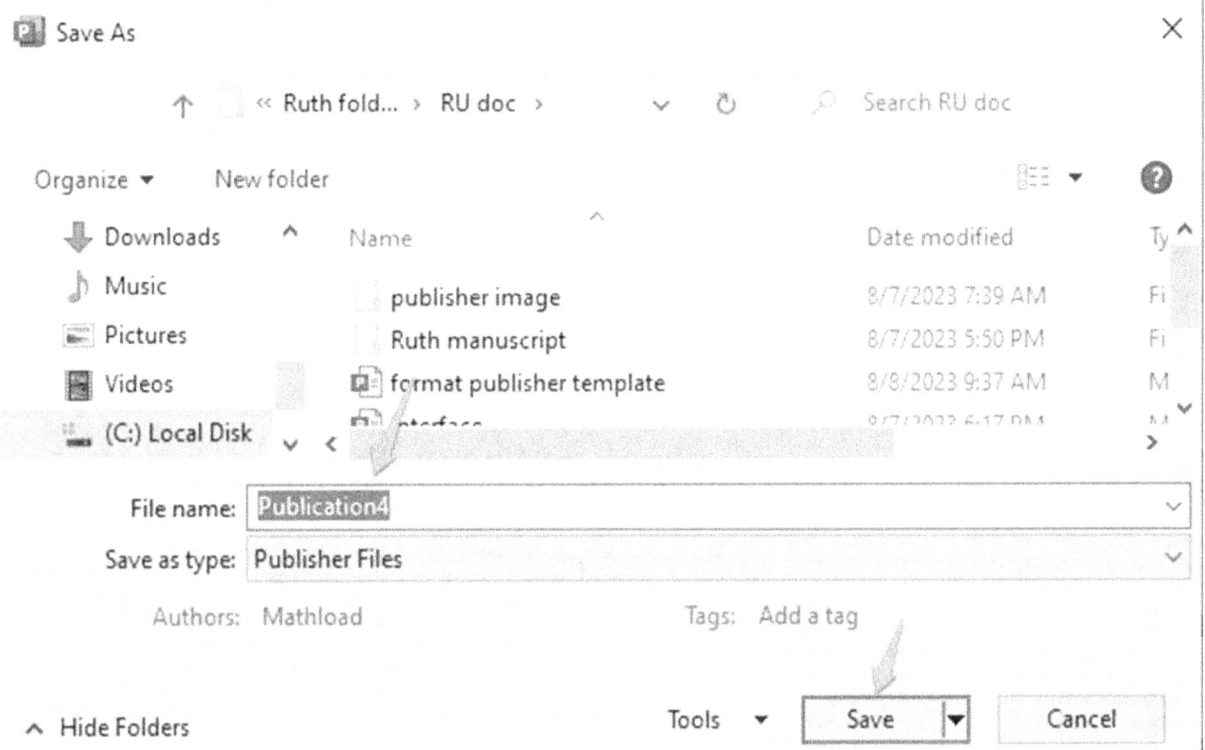

CHAPTER EIGHT
MANAGING YOUR PUBLICATION

This chapter deals with various ways of managing one's publication such as saving your work, page setup, page master, and so on.

SAVING DOCUMENTS

Follow the steps itemized below to save your work.

1) Click the **File** tab and click **Save As** on the File Backstage.

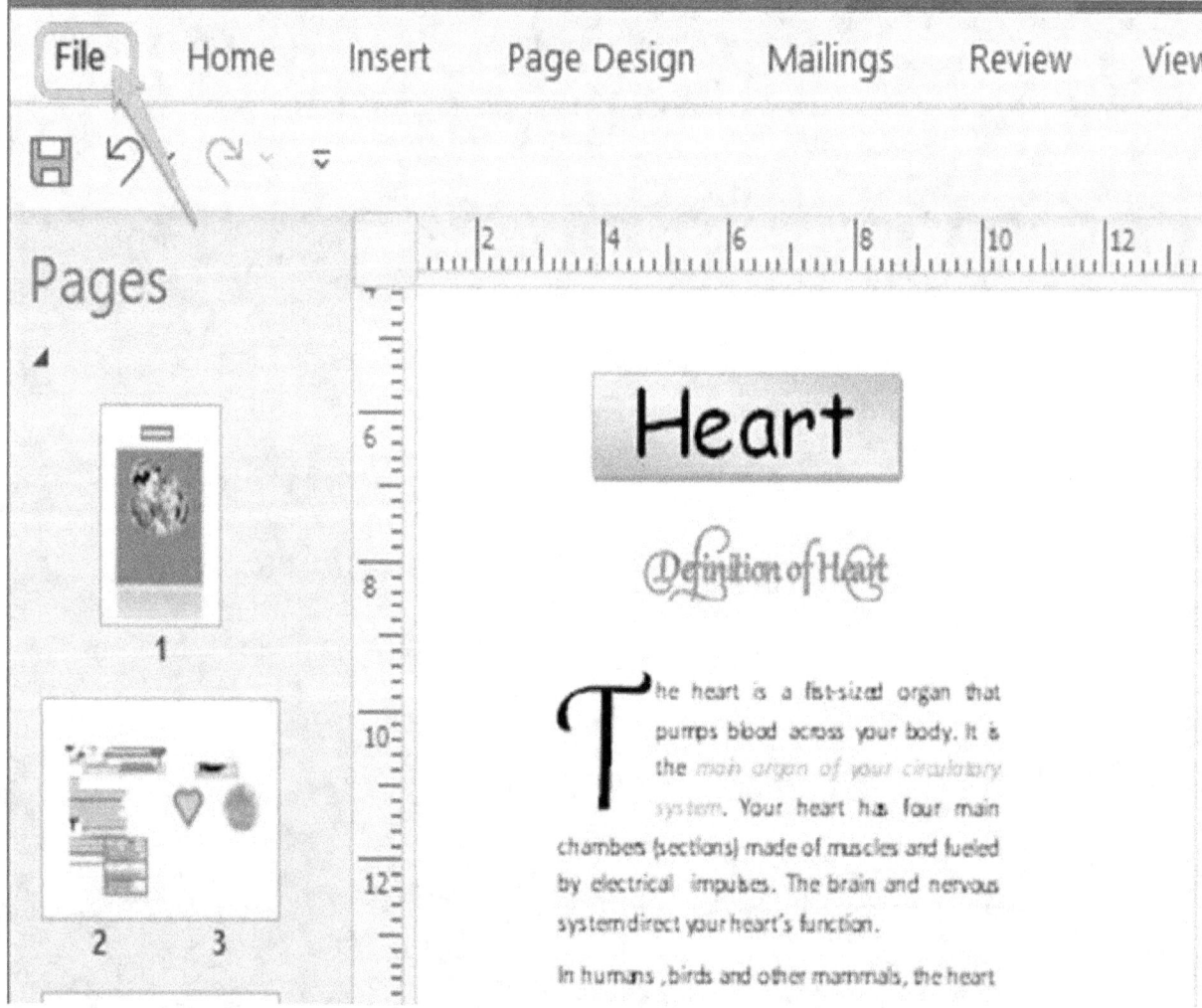

2) Specify the **folder** where you want the Publisher to save your document, provide a file name in the **File Name** text box, and click **Save**.

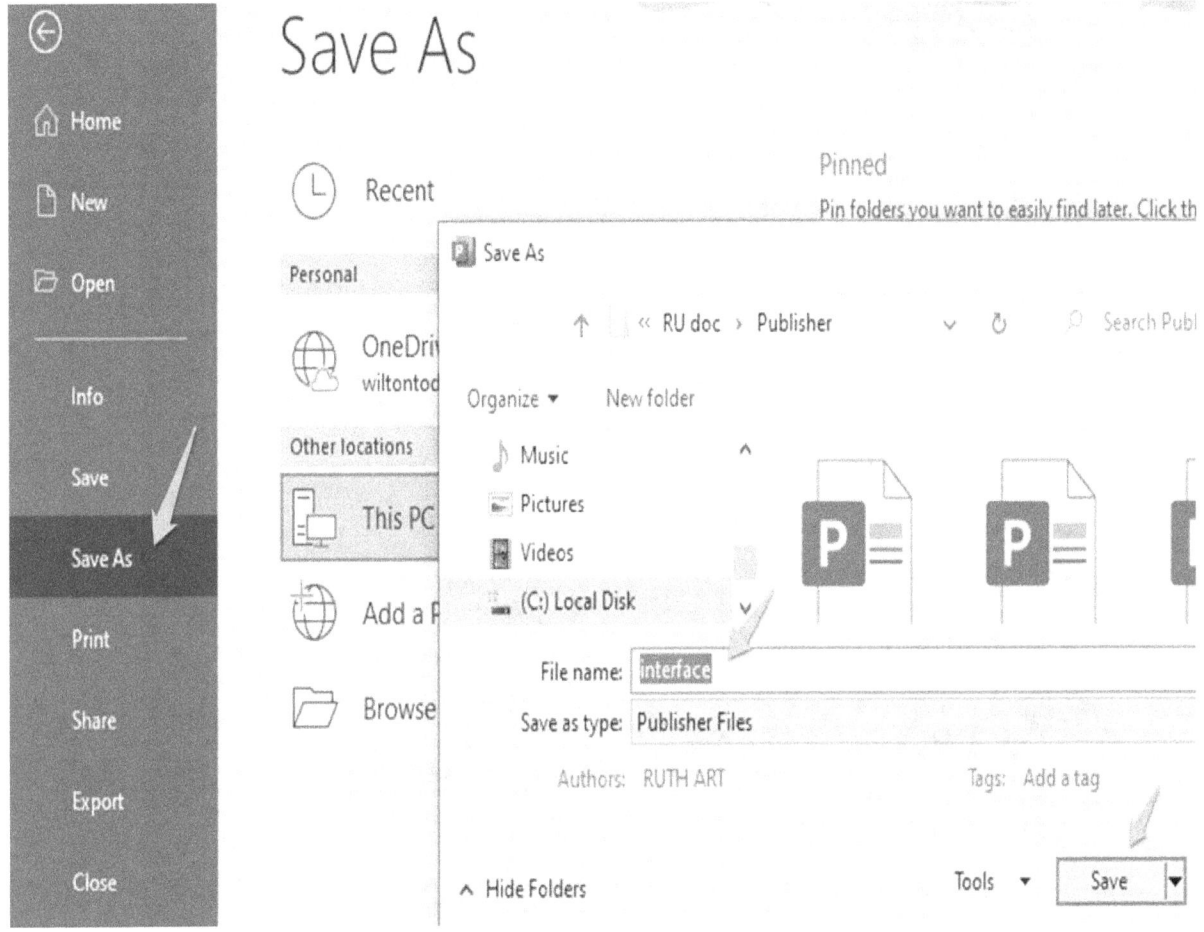

SAVING DOCUMENT AS A DIFFERENT FORMAT

Occasionally, you may want to save a document in a different format, particularly if you want to send the document to a person who does not use Publisher or Microsoft Office.

Publisher lets you save your document in different formats. A typical example is saving files as PDFs, it is a portable format that can be read on any type of computer, phone, or tablet without a need to use Microsoft Publisher. Follow the steps below to save your document in a different format.

1) With the document still open, Click the **File** tab and select **Save As** on the File Backstage.
2) Specify the **folder** where you want the Publisher to save your document and provide a file name in the **File Name** text box.
3) Click the "**Save as type**" menu and choose "**PDF**".

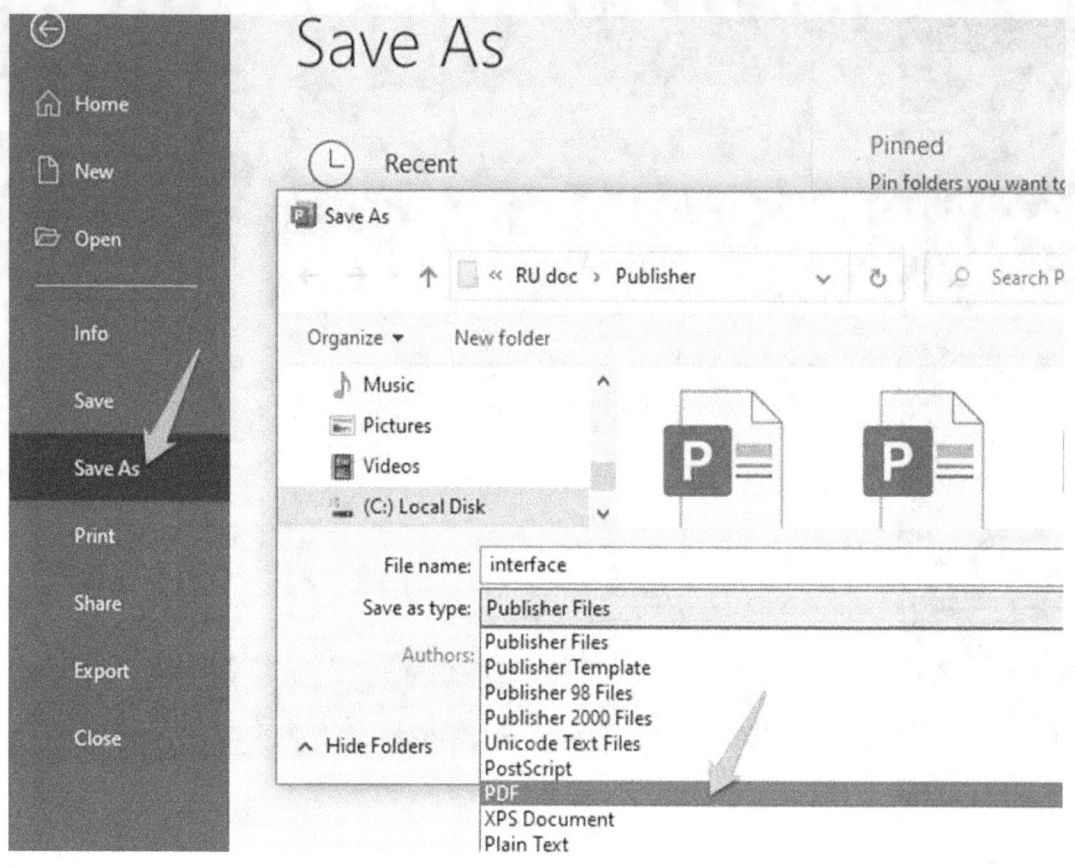

4) Click "**Options**" on the lower left of the dialog box and choose **high-quality printing**.
5) Click "**Save**" on the Save As dialog box to complete the process.

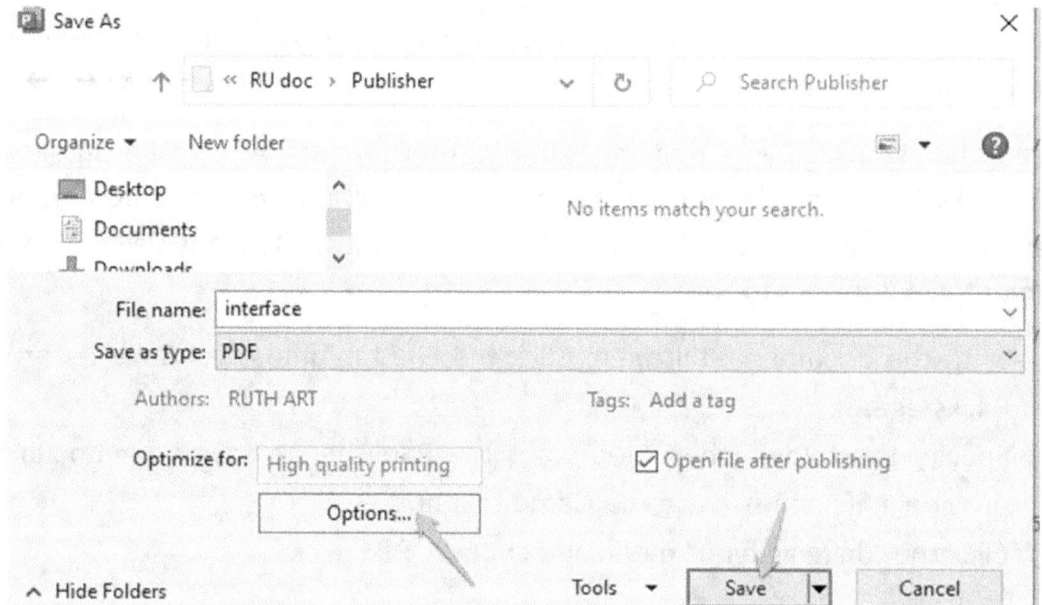

OPENING SAVED DOCUMENTS

1) Click the **File** tab and select **Open** on the File Backstage.
2) Choose the **document** you want to open on the list on the right side.

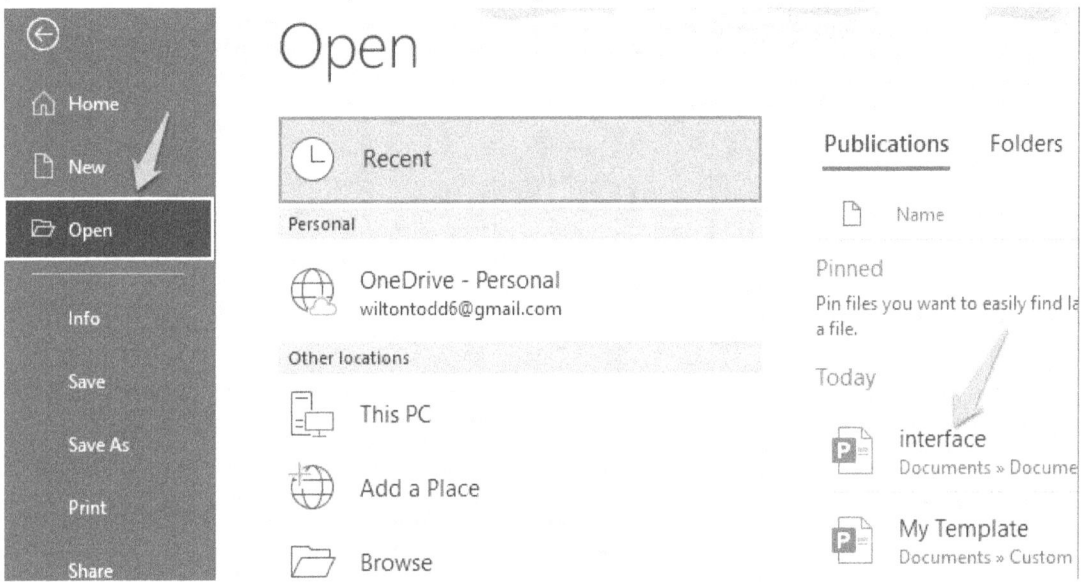

3) Microsoft Publisher lists all the most recently opened documents. The newest file is listed first. Double-click any **file** on the **Recent** tab to open it.
4) If the document you want to open is not listed on the Recent tab, click the **Browse** button to locate the folder where it is saved. When you get the file **select it** and click **Open**.

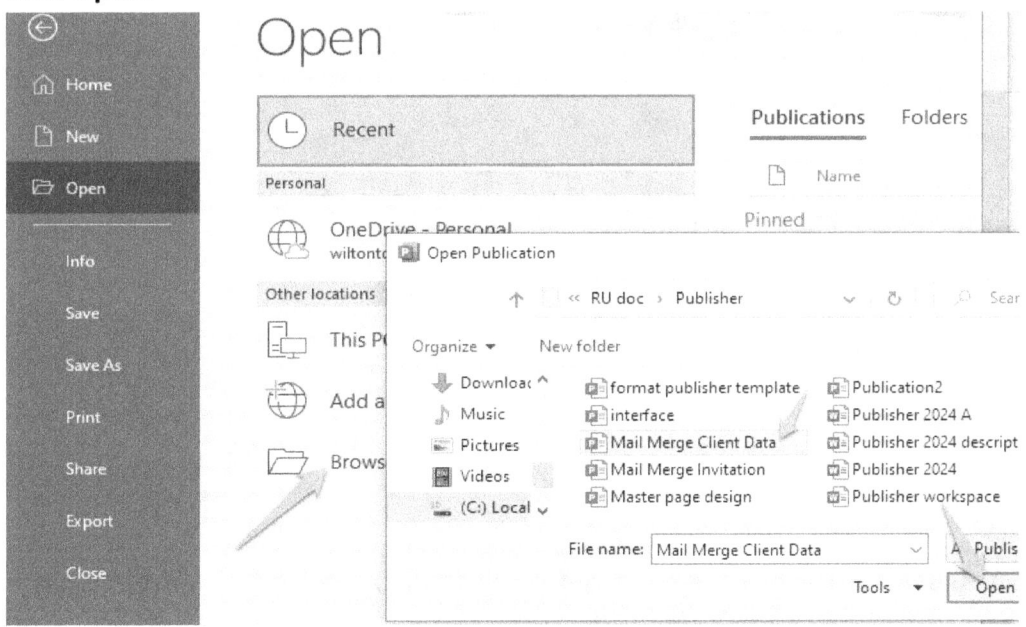

PAGE SETUP

Page setup lets you adjust the margins, orientation, paper size, and general layout of the document. follow the steps itemized below to adjust your page setup.

1) Click the **Page Design** tab and click the **Page Setup dialog box launcher**. The Page Setup dialog box appears.

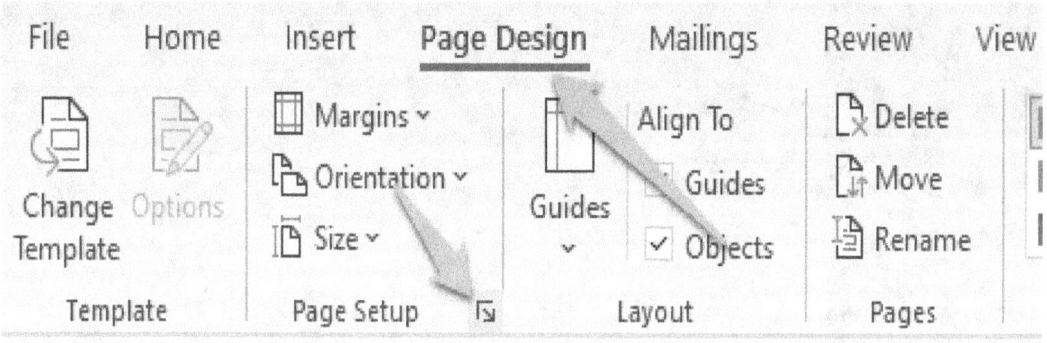

2) The dialog box allows you to adjust the layout type. For instance, you can create **envelopes**, **booklets, folded cards**, and so on.

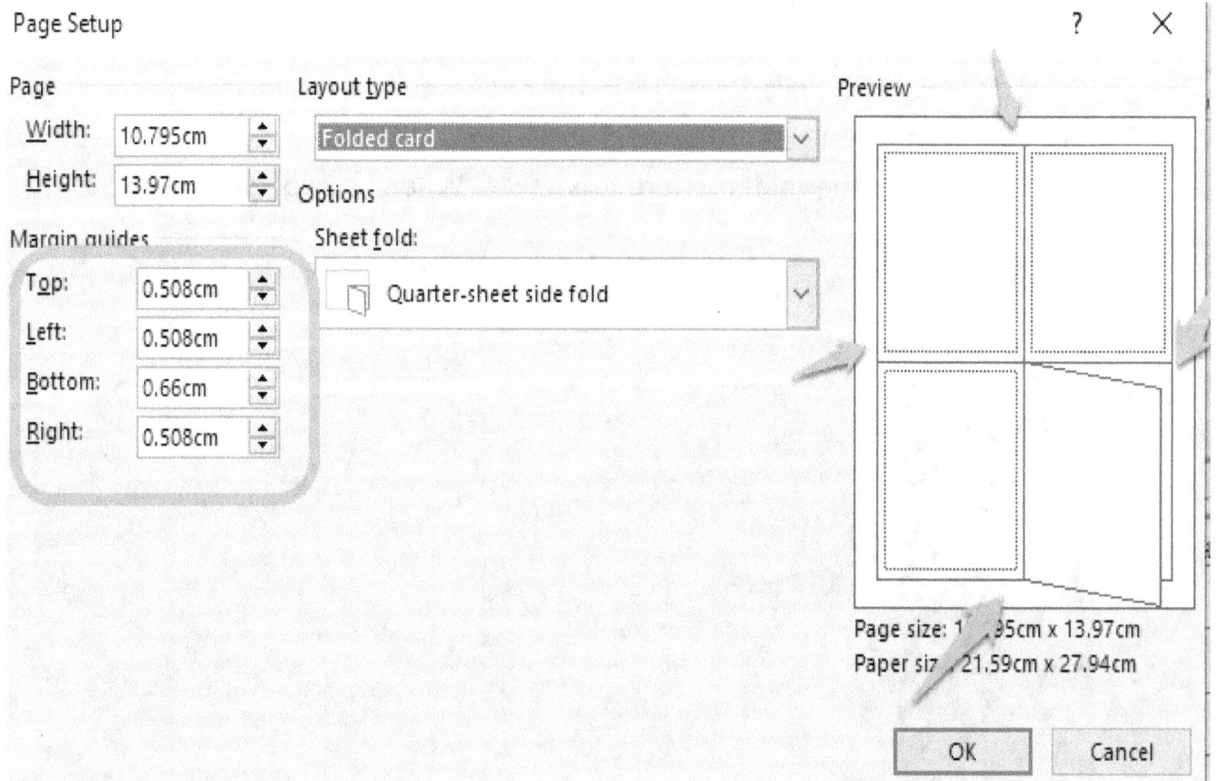

3) You can adjust the margin guides that are displayed in the **Margin Guides** section.

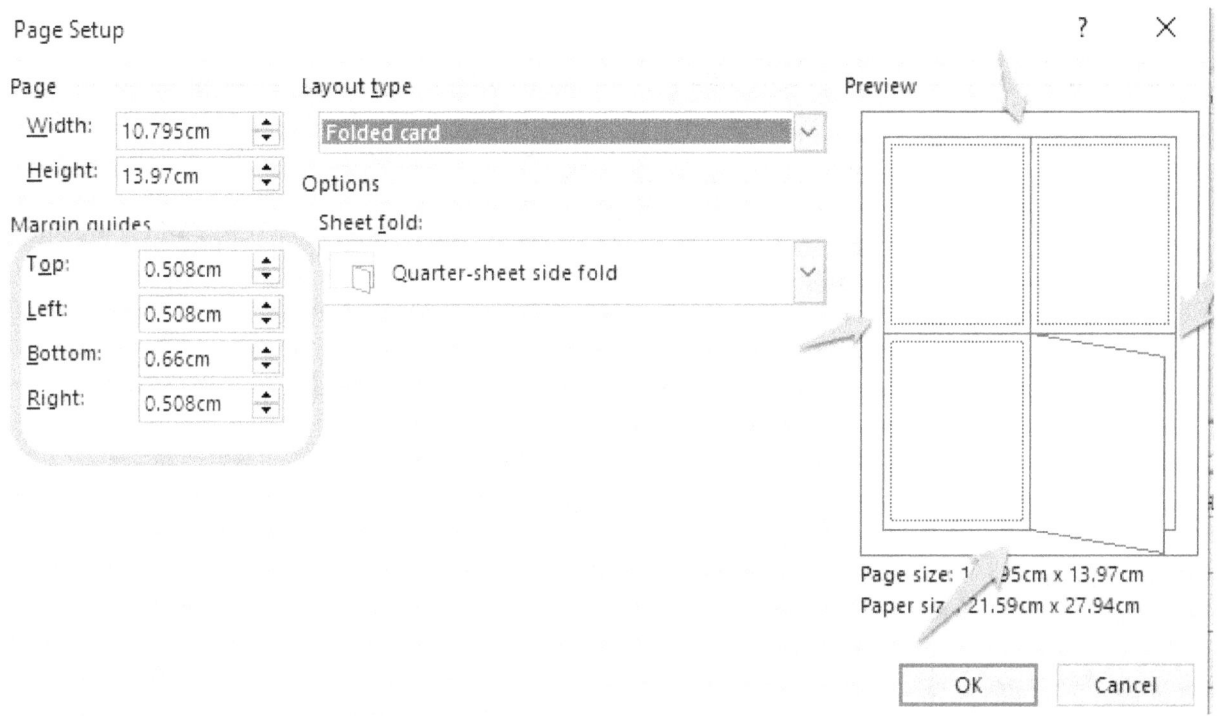

4) You can also adjust the page size of your document in the **Page** section.

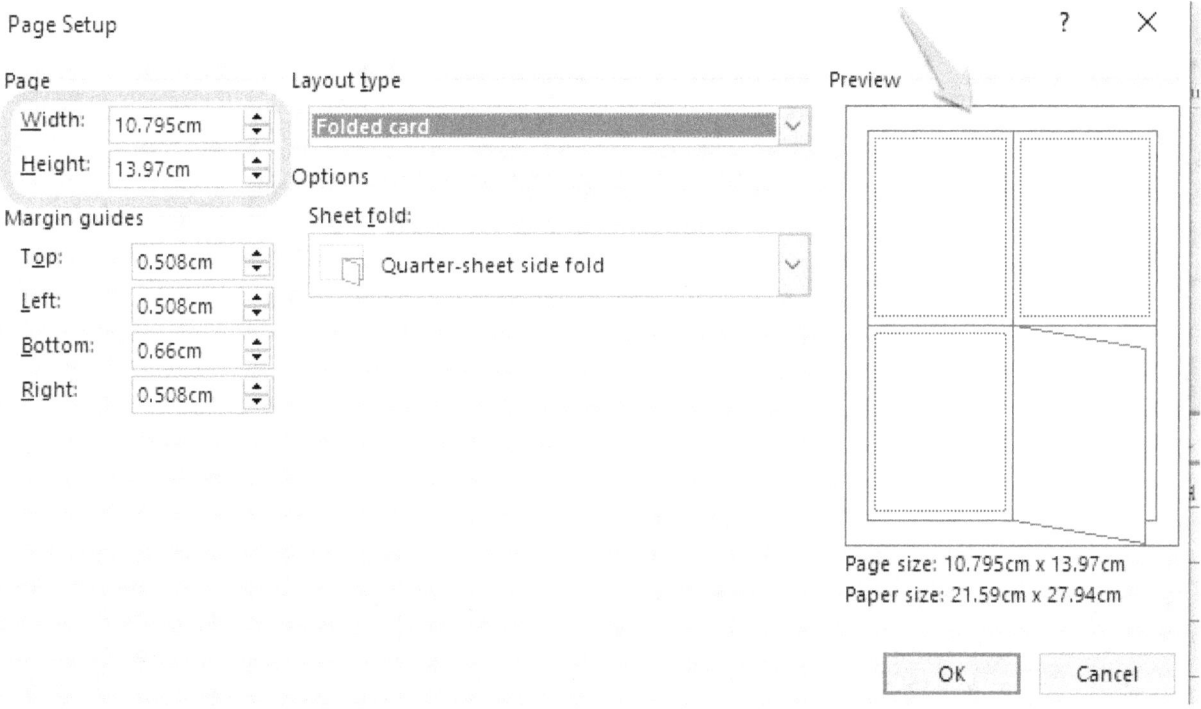

CREATING BOOKLETS

You can create a booklet layout in Publisher using the steps itemized below:

1) Open a **blank publication,** click the **Page Design** tab, and click the **Page Setup launcher.** The Page Setup dialog box appears.

2) Click the **menu** in the **Layout type** heading and choose **Booklet**.

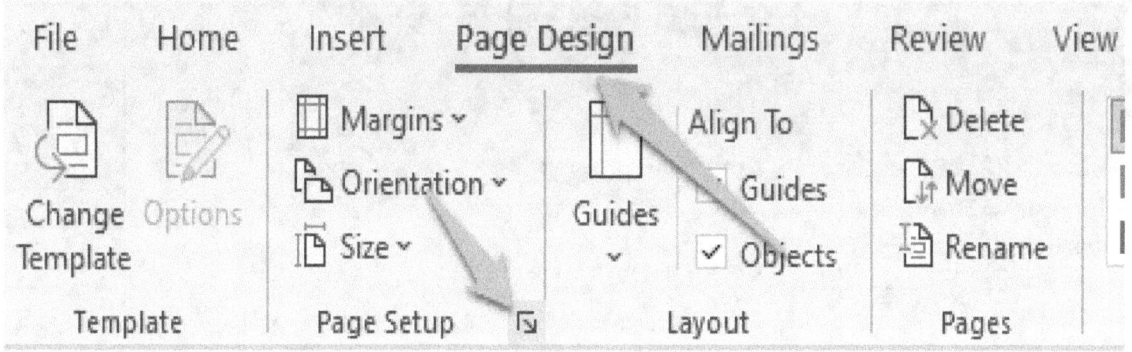

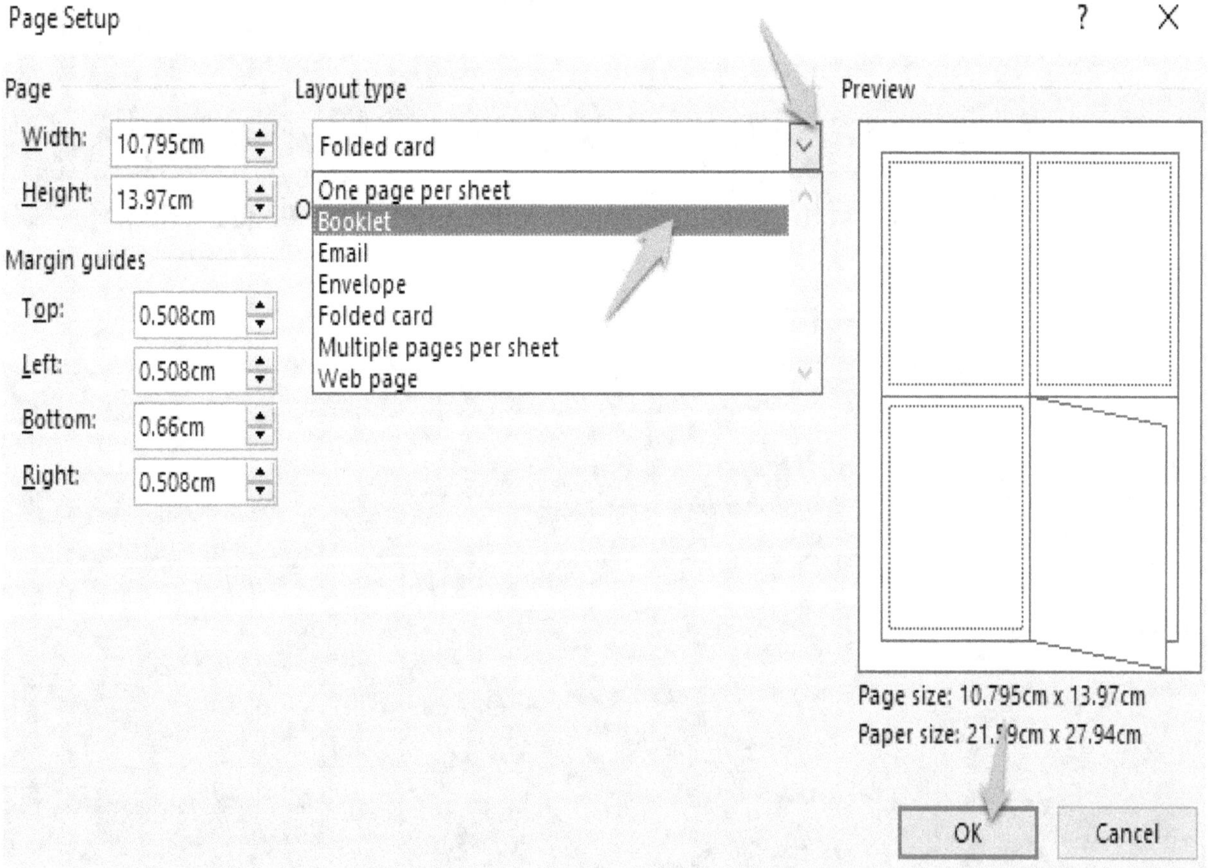

3) Click **OK**, Publisher automatically creates a booklet layout for you. your booklet pages are arranged on the left side of the screen in the navigation pane. In this case, you only have the **front page, the inside spread, and the back page**. You can begin to add more pages and build up your booklet.

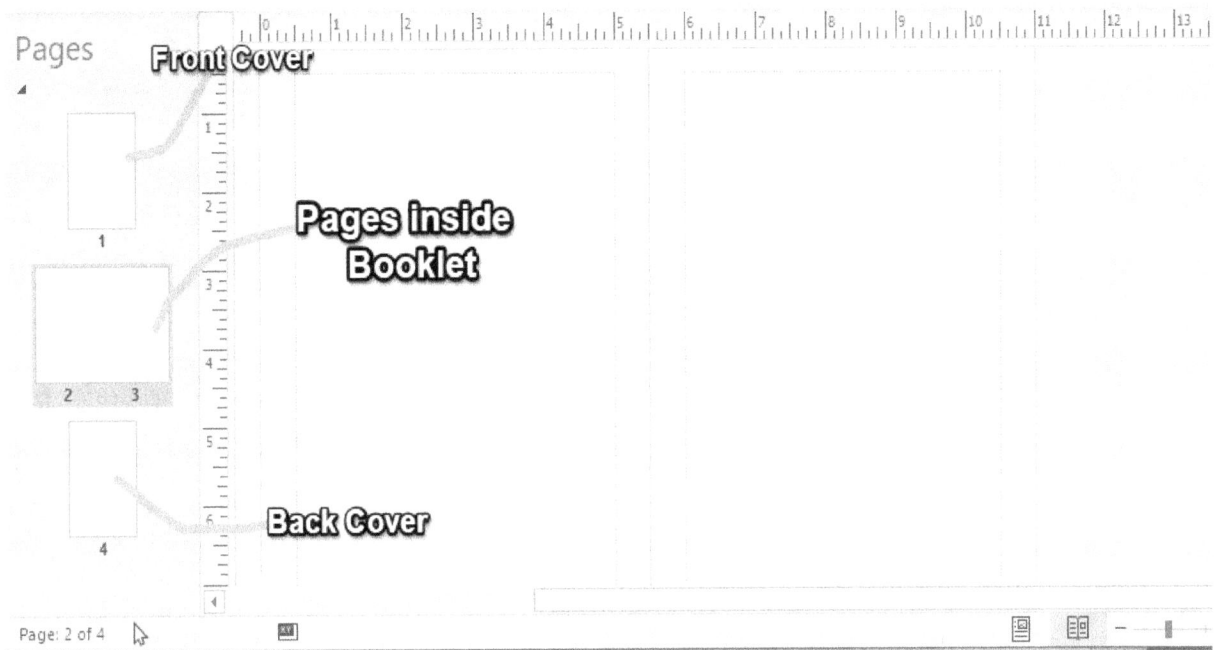

Note: This is the perfect way to start. Converting a publisher document to booklet form can sometimes bring layout problems if there is a need to resize your pages.

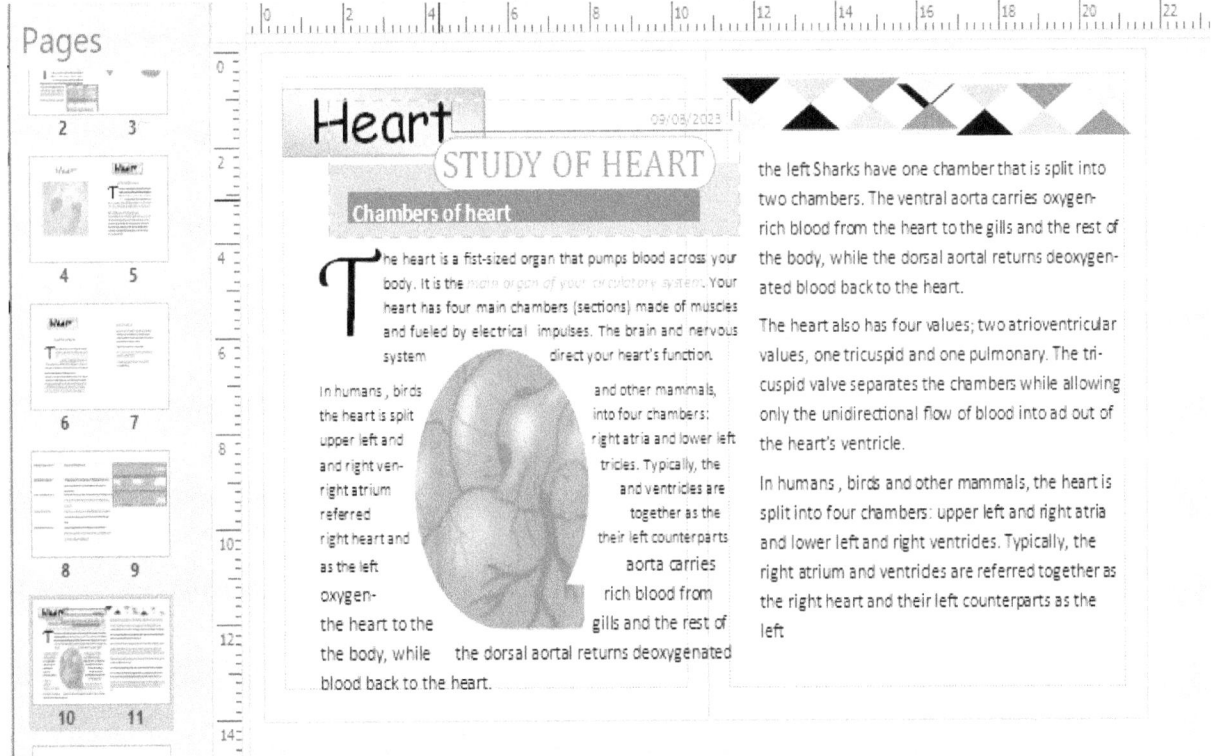

CHAPTER NINE
GETTING STARTED WITH THE PARENT PAGE

Master Page (Parent page) enables you to replicate layout elements and design on several pages in a publication. It creates a uniform appearance across your design and lets you update the design in one place, instead of changing them on each page.

EDITING MASTER PAGES

For instance, if you are working on a booklet, you can use the page master to add a page header or page number to each page.

1) Click the **Page Design** tab, click the **Master Page** menu, and select **Edit Master Page**.

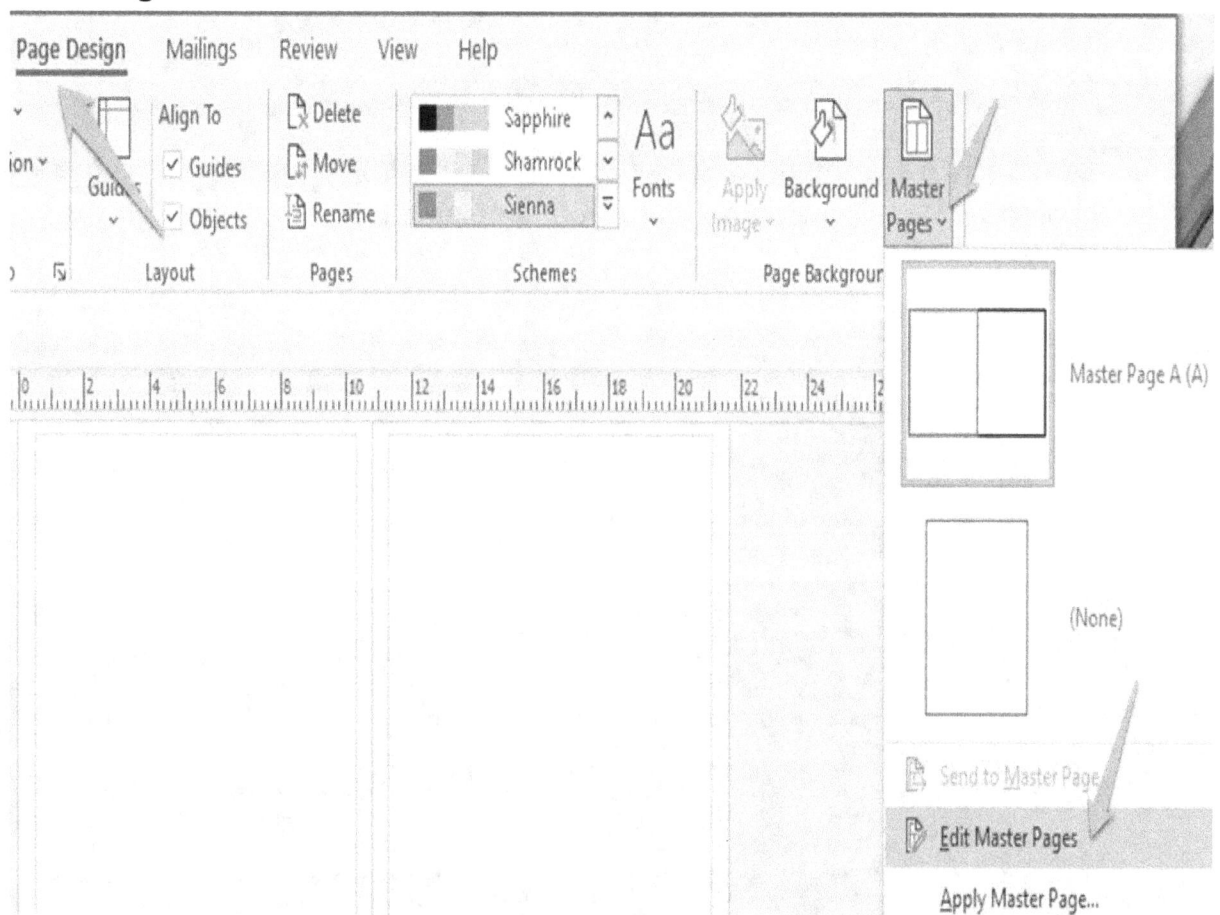

2) Click **Show Header/Footer**, and click **Top** of the page to add a header that can serve as a title such as "**Anatomy of the Heart**".

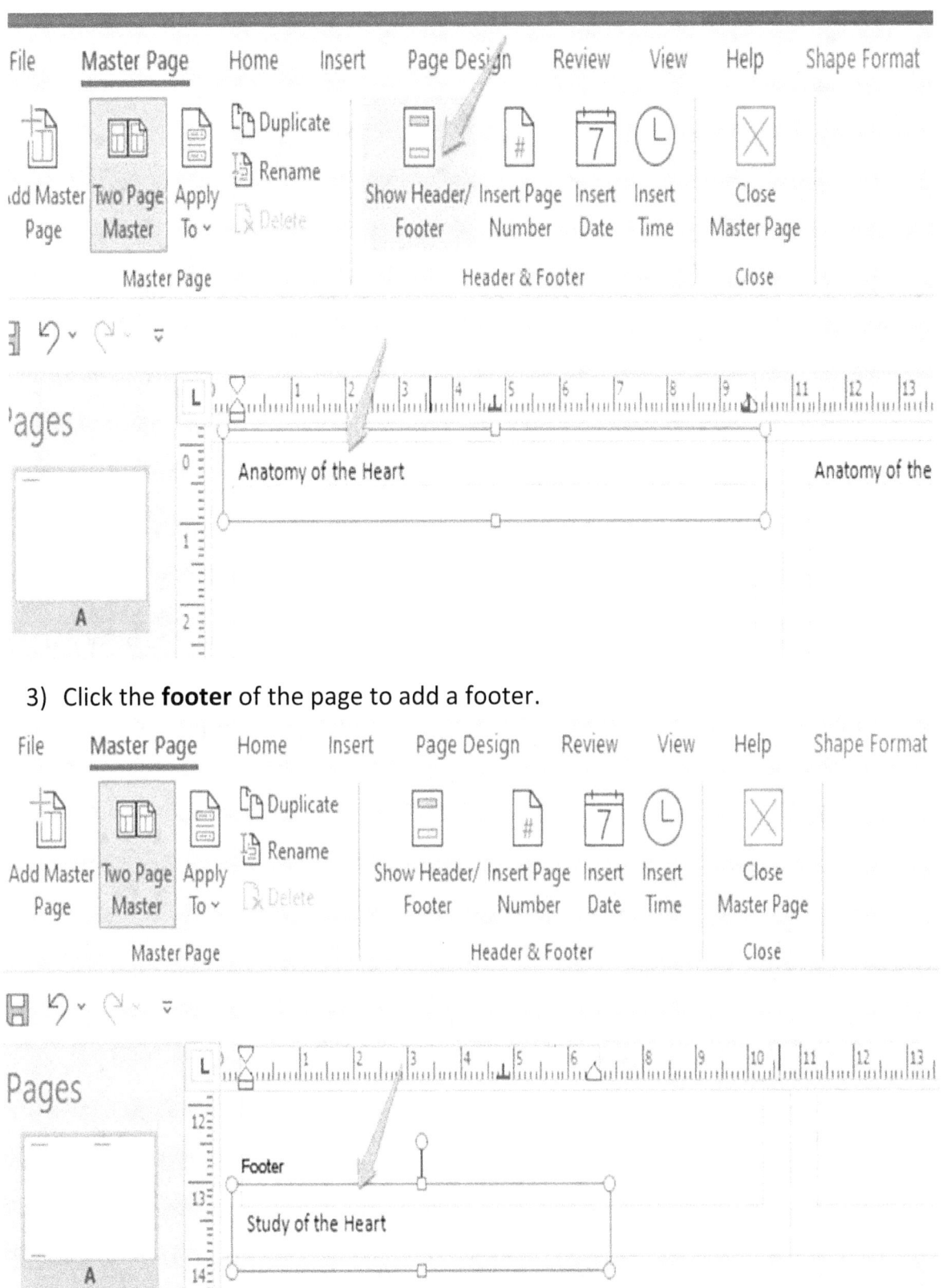

3) Click the **footer** of the page to add a footer.

4) Click the **"Insert Page Number"** to add a page number.

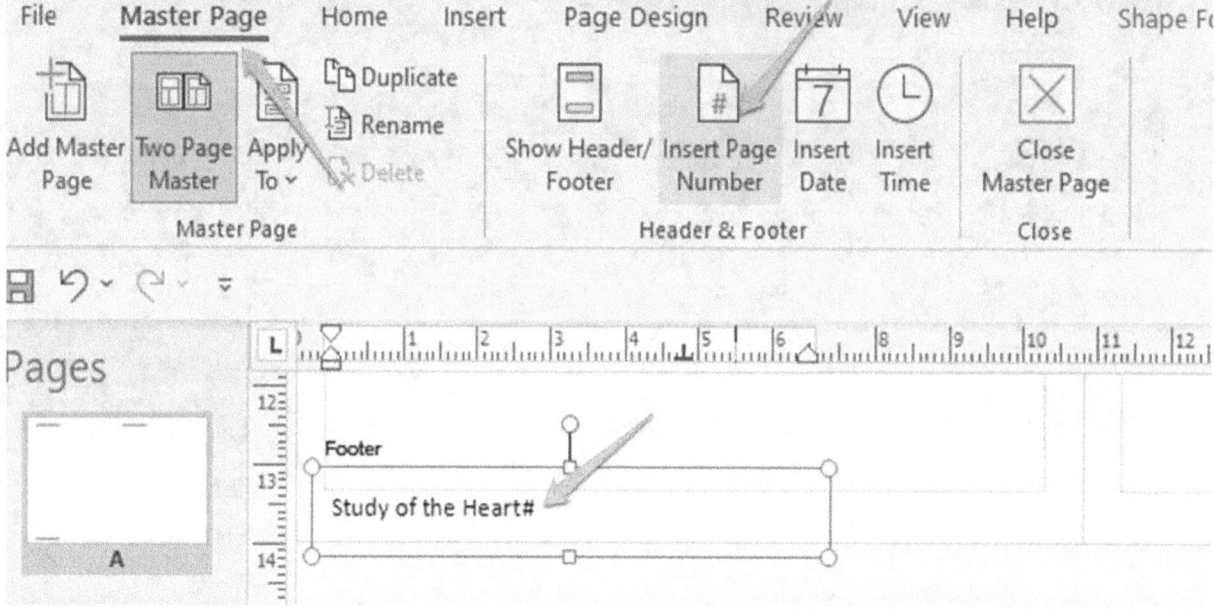

CREATING MASTER PAGES

Perhaps you need to create more master pages, follow the steps itemized below to create a new master page.

1) Click the **"Page Design"** tab and click the **"Add Master Page"**. The Master Page dialog box appears.
2) Type a concise name as the master page name into the **Descriptive** text box.

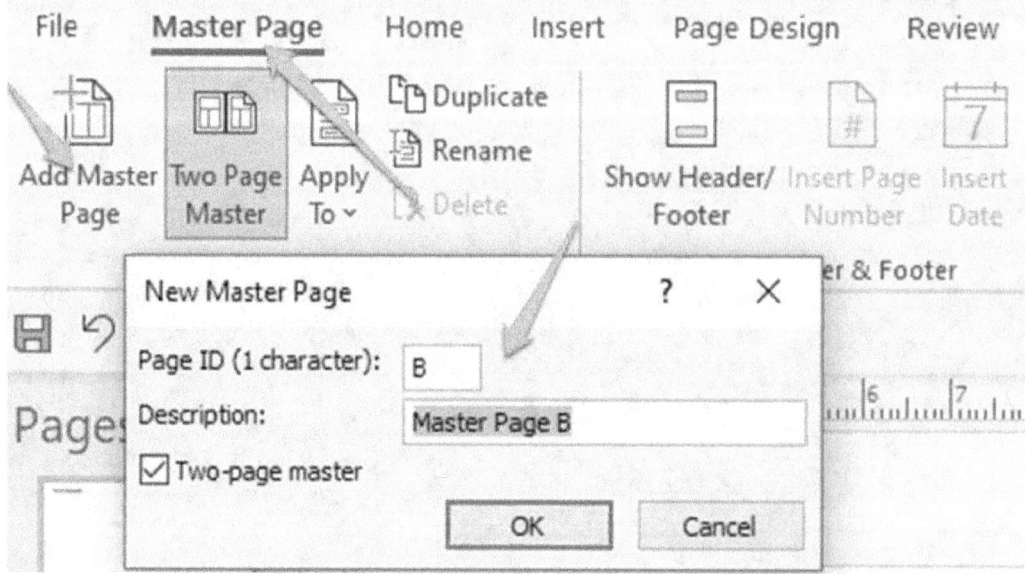

3) Leave the **Two-page master** check box **marked** if you want a two-page spread in the middle of a booklet, otherwise, **unmark** the **Two-page master** check box to make it an individual page.

After the creation of the parent page such as **B parent** in this case, you can format the master page, the way you want it.

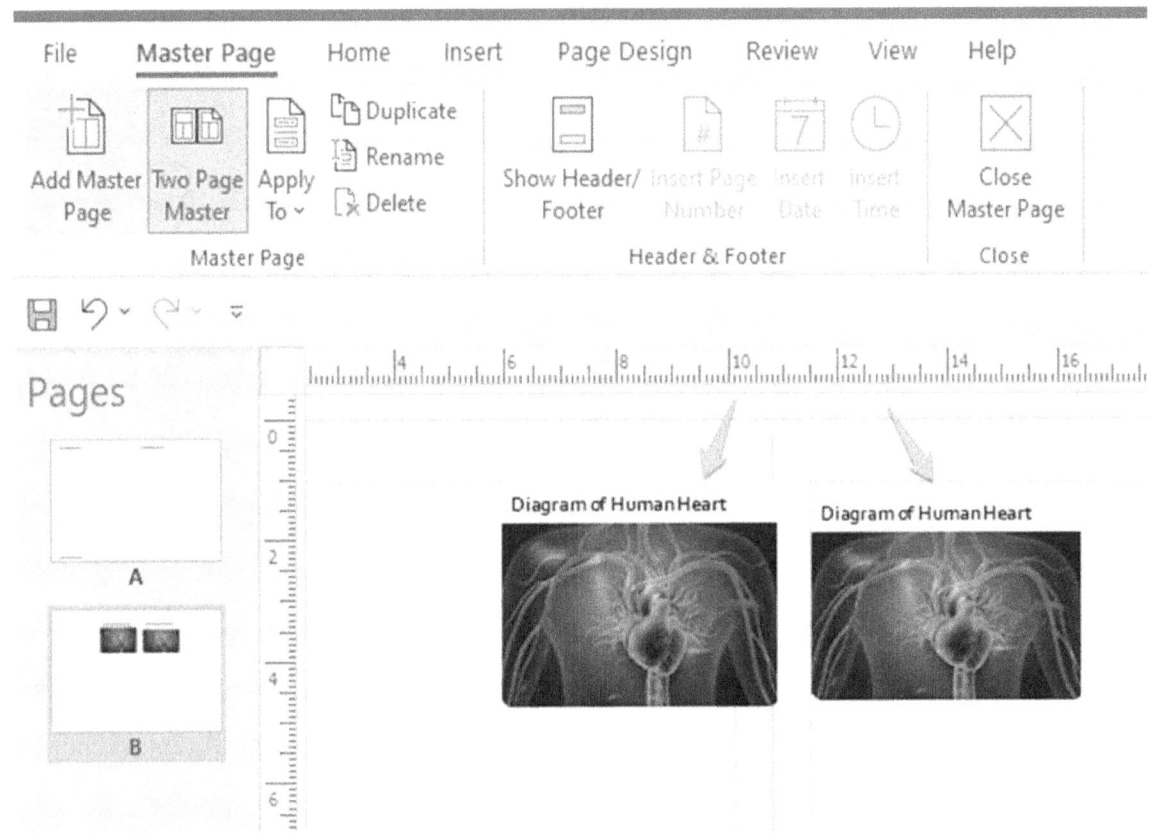

Note: Next, you can build your master page as we have done in the above screenshot. You can add pictures or text boxes that you want to apply across two or more pages using the Insert tab.

APPLYING MASTERS

Follow the steps itemized below to apply a master to a page.

1) Right-click the **spread or page** in the navigation pane on which you want to apply the master page.
2) Click the **Master Page** menu and choose the master you want to apply on the fly-out.

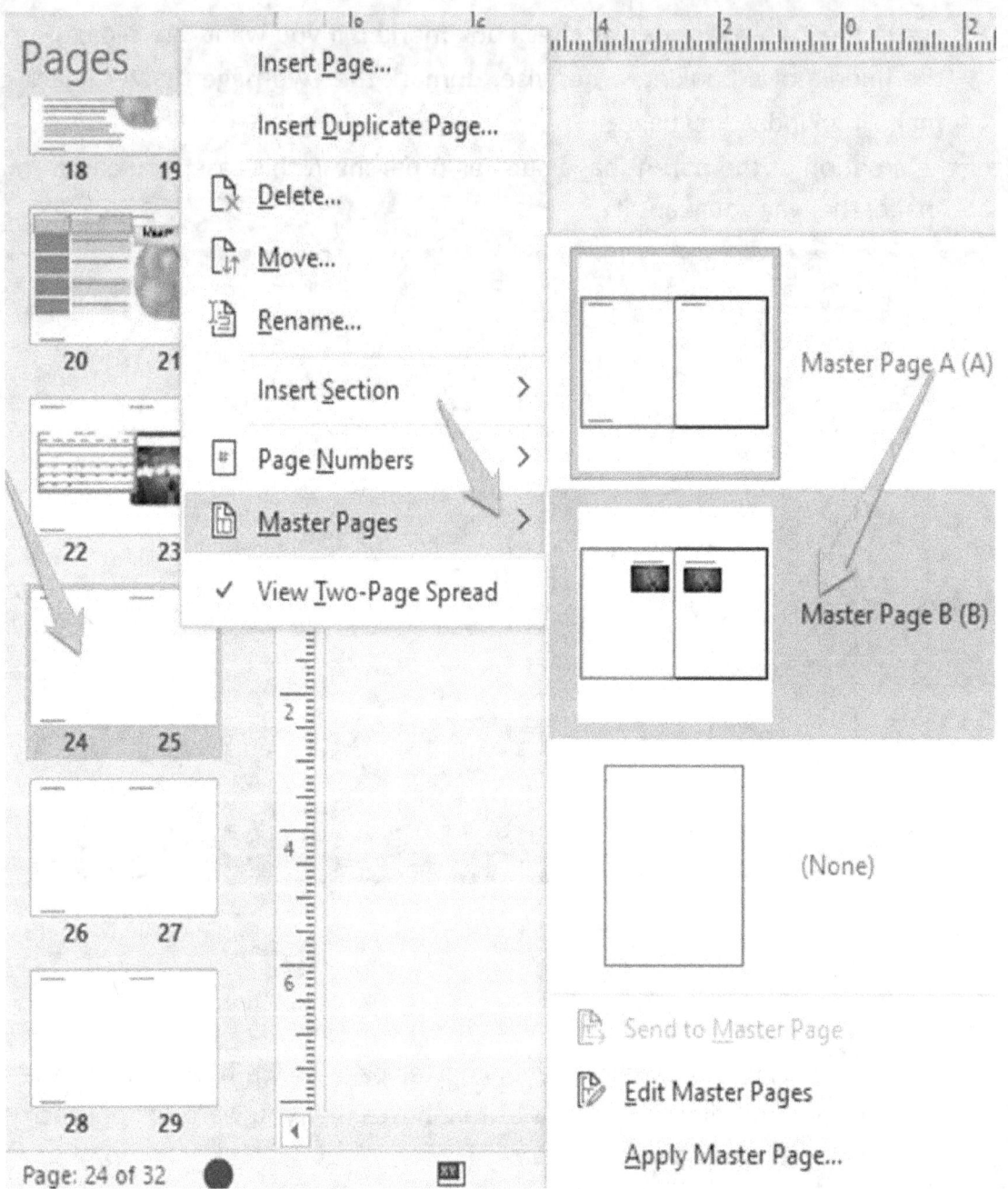

3) If you wish to apply a master to several pages, right-click on any page in the navigation pane and choose "**Apply Master Pages**" on the fly-out menu. The Apply Master Page dialog box appears.

4) Choose the **Master** you want to apply and specify the **pages** on which you want to apply the selected master such as **All pages**, **Pages from to**, or **Current page(s)**, and click **OK**.

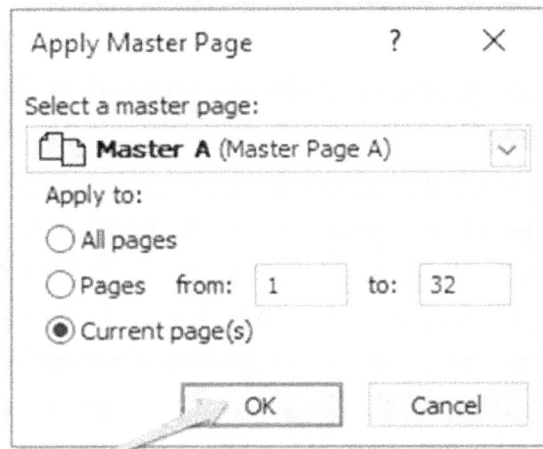

USING THE LAYOUT GUIDES

Layout guides come in handy for spacing your publication, aligning text boxes, align pictures, tables, and shapes. Layout guides are displayed on the page as a grid or line.

There are built-in guides you can use to arrange your publication. Follow the steps itemized below to enable the layout guides.

1) Click the "**Page Design**" tab, and click the **Guides** menu.
2) Choose the **layout** you want on the drop-down menu. For instance, you can choose **three or two-column layout guides** for a magazine or newsletter.

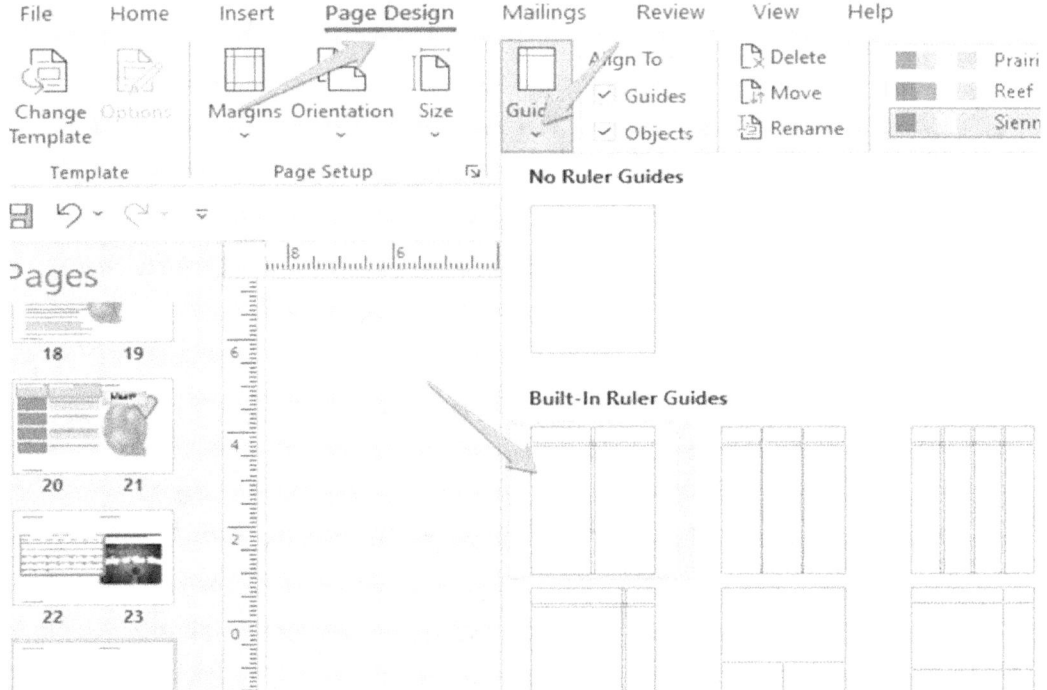

3) Align your **pictures**, **headings**, and text box to the grid lines.

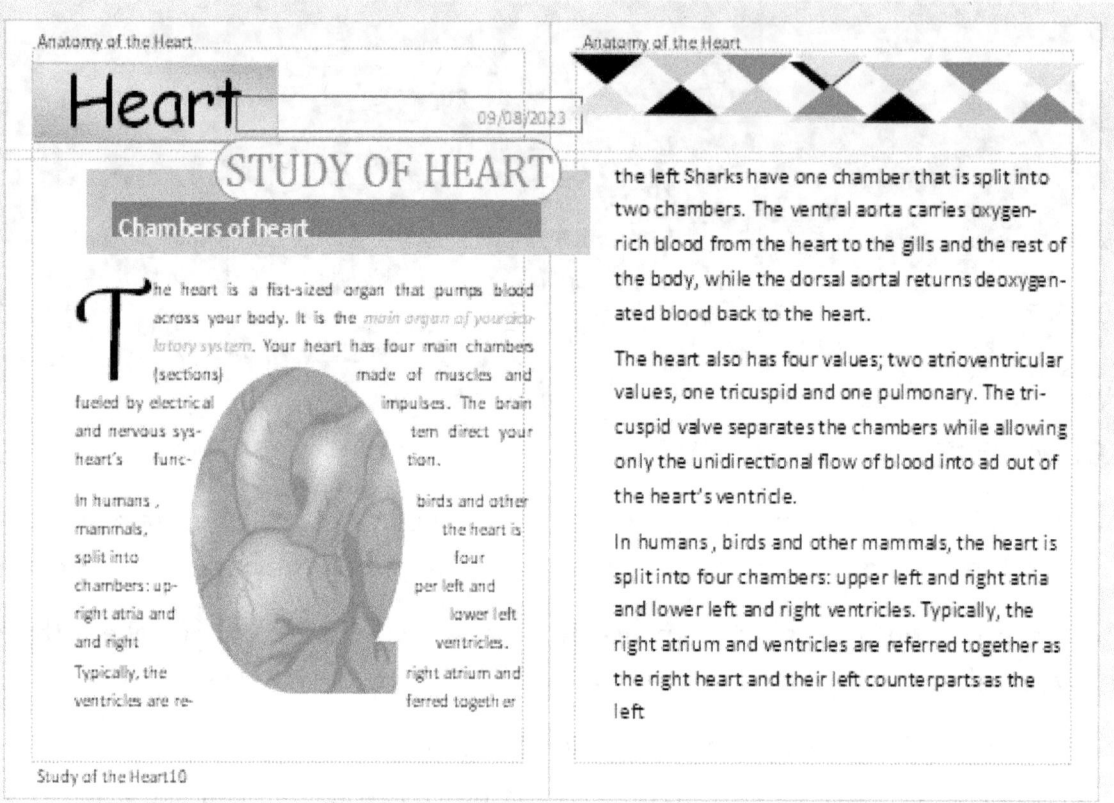

4) To move a guideline, **click and drag** it to a new location within the page.

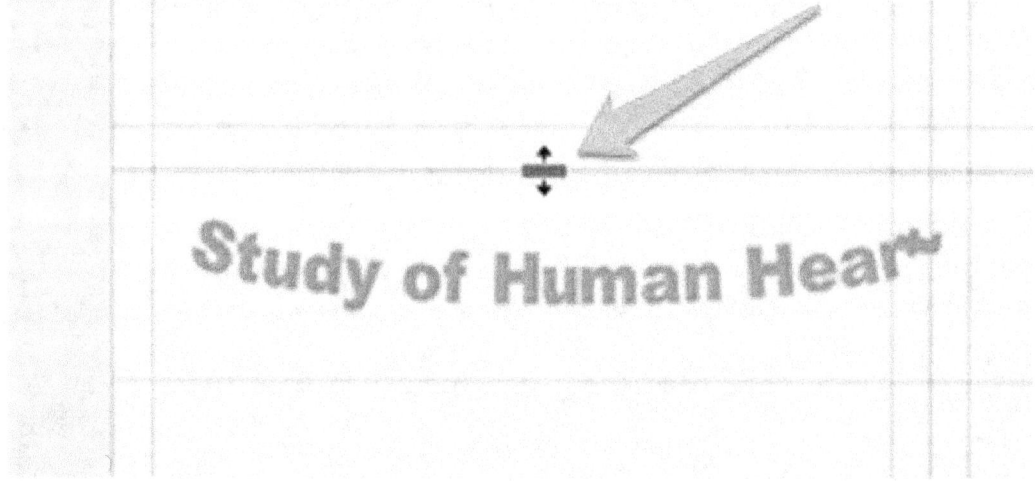

5) To add a horizontal guide line, click and drag the **horizontal ruler** into position on the publication page.
6) To add a vertical guide line, click and drag the **vertical ruler** into position on the publication page.

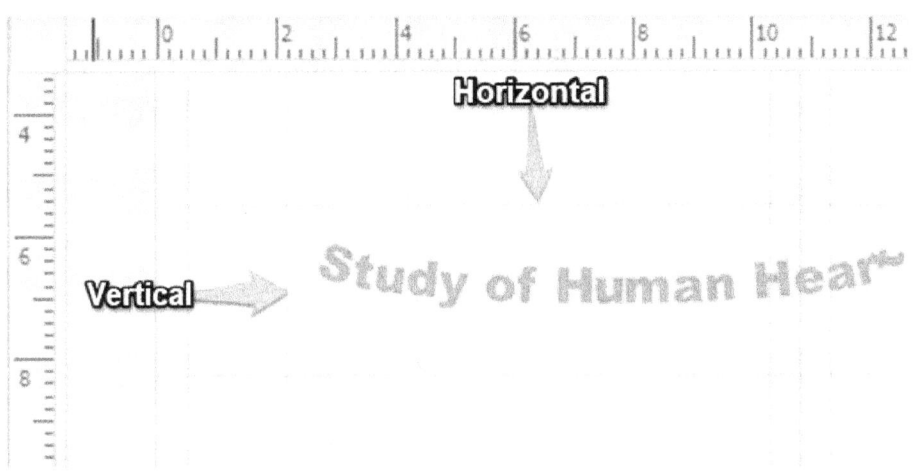

7) To delete a guide line, right-click the guide line and choose "**Delete Guide**".

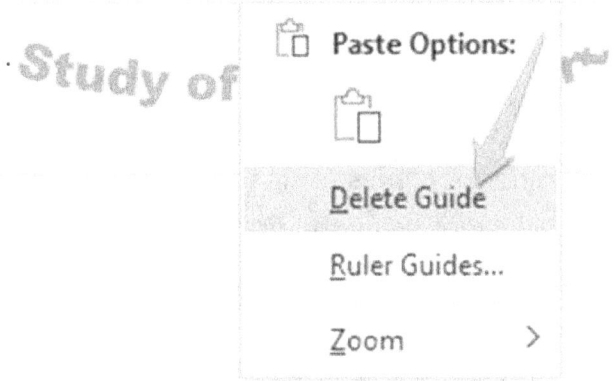

CHAPTER TEN
PUBLISHING YOUR PUBLICATION

In this last chapter, we shall be looking at various ways of printing publications, how to share and export your publications, and so on.

PRINTING YOUR DOCUMENT

Follow the steps itemized below to print your publication document.

1) Click the **File** tab and choose **Print** on the File backstage.

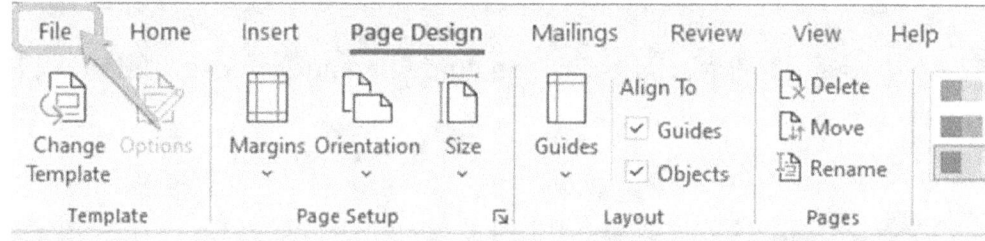

2) Specify the number of **copies** using the **Copies of Print Job** field. **Print individual pages or print all pages** using the **first** menu on the Settings heading.

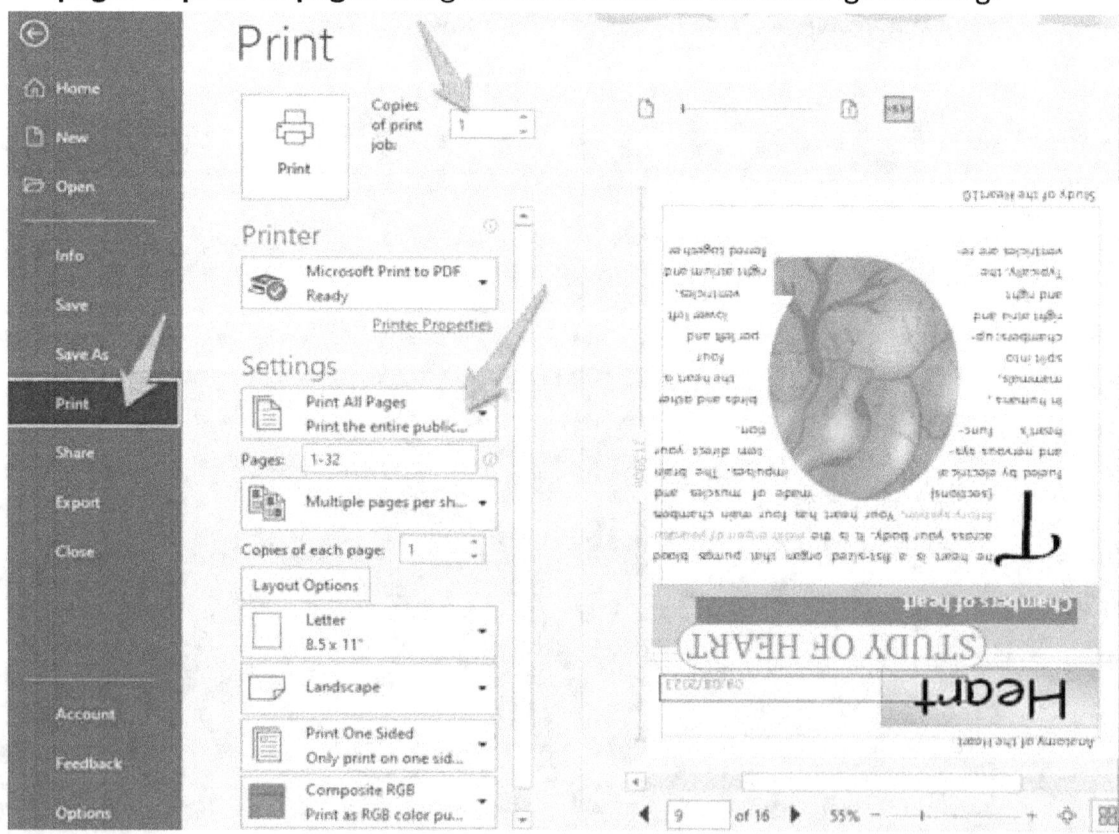

3) Choose an **option** to print the page on "**one sheet of paper**" or scale it up to **multiple sheets**. Or you may print multiple pages on a single sheet.

4) You can also print the pages into a booklet. To alter this setting, click the **One Page per Sheet** menu.

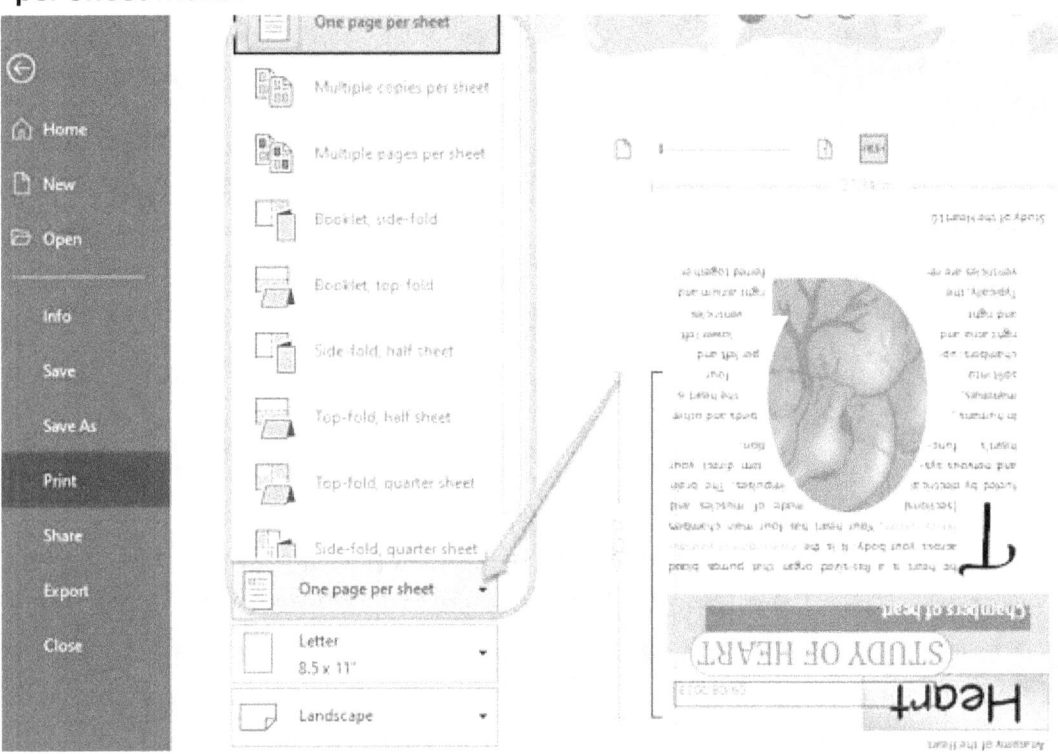

5) When you are done specifying all options, click the **Print** button at the top left side of the Print pane.

PRINTING AS A BOOKLET

Follow the steps itemized below to print the book as a booklet.

1) Click the **File** tab and click **Print** on the File Backstage.

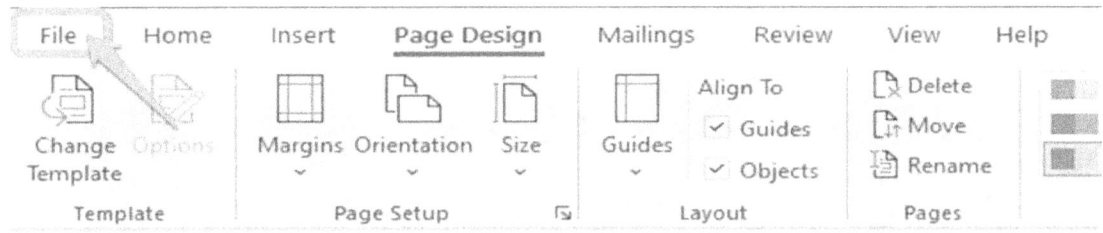

2) Click the "**One Page per Sheet**" menu and choose "**Booklet side fold**" on the fly-out menu.

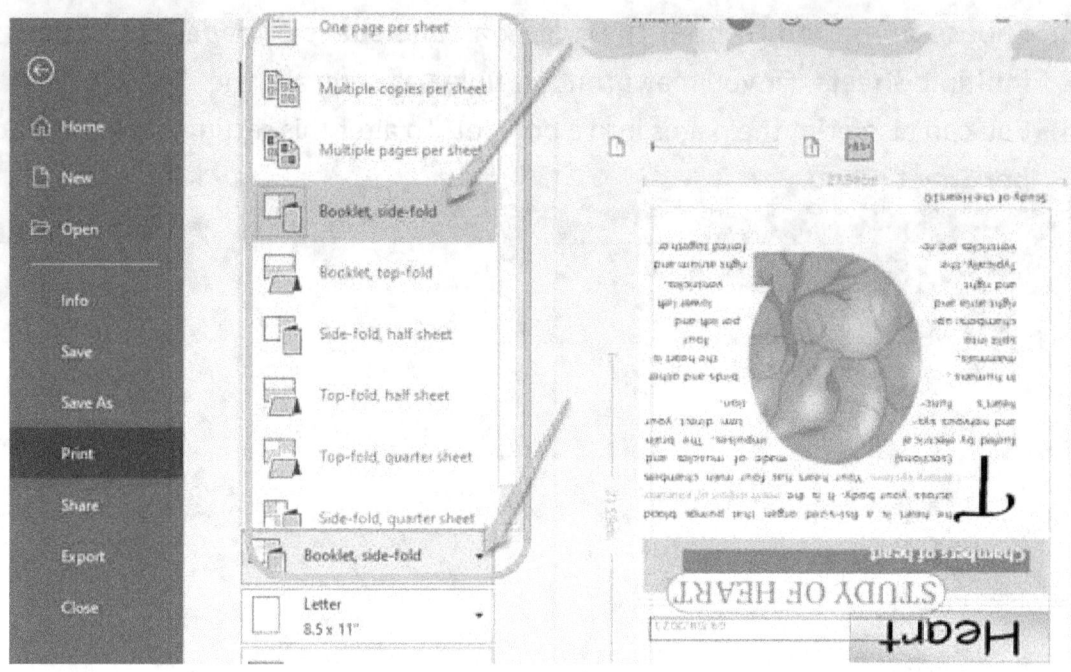

Note: Most of the current printers support duplex printing. For instance, they can print on both sides of the paper. With some desktop printers, selecting duplex means your printer will print all of the copies of the first side of a page, afterward pause and Printer will request you to flip the sheets that it just prints and returns them to the printer to print all of the copies of the second side.

3) To print on both sides, click the **menu** beside "**Print One Sided**" and choose **Print On Both Sides or Manual 2-Sided Print**.

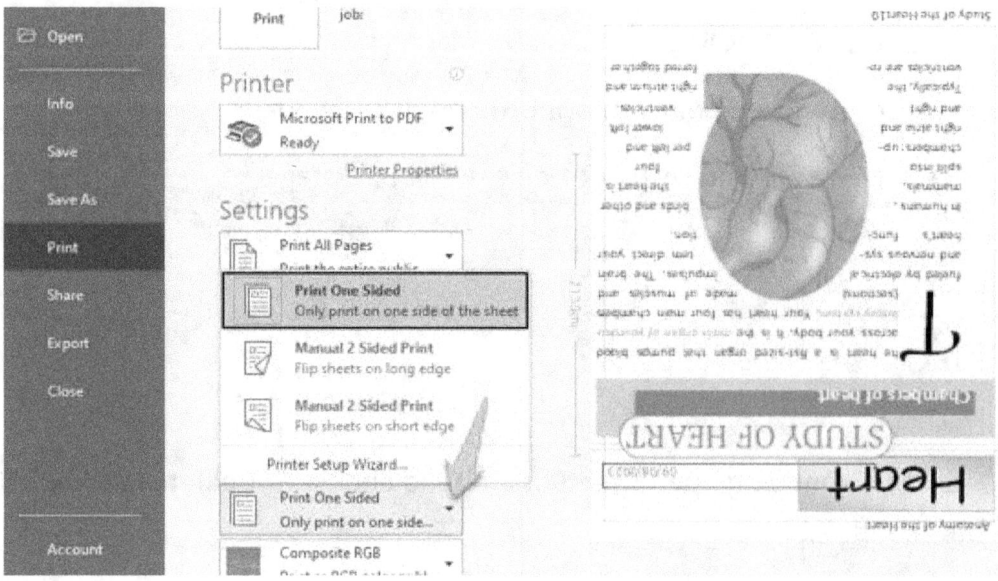

4) Then click the "**Print**" button at the top left side of the Print pane.

If you are using a manual machine, immediately the printer prints all the first side, turns the stack of the printed sheets over, and returns them to the paper tray for second-side printing.

SHARING A FILE

1) Click the **File** tab and choose **Share** on the File Backstage.
2) Specify how you want to attach the file to your email. you can forward the current page as an **email, you can share your file as a PDF, or you can share your publication as a publisher file(.pub).** if you are sharing the file with a person who doesn't use Publisher, you should consider sharing the file as PDF.
3) I will be sharing this file as PDF, so I will click "**Send as PDF**". The email will come up, the attached file will appear in the email.

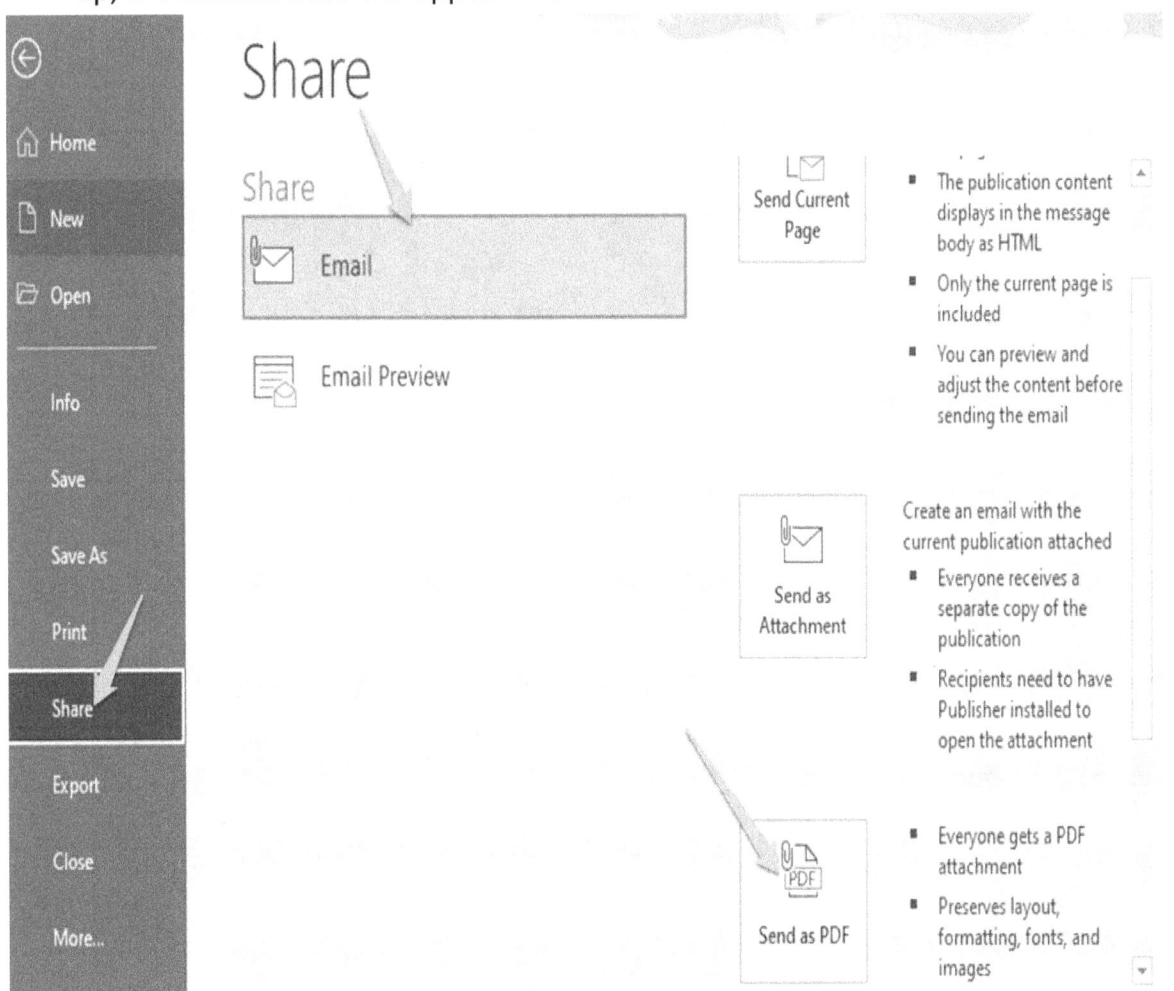

4) Add the **email address of the recipient** of the file, you can also add a **subject** and **message**.
5) Then click the **Send message** to send the file.

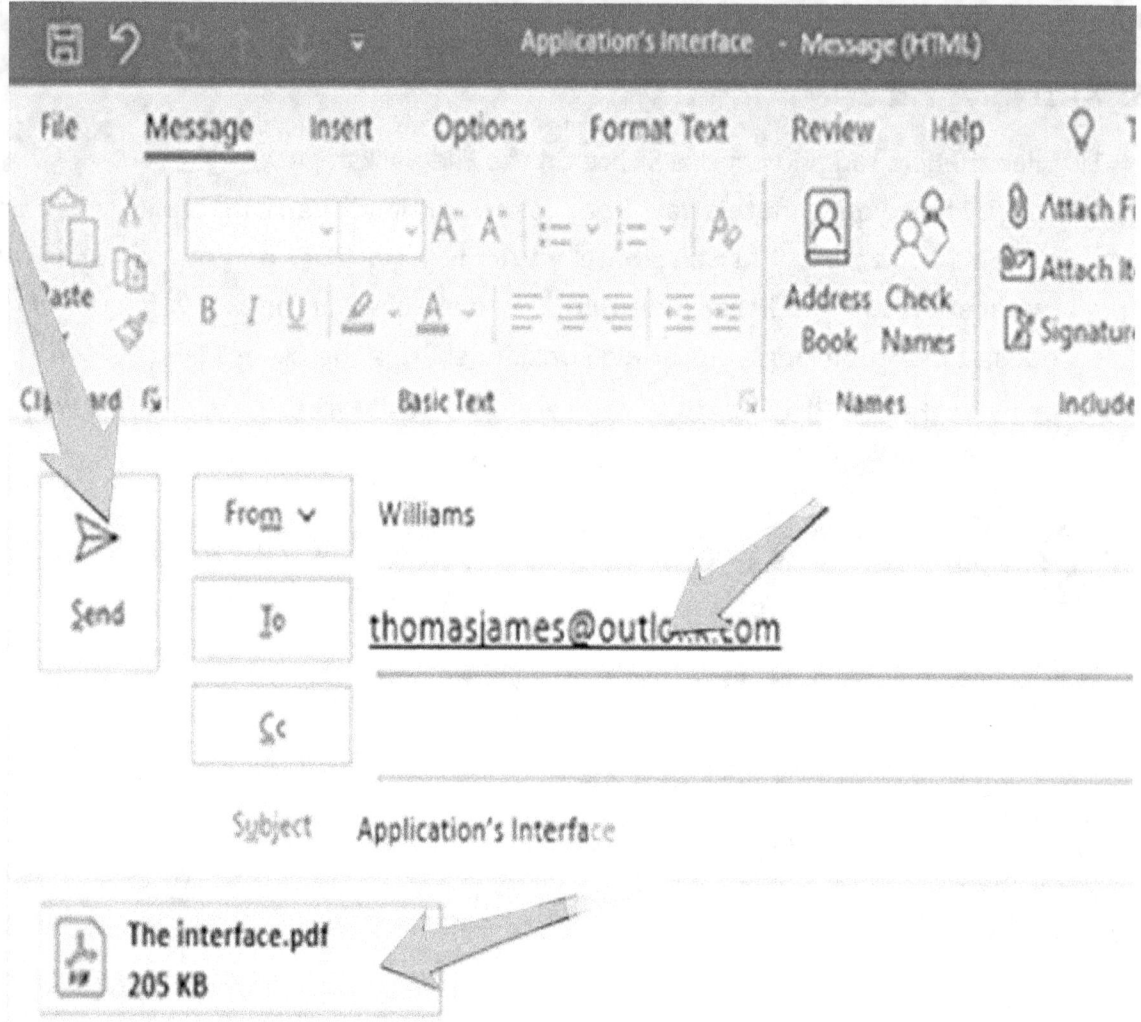

EXPORT DOCUMENT AS PDF

PDF is the acronym for Portable Document File. It is a file that can be displayed and printed in Adobe Acrobat Reader and Web browser. Follow the steps itemized below to export your document as a PDF

1) Click the **File** tab, and click the **Export** on the File Backstage to access the Export window.
2) Click the Create **PDF/XPS** button.

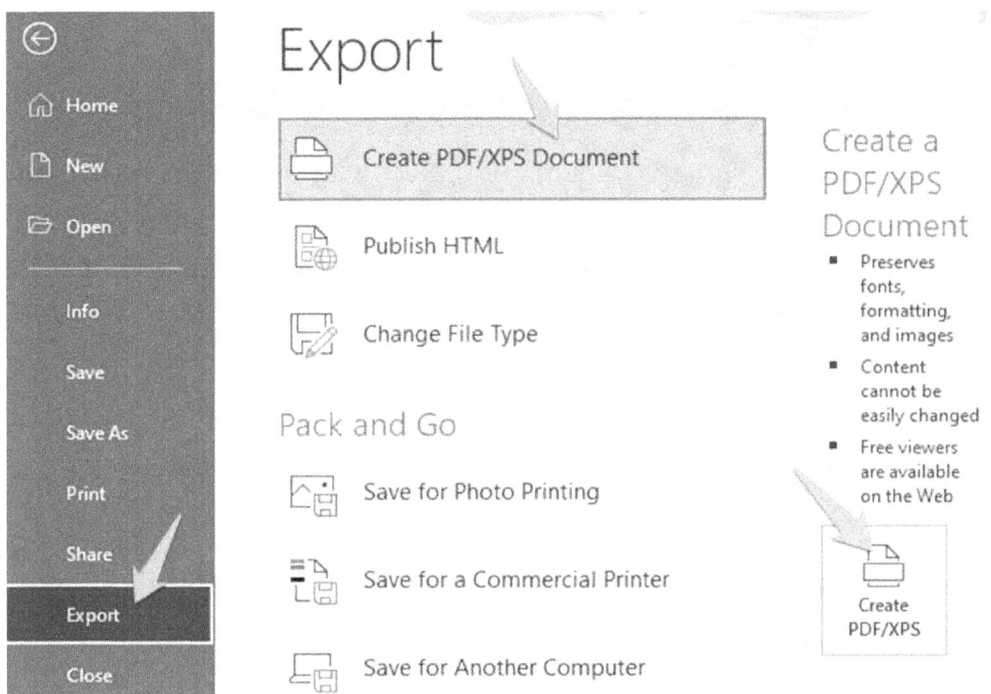

3) The Publish as PDF or XPS dialog box comes forth, type the **name** of the **file** and specify the **folder** location where you want to store the file.
4) Click the **Publish** button.

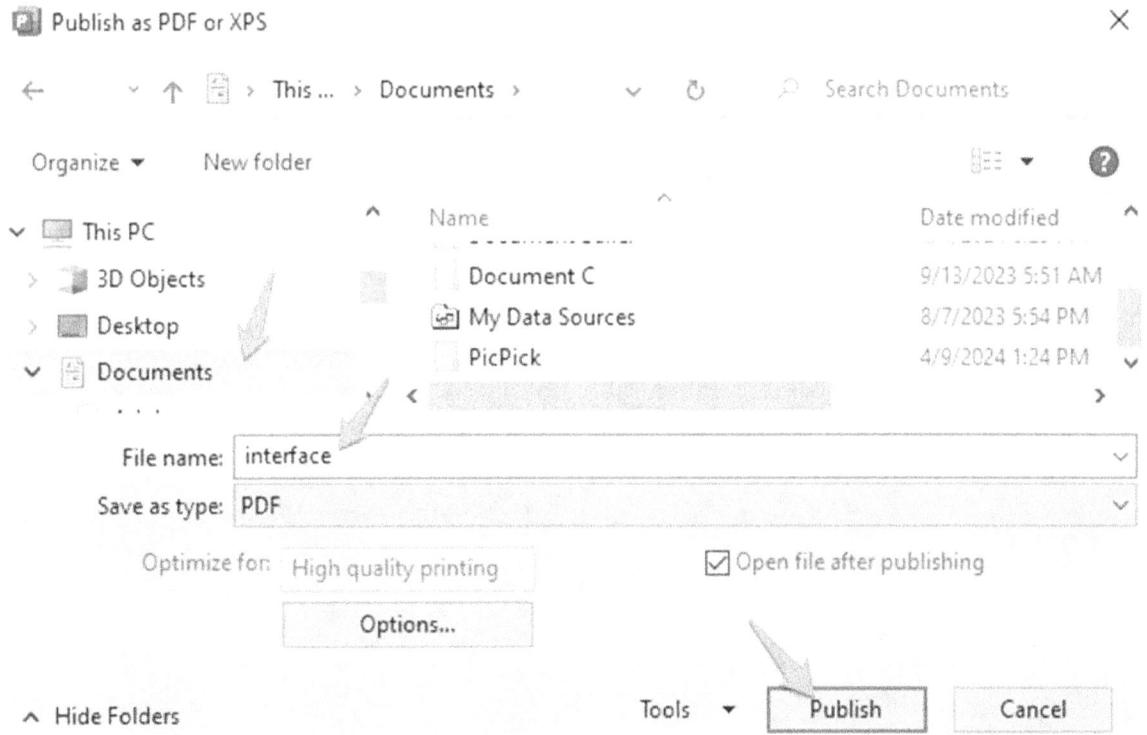

CHAPTER ELEVEN
MICROSOFT PUBLISHER TIPS AND TRICKS

At its core, MS Publisher serves as a dynamic platform for designing and arranging diverse visual materials. Its user-friendly interface caters to both seasoned professionals and novices alike, fostering continuous navigation and operation. It includes a rich array of templates and customization options, MS Publisher empowers users to fashion stunning publications without the need for extensive design expertise. To enjoy each of Publisher's features, the following tips and tricks will help you on the go.

CHANGING INTERFACE SCRATCH AREA TO DARK GRAY

You can set up a publisher interface to make it easier to use and give a better and exact preview of how your publication looks like. It helps to better see the contrast of your design during publication.

1) Go to the **File** menu and click **Options** on the File backstage.
2) Move to **General** subgrouping in the **Publisher Options** dialog box, find your way to the "**Personalize your copy of Microsoft Office**" section, and change **Office Theme** to a color that suits your publication.

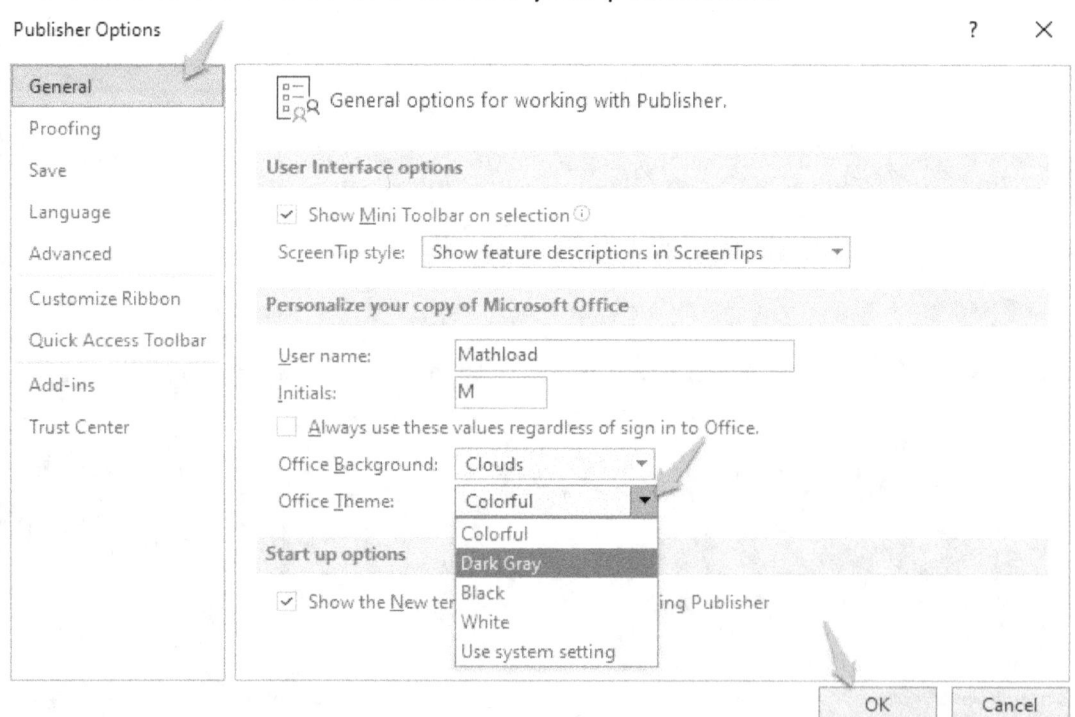

3) You can select **Dark Gray**, it gives a little bit higher contrast, and it helps to see the contrast on the page accurately. You can try other colors as well.

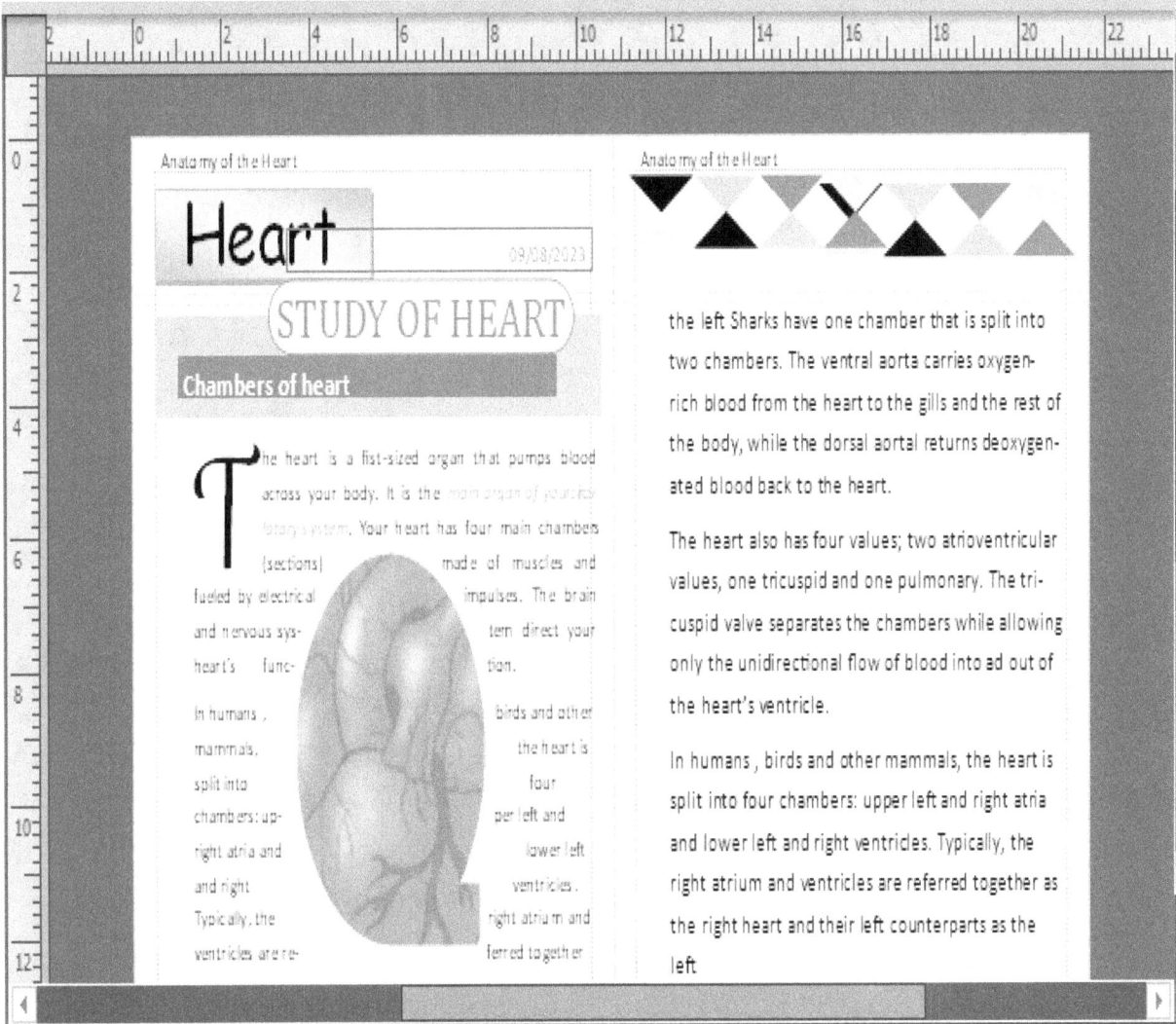

TIPS ON WORKING WITH SHAPES

If you open the **Shapes** menu from the **Home** or **Insert** tab, there are a lot of shapes that you can create. Whether you are working with a line, square, rectangle, or whatever shape you are drawing If you hold down the **Shift** key whenever using those shapes, it is going to affect the shape you are drawing. Holding the Shift key helps to stay straight on a specific angle.

Another tip is that If you drag or move the yellow diamond handles on any shape, it is going to help alter such shape.

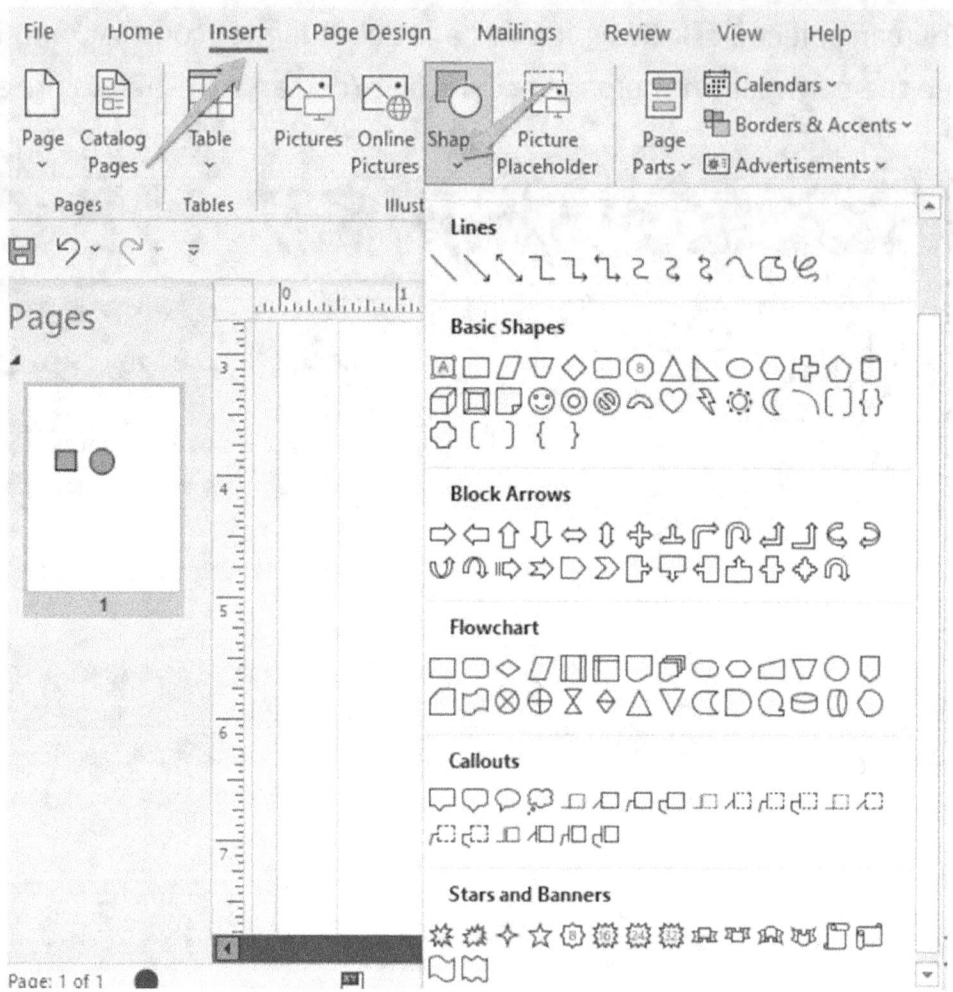

We shall consider them one after the other in this section.

✓ Holding down the **Shift** key while drawing a straight line helps to draw a straight horizontal, vertical, or 45-degree line.

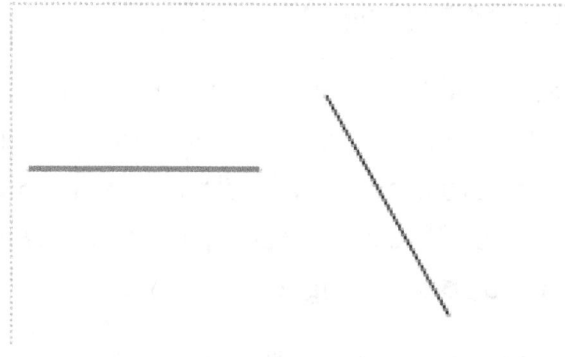

- ✓ Holding down the **Shift** key while drawing a **rectangle** or **sphere** helps to draw a perfect **square** or **circle**.

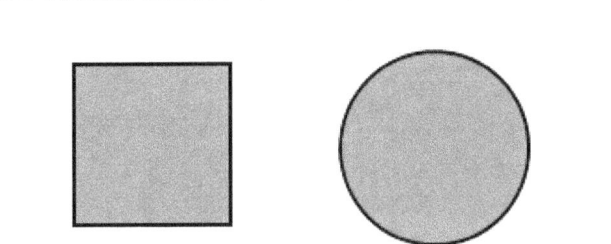

The yellow diamond handle on any of the shapes you draw on Publisher helps to alter the concerned shape. We will unveil this in the following section.

- ✓ If you draw any **shapes** from the **Callout** group, you can move the callout to any area around the shape by dragging the yellow diamond handles around the shape. That is pretty cool for your creative work.

- ✓ If you draw a banner from the **Stars and Banners** group, you can alter the banner areas by dragging up or down the yellow diamond handles around the shape. That is pretty cool for your creative work also.

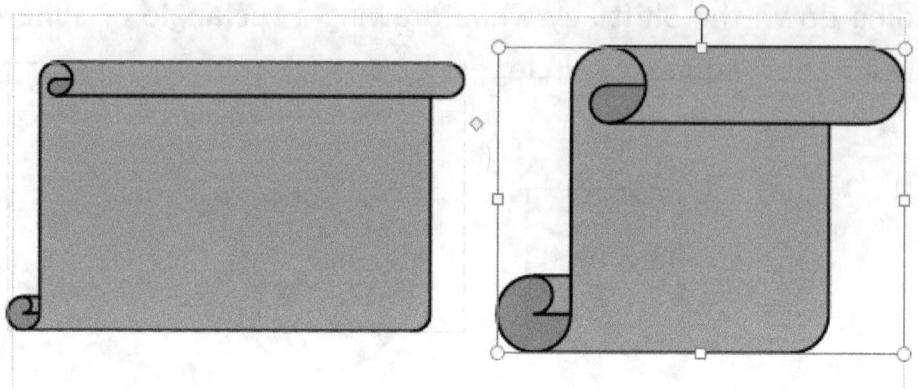

✓ If you draw an arrow from the block arrows group, you can drag the yellow diamond handle around to alter the arrow shape or twist its coverage.

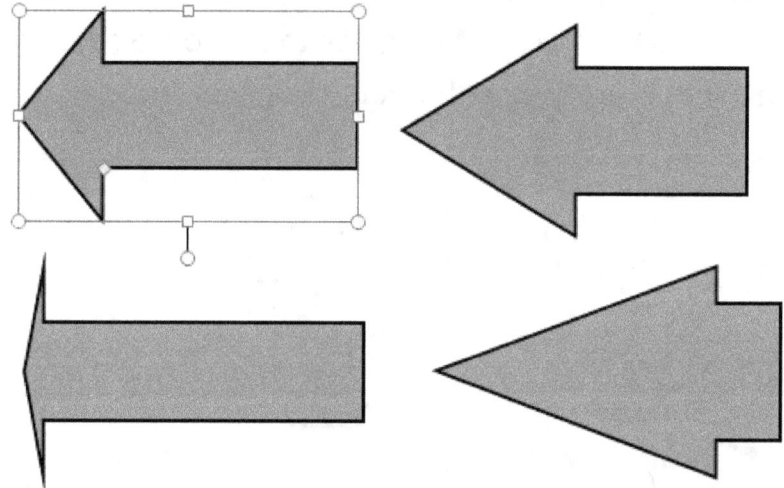

Note: there are a lot of creatives you make on Microsoft Publisher by drawing with shapes and altering them using the yellow diamond handle. Kindly play around with the shapes and twist or alter them with the yellow diamond handles.

CHAPTER TWELVE
SHORTCUT KEYS FOR ENHANCED EFFICIENCY

Microsoft Publisher, nestled within the robust MS Office suite, stands as a powerhouse desktop publishing software. With its user-friendly interface, it empowers users to craft an array of polished publications, spanning from brochures to greeting cards. Embracing this tool unveils boundless creativity. Yet, to truly explore its capabilities, mastering its shortcut keys is key, to elevating efficiency and simplifying workflows.

COPYING, CUTTING, PASTING OR DELETING OBJECTS

USES	SHORTCUTS
Copy the selected object or text	Ctrl + C or Ctrl + Enter
Cut the selected object or text	Ctrl + X or Shift + Delete
Paste objects or text	Ctrl + V or Shift + Insert
Delete selected object	Ctrl + Shift + X

NUDGING AN OBJECT

USES	SHORTCUTS
Nudge a selected object left, right, up, or down	Arrow keys
If the selected object has an insertion point in its text, nudge the selected object right, left, up, or down	Alt + arrow

ZOOMING

USES	SHORTCUTS
Switch between the actual size and the current view	F9
Zoom to full-page view	Ctrl + Shift + L

EDITING AND FORMATTING SHORTCUTS

USES	SHORTCUTS
Show the Find and Replace task pane, with the Find option selected under Find or Replace. These keyboard shortcuts might not work if any other task pane is opened	F3, or Shift + F4, or Ctrl + F
Show the Find and Replace task pane, with the Replace option selected under Find or Replace. These keyboard shortcuts might not work if any other task pane is opened	Ctrl + H
Underline Text	Ctrl + U
Bold Text	Ctrl + B
Italicize text	Ctrl + I
Check Spelling	F7
Copy Formatting	Ctrl + Shift + C
Paste Formatting	Ctrl + Shift + V
If the insertion pointer is active in the text box, all the text in the text frame or story are selected. If the insertion pointer is not active in any text box, all the objects on the page are selected	Ctrl + A
Select the Font Size box on the Formatting toolbar	Ctrl + Shift + P
Select the Font box on the Formatting toolbar	Ctrl + Shift + F
Select the Style Size box on the Formatting toolbar	Ctrl + Shift + S
Apply or Remove superscript formatting	Ctrl + Shift + =
Apply or Remove subscript formatting	Ctrl + =
Return character formatting to the current text style	Ctrl + Spacebar
Switch on or off Special Characters	Ctrl + Shift + Y

Increase font size by 1.0	Ctrl +]
Decrease font size by 1.0	Ctrl + [
Align the paragraph to the center	Ctrl + E
Align paragraph to the left	Ctrl + L
Align paragraph to the right	Ctrl + R
Justified align the paragraph	Ctrl + J
Insert the current page number	Alt + Shift + P
Insert the current time	Alt + Shift + T
Insert the current date	Alt + Shift + D
Insert a zero-width non-breaking space	Ctrl + Shift + 0
Set the active paragraph to single-spacing	Ctrl + 1
Set the active paragraph to double-spacing	Ctrl + 2
Set the active paragraph to 1.5 line spacing	Ctrl + 3
Undo the last action	Ctrl + Z or Alt Backspace
Redo the last action	Ctrl + Y or F4
If text is selected, deselects the text, but the object that holds the text remains selected	Esc

LAYERING OBJECTS

USES	SHORTCUTS
Bring an object to the front	Alt + 6
Send an object to the front	Alt + Shift + 6

SELECT OR GROUP OBJECT

USES	SHORTCUTS
Select all objects on the page	Ctrl + A

To group selected objects, ungroup the grouped object	Ctrl + Shift + G

SNAP OBJECTS

USES	SHORTCUTS
Switch Snap to Guides on and off	Ctrl + Shift + W

SHOW OR HIDE BOUNDARIES OR GUIDES

USES	SHORTCUTS
Switch Boundaries and Guides on or off	Ctrl + Shift + O
Switch horizontal Baseline Guides on or off. This shortcut is not working in the Web view	Ctrl + F7
Switch vertical Baseline Guides on or off. This shortcut is not working in the Web view	Ctrl + Shift + F7

DEALING WITH PAGE SHORTCUTS

USES	SHORTCUTS
Display Go To Page dialog box	Ctrl + G or F5
Insert a page after the selected page	Ctrl + Shift + N
Insert a duplicate page after the selected page	Ctrl + Shift + U
Go to the next page	Ctrl + Page Down
Go to the previous page	Ctrl + Page UP
Switch between the current page and the master page	Ctrl + M

CREATING, OPENING, SAVING OR CLOSING A PUBLICATION

USES	SHORTCUTS
Create a new blank publication	Ctrl + N
Open a publication	Ctrl + O
Save the current publication	Ctrl + S
Close the current publication	Ctrl + W or Ctrl + F4

WHEN USING PRINT PREVIEW

USES	SHORTCUTS
Print publication	Ctrl + P
Switch between the current view and the actual size	F9
Scroll left, right, up or down	Arrow keys
Scroll up in large increment	Page Up or Ctrl + Up arrow
Scroll down in large increment	Page Down or Ctrl + Down arrow
Scroll left in large increment	Ctrl + Left arrow
Scroll right in large increment	Ctrl + right arrow
Scroll to the lower right side of the page	End
Scroll to the upper right side of the page	Home
Go to the next page	Ctrl + Page Down
Go to the previous page	Ctrl + Page Up
Exit Print Preview	Esc

WHEN USING DIALOG BOXES

USES	SHORTCUTS

Move to the next option or group of option	Tab
Move to the previous option or group of option	Shift + Tab
Switch to the next tab in a dialog box	Ctrl + Tab
Switch to the previous tab in a dialog box	Ctrl + Shift + Tab
Carry out the action assigned to the selected button; check or clear the selected check box	Spacebar
Move between options in an open drop-down list, or between options in a group of options	Arrow keys
Open a selected drop-down list	Alt + Down Arrow
Enter	Carry out the action assigned to a default button in a dialog box
Esc	Close a selected drop-down list; cancel a command and close a dialog box

CONCLUSION

As we wrap up this remarkable user guide, I trust that the straightforward illustrations provided have equipped you with a wealth of knowledge about Microsoft Publisher. With this brand-new confidence, tackling any publication project, whether it's greeting cards, brochures, magazines, newsletters, party invitations, or beyond, should no longer pose a challenge for you.

I firmly believe that this book will empower you to overcome any obstacles you may encounter while navigating Microsoft Publisher. The key to maximizing your proficiency lies in revisiting any areas where you face difficulty, allowing you to extract the utmost value from this powerful tool. I visualize you growing into a proficient desktop publisher and reaching new heights of success.

If this guide has proven valuable to you, I encourage you to share your positive feedback and recommendations with others. The world eagerly awaits the emergence of your talents and capabilities. Wishing you the very best of luck on your journey ahead.

INDEX

A

Add Master Page"., 108
ADDING PHOTOS, 49
ADJUSTING TEXT BOXES, 33
Align Bottom, 68
Align Center, 68
Align Left, 68
Align Middle, 68
ALIGN OBJECTS, 67
Align Right, 68
Align Top:, 68
APPLYING MASTERS, 109
ARRANGING OBJECT LAYERS, 70

B

Best Fit, 35
BOOKLETS, 103

C

CAPTION, 55
CLIPART, 53
CREATING MASTER PAGES, 108
CREATING YOUR OWN TEMPLATE, 94
CUSTOMIZING WRAP POINTS, 62

D

Do not Autofit, 35
DROP CAP, 23

E

EDITING MASTER PAGES, 106
EXPORT DOCUMENT AS PDF, 118

F

FILE TAB, 10

G

GROUPING AND UNGROUPING OBJECTS, 69
Grow text box, 35
GUIDES, 16

H

HOME TAB, 9

I

INSERT TAB, 10
INSERTING CALENDARS, 76
INSERTING TABLES, 39

L

LAYOUT GUIDES, 111
LINKING TEXT BOXES, 37

M

MAIL MERGE AN INVITATION, 88
MAIL MERGE ENVELOPES, 83
MAILING TAB, 10
Margin Guides, 102
MARGINS, 13
MERGING CELLS, 44

P

PAGE DESIGN TAB, 10
PAGE SETUP, 102
picture placeholders, 18
PRINTING YOUR DOCUMENT, 114

PUBLISHER MAIN SCREEN, 8

R

REVIEW TAB, 10

S

SAVING DOCUMENT AS A DIFFERENT FORMAT, 99
SHADOW/REFLECTION/GLOW, 27
Shrink Text, 35
SPECIFY ORIENTATION, 13
STYLISTIC SETS, 24

T

TEXT ALIGNMENT, 21
TEXT AUTOFIT, 35
TEXT BOX MARGIN, 35
text boxes, 17
TEXT COLOR, 21
TYPOGRAPHY FEATURES, 23

U

USING AN IN-BUILT TEMPLATE, 92

V

VIEW TAB, 10

W

WORDART STYLES, 28
WRAPPING TEXT AROUND PICTURES, 61

www.ingramcontent.com/pod-product-compliance
Lightning Source LLC
Chambersburg PA
CBHW062107220526
45471CB00010B/3631